Palgrave Studies in the History of Social Movements

Editors:
Stefan Berger (Institute for Social Movements, Ruhr-University Bochum)
Holger Nehring (University of Stirling)

Editorial board:
John Chalcraft (London School of Economics)
Andreas Eckert (Humboldt-University, Berlin)
Susan Eckstein (Boston University)
Felicia Kornbluh (University of Vermont)
Jie-Hyun Lim (Research Institute for Comparative History, Hanyang University, Seoul)
Marcel van der Linden (International Institute of Social History, Amsterdam)
Rochona Majumdar (University of Chicago)
Sean Raymond Scalmer (University of Melbourne)

RUHR
UNIVERSITÄT
BOCHUM
INSTITUT FÜR SOZIALE BEWEGUNGEN

Around the world, social movements have become legitimate, yet contested, actors in local, national and global politics and civil society, yet we still know relatively little about their longer histories and the trajectories of their development. This new series seeks to promote innovative historical research on the history of social movements in the modern period since around 1750. We bring together conceptually-informed studies that analyse labour movements, new social movements and other forms of protest from early modernity to the present. We conceive of 'social movements' in the broadest possible sense, encompassing social formations that lie between formal organisations and mere protest events. We also offer a home for studies that systematically explore the political, social, economic and cultural conditions in which social movements can emerge. We are especially interested in transnational and global perspectives on the history of social movements and in studies that engage critically and creatively with political, social and sociological theories in order to make historically grounded arguments about social movements. This new series seeks to offer innovative historical work on social movements, while also helping to historicise the concept of 'social movement'. It hopes to revitalise the conversation between historians and historical sociologists in analyzing what Charles Tilly has called the 'dynamics of contention'.

Titles in the Series:

Helena Dawes
CATHOLIC WOMEN'S MOVEMENTS IN LIBERAL AND FASCIST ITALY

Tamar Groves
TEACHERS AND THE STRUGGLE FOR DEMOCRACY IN SPAIN, 1970–1985

Inna Shtakser
THE MAKING OF JEWISH REVOLUTIONARIES IN THE PALE
Community and Identity in the Russian Revolution, 1905–1907

Kyle Harvey
AMERICAN ANTI-NUCLEAR ACTIVISM, 1975–1990
The Challenge of Peace

Tara Povey
SOCIAL MOVEMENTS IN EGYPT AND IRAN

Matthias Reiss
BLIND WORKERS AGAINST CHARITY
The National League of the Blind of Great Britain and Ireland, 1893–1970

Palgrave Studies in the History of Social Movements
Series Standing Order ISBN 978–1–137–30423–0 hardcover
(*outside North America only*)

You can receive future titles in this series as they are published by placing a standing order. Please contact your bookseller or, in case of difficulty, write to us at the address below with your name and address, the title of the series and one of the ISBNs quoted above.

Customer Services Department, Macmillan Distribution Ltd, Houndmills, Basingstoke, Hampshire RG21 6XS, England

Blind Workers against Charity

The National League of the Blind of Great
Britain and Ireland, 1893–1970

Matthias Reiss

Senior Lecturer, University of Exeter, UK

palgrave
macmillan

First published 2015 by
PALGRAVE MACMILLAN

Palgrave Macmillan in the UK is an imprint of Macmillan Publishers Limited, registered in England, company number 785998, of Houndmills, Basingstoke, Hampshire RG21 6XS.

Palgrave Macmillan in the US is a division of St Martin's Press LLC, 175 Fifth Avenue, New York, NY 10010.

Palgrave Macmillan is the global academic imprint of the above companies and has companies and representatives throughout the world.

Palgrave® and Macmillan® are registered trademarks in the United States, the United Kingdom, Europe and other countries.

ISBN 978–1–137–36446–3

This book is printed on paper suitable for recycling and made from fully managed and sustained forest sources. Logging, pulping and manufacturing processes are expected to conform to the environmental regulations of the country of origin.

A catalogue record for this book is available from the British Library.

A catalog record for this book is available from the Library of Congress.

For my parents

O charity, thy bitter bread,
Is hateful to the brave and free,
Better numbered with the dead,
Than living death, on charity.

Why should this beauteous world of ours,
In such confusion ever be,
The wealthy, waste their precious hours,
While others pine on charity.

A better system must be found,
More justice, and equality,
A fairer distribution round,
And less of this cold charity.

(From the poem 'Charity', composed by
Charles G. Lothian,printed in the
Blind Advocate (March 1918), p. 10.)

Contents

Figures

Acknowledgements

Research for this study has been made possible by British Academy Small Research Grant SG110575 and I would like to express my profound gratitude to the British Academy for its support. I would also like to thank the staff of the Working Class Movement Library in Salford as well as Joe Mann, Gareth Davies and Robert Mooney from the National League of the Blind and Disabled for their help and generosity. Tony Baldwinson very kindly gave me access to images from the National League of the Blind and Disabled. Andrew Thorpe provided much appreciated encouragement and advice. My wife Iris lived with this project for a long time and I am deeply grateful for her patience and crucial support during this period.

Some of the material presented in Chapters 2 and 4 has been previously used for the article 'Forgotten Pioneers of the National Protest March: the National League of the Blind Marches to London, 1920 and 1936', *Labour History Review* Vol. 70(2) (2005): 131–65.

Acronyms and Abbreviations

AEU	Amalgamated Engineering Union
ASW	Amalgamated Society of Woodworkers
AUBB	Amalgamated Union of British Blind
BA	*Blind Advocate*
COS	Charity Organisation Society
CPGB	Communist Party of Great Britain
CRP	Conference Reports and Papers
EC	Executive Council
Gen. Sec.	General Secretary
GFTU	General Federation of Trade Unions
Hon. Gen. Sec.	Honorary General Secretary
IFB	International Federation of the Blind
ILP	Independent Labour Party
Insp.	Inspector
ISTC	Iron and Steel Trades Confederation
LHA	Labour History Archives
MoH	Ministry of Health
MoNI	Ministry of National Insurance
MRC	Modern Record Centre, University of Warwick
NABW	National Association of Blind Workers
NAULAW	National Amalgamated Union of Life Assurance Workers
NI	National Insurance
NLB	National League of the Blind
NLBD	National League of the Blind and Disabled
NLB, SWD	National League of the Blind, South-Western District
NUPIB	National Union of the Professional and Industrial Blind of Great Britain and Ireland
NUR	National Union of Railwaymen
NUS	National Union of Seamen
NUWM	National Unemployed Workers' Movement
NUWSS	National Union of Women's Suffrage Societies
ODNB	*Oxford Dictionary of National Biography*
PM	Prime Minister

P.S.	Police Sergeant
RCA	Railway Clerks' Association of Great Britain and Ireland
RCBDD	Royal Commission on the Blind, the Deaf and Dumb
SB, MePo	Special Branch, Metropolitan Police
SDF	Social Democratic Federation
Sec.	Secretary
TC	Trades Council
TNA	The National Archives, Kew
TUC	Trades Union Congress
TUCL	TUC Library
WBU	World Blind Union
WCir	WCML, NLBD Circulars 1918–45, 1969–71
WCML	Working Class Movement Library, Salford
WNJC	NLB London and Home Counties, National Joint Council for Workshops for the Blind

Introduction

This book is not about blindness but about a unique social movement organisation and its campaign to replace all charitable aid for blind people with an entitlement to statutory provisions. It is a work of history and as such is predominantly concerned with challenging assumptions about the past. Nevertheless, it is hoped that this book will also be of interest to disability scholars and activists as it examines how a relatively small organisation with limited resources has managed to influence policy-making as well as public opinion from the late nineteenth century onwards. All members of the National League of the Blind were partially sighted or completely blind, but it was not this fact which led them to organise in the 1890s. What united them was a perception that they were marginalised in British society because their standard of living depended on the benevolence of others. In addition, they objected to the fact that sighted officials who controlled the funds donated for the benefit of blind people assumed the right to speak for them. The story of the National League of the Blind is therefore part of a much larger narrative. It illustrates how notions of democracy, economic performance and social entitlement became increasingly interwoven from the late nineteenth century onwards. The goals of economic security, civil rights and independence were inextricably linked in the eyes of the League's leaders, and these goals had to be won through struggle. As one of the League's founders put it in January 1899: 'Our mission is to preach the gospel of discontent amongst the blind, to lead them to the conception of a higher social status than which they occupy to-day, to teach them, if we may presume, so much, that their freedom must be won, not bought.'[1]

The enemy in this struggle was not a particular class. As will be shown, membership in the League was open to every blind or partially sighted

1

individual of working age, regardless of their employment status or social standing. While the League's long-term affiliation with both the Trades Union Congress (TUC) and the Labour Party most likely deterred some people from joining, its rhetoric was not focused on class. Instead, the League's enemy was a principle: Charity, i.e. aid provided on the basis of individual need.

Charity has a long tradition in Britain and has always been intertwined with the state in a complex and ever-changing partnership. The state has tried to regulate and control charitable activities since the sixteenth century, and what constitutes 'charity' was first defined under English law in 1601. British monarchs have been associated with voluntary organisations, including many devoted to charitable causes, since the eighteenth century.[2] The current dominant form of 'associated philanthropy' which originated in the late seventeenth century flourished especially during the Victorian era, even though the notion of a 'golden age of philanthropy' in that period has been sharply disputed by some scholars. The voluntary sector further expanded during the nineteenth century in response to the challenges and problems created by industrialisation and urbanisation. Middle-class volunteers linked philanthropy to moral reform and social control, while the working classes created self-help organisations such as trade unions, cooperative or mutual aid societies.

The introduction of mass franchise and the First World War triggered a shift in the relationship between the state and the charitable organisations. While the former assumed a growing responsibility for the problems of modern society it also began to discharge some of these responsibilities through the voluntary sector. This relationship was described as 'New Philanthropy' by Elizabeth Macadam in 1934 when registered charities already received over a third of their income from the state.[3] The Second World War once and for all established the inability of voluntary organisations to deal with problems such as health care, poverty or education in a comprehensive and equal way. The 'people's war' also created a sense of entitlement in broad sections of the population which was at odds with the spirit of charity in its traditional form. Politicians of all parties responded to this change with the welfare state legislation of the 1940s which built on, as well as consolidated, the existing trend towards comprehensive statutory services.[4] The prestige and often also the fortunes of many charitable organisations went into brief decline thereafter, until the 'rediscovery of poverty' and the appearance of pressure groups and the so-called New Social Movements revitalised the sector in the 1960s.[5] State funding for charitable organisations began to increase again in the following decade and they are today an integral and omnipresent part of British society.[6] High-profile fundraising campaigns receive extensive media coverage and widespread support from all levels of society, and opinion polls show that the British public trusts private organisations which help those in need more than political parties, the government or other political institutions.[7]

Charitable organisations are part of the wider voluntary sector.[8] Following Alexis de Tocqueville's thesis that voluntary organisations serve as training grounds for active citizenship the state of the voluntary sector is often used to assess the health of a country's civil society. The theory is that voluntary organisations, including charities, are not just providing services but also reflect the civic-mindedness of a population. Academics as well as politicians have therefore found significance in the steadily growing number of voluntary associations in Britain, even though the nature of people's involvement in these organisations has changed over time. Voluntary associations were frequently praised, in the words of William Beveridge, the architect of the British welfare state, as 'the distinguished marks of a free society' and 'outstanding features of British life'.[9]

It is therefore increasingly difficult to realise that in the past voluntarism, and especially charity, always had its enemies. Even the notion that the Labour Movement was unrelentingly hostile towards charity and voluntary action has now been described as a 'crude stereotype' and 'a myth'.[10] This book will try to establish a more balanced picture by looking at the League's fight against charity and for statutory provisions. Using the National League of the Blind as a case study, this book argues that militant self-representation groups helped to create and shape the British welfare state well before the emergence of the so-called New Social Movements in the 1960s. This decade is often presented as a watershed moment in the history of activism in Britain as new self-representation groups such as the Disability Income Group provided a voice for those hitherto marginalised and began to campaign for the civil rights of disabled people.[11] As will be discussed below, most disability scholars have treated the League as a mere forerunner to this development. This book argues that it was much more than that. In the field of blind welfare, the League, together with the TUC, acted as a third player next to the state and the voluntary sector. 'The term "self organisation" is one that has come to the fore in recent years for a number of different groups who for one reason or another suffered discrimination', the TUC's Deputy General Secretary Brendan Barber told the League's Centennial Anniversary Conference in 1999: 'But it was a concept that you created a century ago.' According to Barber the members of the League 'were the pioneers of the parliamentary lobby' as well as 'to the fore in devising that other weapon of the effective campaigner – taking your message onto the streets'.[12] The League's 'pioneering methods were acknowledged at the time', Barber concluded, and 'emulated on many occasions since'.[13]

Barber's comments capture in a nutshell the innovative character of the League. Many organisations dedicated to the welfare of blind people also originated from the initiative of individuals who were themselves without sight and a number of them were significantly older than the League. The Liverpool School for the Indigent Blind founded in 1791, the Association for Promoting the General Welfare of the Blind (1854) and the British and Foreign Blind Association (1868) which was to become the Royal National Institute of the Blind are just the most prominent examples.[14] Partly as a result of their work, blind people began to emerge from the larger group of the 'deserving poor' during the nineteenth century and acquire a distinct identity. The state responded by recognising the special needs of blind people, even though they were initially grouped together with the – in the language of the time – 'deaf and dumb'. Starting with the Ballot Act of 1872, blind people became the subject of special measures and legislation which gave them a privileged position within the wider disabled community in Britain.[15] The League was, to some degree, the product of this development but also a new phenomenon. It was the first self-presentation group of blind people which combined lobbying for legislative change with direct action campaigning on a national scale. This comprehensive and militant approach also separates it from the British Deaf and Dumb Association (renamed the British Deaf Association in 1971) which was founded in 1890 mainly to promote the use and acceptance of British Sign Language.[16]

Founded in the 1890s the League became a registered trade union in 1899 and affiliated with the TUC in 1902. Rather than restricting itself to industrial questions, however, it explicitly aspired to organise and represent all blind people in Britain over the age of sixteen and to improve their economic conditions as well as change their social status and individual attitudes. It was a true self-advocacy group as only blind individuals could become members until 1968 when it also opened membership to sighted disabled individuals and became the National League of the Blind and Disabled of Great Britain and Ireland.[17] It campaigned vigorously for replacing charitable services with an entitlement to direct state aid and the abolition of all charitable organisations.

Its hostility towards charity was shared by significant sections of the Labour Movement, and by 1905 the League was also affiliated with the Labour Representation Committee. In the following year it was represented at the annual Labour Party Conference as well as the Trades Union Congress and 'resolutions in favour of the objects of the League' and pledging active assistance 'were passed with unanimity' at both meetings.[18]

Somewhat ironically, however, the League was eventually forced to register as a charitable organisation in 1933 in order to continue its fundraising activities without breaking the law. British courts forced the League to become a charity despite the fact that charitable organisations were banned from being politically active under Common Law.[19] Nevertheless, the League remained very active in the field of politics. Like a modern pressure group it tried to achieve its aims by working from within the political system and drafted legislation and policy statements, gave evidence to committees, lobbied politicians, sent deputations and gained representation on crucial advisory bodies. It also understood the power of statistics and created an Information Bureau within its Central Office in February 1925 to systematically collect data on the condition of blind people in Britain. Twelve years later it even decided to issue a standardised annual questionnaire to its branches on this question.[20] It is not clear how thoroughly both decisions were actually implemented, but the League's official organ frequently published statistical information on the economic situation of the blind community. When the British government began to consolidate the welfare state in the 1940s it also relied on the data collected by the League. At the same time the League also employed extra-parliamentary methods. The most high-profile events were without doubt the League's two marches to London in 1920 and 1936, but it also organised countless local protest events and was very conscious of the need to rally public opinion behind its cause. 'At no time in our history have we had any economic power to enforce our wishes', the League's General Secretary stated in 1969. 'All our Members were able to do was use propaganda measures to try to focus public opinion on their side.'[21]

The League's own resources were not sufficient to fund all its activities. It was a genuine poor people's movement but nevertheless managed to create branches in every part of the United Kingdom during the first decade of the twentieth century.[22] In the 1920s and 1930s it also developed a rigidly centralised administrative structure which created substantial conflict within the organisation. The League's Executive Council was frequently accused of undemocratic practices and the organisation experienced a series of internal disputes throughout its existence. Disagreements over policy led to breakaways, while Irish independence triggered the separation of the League's Dublin branch in 1925 and its development into the National League of the Blind of Ireland.[23] Its parent organisation remained an independent entity until it merged with the Iron and Steel Trades Confederation (ISTC) trade union in February 2000 to help form the new trade union Community four years later.[24] While its Irish counterpart became a charity in 2008, the British organisation still campaigns as a distinct section within Community 'for full civil rights and an end to discrimination against disabled people'.[25]

Campaigning for rights only covered a part of the League's activities. Branches of the League organised activities such as picnics or outings, or held social events to bring members together.[26] Almost from the moment the organisation was born, it tried to negotiate concessions and better facilities for blind people on railways and buses.[27] Claiming that its aims also included the widening of 'the mental horizon of blind men and women' the League advocated special museums for blind people after two successful exhibitions at the Science Museum in South Kensington, London, in 1950.[28] Shortly afterwards, it joined the protest when the Football League decided that the BBC would not be allowed to broadcast matches live.[29] When the problem of 'vehicles parked on verges and pavements' was becoming 'a nightmare to blind pedestrians throughout the country', the League felt entitled to approach the Minister of Transport on this issue, and it also campaigned for a law to have visual markings on all clear glass doors in order to protect partially sighted people from accidents.[30] The League also had a long-standing interest in the prevention of blindness, and its ink journal the *Blind Advocate* reported regularly on medical efforts to cure sight loss as well as on new technological devices to help blind individuals.[31]

In addition to campaigning for issues affecting all visually impaired people, the League also provided a range of services for its members. It granted legal aid as well as distress grants, death benefits and dispute or victimisation pay under certain conditions. It fought hard for individual members such as George Edge, who was dismissed from Henshaw's Institution in Manchester in 1901 for marrying a fellow blind woman.[32] The case of M. Tone who was dismissed from the Greenwich workshop after calling the manager 'a despicable cur' in September 1930 was only won in January 1935. The manager had refused to allow another worker, who was 'the worse for drink' after an outing, permission to wait in the workshop for a cab to take him home.[33] When six members of the League at the Carlisle workshops were accused of homosexual activities by a sighted female supervisor in 1973, the League organised a one-day strike to have the woman dismissed.[34] By that time the organisation already had considerable experience in organising industrial action. It had called its first strike in Bristol in 1912 and many more followed.[35] Most of them were fought over working conditions and pay, but the League also called strikes to have workers reinstated.[36] Members of the League at the Birmingham Royal Institution for the Blind even staged a two-and-a-half hour token strike in 1951 to prevent the dismissal of a popular workshop manager.[37]

In other words, the League was a complex and multi-faceted organisation. It is worth studying because it helped to shape the living conditions as well as the image of blind and partially sighted people in Britain. It also provides an interesting case study into how an economically and socially marginalised group was able to build and maintain a hierarchically organised social movement organisation with very few resources, and how this organisation worked to transform its constituents from objects of charity into citizens with a statutory entitlement to state welfare. This status has come under threat again in recent years. In 2010, the coalition government under Prime Minister (PM) David Cameron began to promote voluntarism, under the slogan of the 'Big Society', as an alternative to the comprehensive welfare state. Umbrella groups such as 'The Hardest Hit' or 'Disabled People Against the Cuts' (DPAC) have organised numerous protest events as well as intensive lobbying campaigns against a policy which Simon Duffy, the Director of the Centre for Welfare Reform, denounced in 2013 as 'unfair and un-British'.[38] This book is concerned with how the notion that government aid to blind people was 'fair' as well as 'British' evolved from the late nineteenth century onwards. Instead of focusing on expert debates and the impact of legislative change it will analyse the ways in which blind people themselves propagated the view that they were entitled to state funds in order to be able to participate in their country's economic and social life to the best of their abilities. While history rarely provides a blueprint for contemporary action this book does carry the message that collective struggle is a major engine for social progress and can be successful even against seemingly overwhelming odds.

Scope and structure of this study

To cover all of the League's activities since its inception in the 1890s would require a much larger and far less accessible book than this one. This study will therefore focus on the League's fight to replace voluntary services with statutory services. Its hostility towards charity set it apart from other organisations for and of blind people, and its constant agitation for state funded welfare services represents its most significant contribution to the British welfare state. The League's industrial or social activities will not be discussed, although both topics would be very worth examining. As a result of the focus on the League's fight against charity, much of this study will be concerned with the period between the late nineteenth century and the consolidation of the welfare state in 1948.

'New Union or Poor People's Movement? Building the National League of the Blind' discusses the League's predecessors, origins and founding narrative. The organisation existed as a federation of branches for a few years before it decided to become a registered trade union in 1899. Although it tried to give this decision in hindsight an air of inevitability, the League's aims always went well beyond negotiating wages and regulating workplace relations, and Chapter 1 explores why it decided to adopt the trade union template at the end of the nineteenth century. It also shows how new legislation and legal challenges eventually forced the League to build a centralised structure between the First and the Second World Wars, and discusses the problems and tensions this process created.

In Chapter 2, ' "Justice not Charity": Framing the Message' outlines how the League and its supporters presented the organisation's political demands in order to win the widest possible support. The League's vilification of charity and demand for direct state aid for all visually impaired people in the form of industrial training, sheltered employment or transfer payments was by no means universally popular in British society. The League's leaders therefore had to devise strategies to encourage public opinion, Parliament and the trade unions to support the League's programme. This was mainly achieved during the first two decades of the twentieth century and the search for a successful frame eventually peaked in the first march to London in 1920 under the banner 'Justice not Charity'.

'Mutually Exclusive Principles? Trade Unionism and Charity' examines the League's position within the trade union movement in Great Britain. The League's claim to be an integral part of this movement and the exclusive voice of blind workers within the TUC faced serious challenges during the 1920s and 1930s. Chapter 3 examines why a significant number of members deserted the League during these decades to form breakaway organisations which they claimed better represented the true spirit of trade unionism. It explains how these conflicts revolved around the League's relationship to charity, places them within the wider framework of trade union history, and explains how the League was able to fend off these challenges with the help of the TUC.

Chapter 4, 'The Limits of Radicalism: Politics and Protest in the 1920s and 1930s' examines how the League tried to maintain the momentum of its campaign for direct state aid after the passing of the Blind Persons Act in 1920. It repeatedly tried to have the Act amended during the interwar years, but its parliamentary strategy failed to produce results. Although Labour formally adopted the League's programme in the 1930s the party's electoral prospects were poor after its crushing defeat in the 1931 General Election and local Labour authorities often ignored the official policy line when dealing with blind or partially sighted people. As a result the League reverted to street politics in 1936 which triggered the passing of another Blind Persons Act in 1938 and it also began to seek wide institutional representation on advisory and decision making bodies.

'Success at Last? The League and the Consolidation of the Welfare State' examines the League's influence on the welfare state legislation of the 1940s. After the failure of its parliamentary strategy the League decided in 1933 to seek wide institutional representation in order to shape policy decisions at both local and regional level. This cooperative approach allowed it to campaign successfully for a minimum wage and higher allowances during the Second World War. It also increased the standing of the organisation within both the blind community and government and enabled it to influence the content and implementation of welfare state legislation between 1944 and 1948. This legislation fulfilled many of the League's core demands but ultimately also contributed to its eventual decline by centralising the system of blind welfare, changing the status of the specialised workshops and starting to erode the special position of blind people under the law.

The final chapter, 'A Changing Relationship: The League and Charity in the Post-War Era' discusses how the organisation struggled to maintain its status and membership numbers after the Second World War. Many people left once the goal of direct state aid had been achieved in 1948, and the League struggled to find an issue which matched the mobilising potential of this slogan. In addition it was also forced to spend more and more time on workshop matters as these institutions experienced serious problems after the war. As a result the League became less attractive to the growing number of visually impaired people who found employment in open industry as they saw no point in joining a trade union which increasingly became associated with sheltered employment only. The decline of trade unionism in Britain after 1979 also affected the League as financial donations from other trade unions became less reliable and generous.[39] From the 1970s onwards the League therefore began to cooperate with charitable organisations to protect or expand the rights of disabled people and eventually merged with other trade unions in order to survive.

Interspersed between these topical chapters are three shorter case studies. Two of them deal with individuals who have significantly shaped the League and also had an impact beyond it. Ben Purse was one of the central figures of the blind community in Britain during the first half of the twentieth century and a leading member of the League from its inception until 1921. Tom Parker began to take a prominent role in the affairs of the League in the 1920s and, focusing especially on the aspect of international cooperation, continued to do so until the 1990s. Their stories bridge almost the entire twentieth century, highlight some of the key themes in the history of the League and illustrate the degree to which charismatic individuals were able to shape the organisation's fate. The third case study tells the story of the League's two periodicals, the ink-journal the *Blind Advocate* and the Braille journal *Horizon*. Neither of them has yet merited scholarly attention and the short case study will hopefully provide an incentive for further research on these unique publications.

Sources and historiography

'Blind people – organised by the National League of the Blind – were the most militant of all disabled groups before the last war', Steve Humphries and Pamela Gordon state in their book *Out of Sight*.[40] However, anyone interested in finding out more about the radicalism of people with visual impairments and the remarkable organisation which channelled it is bound to be disappointed. Despite a rapidly growing interest in the history of disability and disabled people, very little has so far been written about the National League of the Blind or the organisations which competed with it for the claim to be the authentic voice of blind and partially sighted people in Britain.[41]

This lack of interest cannot be explained by a scarcity of primary source material as the League has left a substantial paper trail. Its official archive at the Working Class Movement Library in Salford contains extensive records of meetings and conferences, copies of the League's publications, financial statements, rule books, banners and a host of other material. Most of it dates from the period after the First World War when the League began to develop a centralised and more professional structure. For example, it was only in March 1931 that the League's Executive Council decided that 'in future all reports be submitted in writing for the purpose of filing'.[42] Many documents from the early period were probably also lost when the League's Head Office in London was hit during a bombing raid in 1942.[43] In the early 1970s the General Secretary acknowledged that the League's first 25 years in particular were very poorly documented and issued a call to all members to send privately owned documents from that period to Central Office.[44] From the 1950s onwards, however, the history of the League is well documented, although the most recent material from the last two decades has not yet been transferred to a public archive and has therefore not been available for this study.[45]

The League's correspondence with the TUC and its affiliated organisations is held at the Modern Record Centre at the University of Warwick. The Centre also holds the correspondence between the TUC and other organisations for or of blind people, such as the National Federation of the Blind, as well as files on campaigns in which the League was involved.[46] Further trade union material is located at the TUC Library at London Metropolitan University, which also has a limited number of publications or documents by the League, while the Labour History Archives in Manchester contain the correspondence between the League and the Labour Party as well as numerous newspaper clippings.

The British Library holds the most complete run of the League's official organ the *Blind Advocate* (from 1968 the *Advocate*) as well as numerous books written by Ben Purse. The League's dealings with the Independent Labour Party can be traced in the archives of the London School of Economics. The Parliamentary Archives hold the transcript of the League's deputation to 10 Downing Street in 1920 and provide online access to the relevant bills and resolutions passed by Parliament. The debates in the House of Commons and the Lords are, of course, recorded in *Hansard*, which is now also available online.[47] Finally, the National Archives in Kew have the files of the various government departments and agencies which interacted with the League throughout its history.

This wealth of primary source material has not yet attracted much scholarly interest. From the 1960s to the 1980s, most of the historical research on protest and trade unionism in the modern era was performed by labour historians who often equated size with power. From this perspective the relatively small League was little more than a footnote in the long history of working-class struggles. Studies published by or on voluntary organisations likewise pay little or no attention to the League, which is probably not surprising given its hostility towards all forms of charity. June Rose's book *Changing Focus: The Development of Blind Welfare in Britain*, for example, devotes less than two pages to the organisation and fails to mention that the blind marchers to London in 1920 came from its ranks.[48] Scholars working in the growing field of disability studies have largely focused on contemporary issues and have mostly treated the League as a historical stepping stone to the modern Disability Rights movement. They are 'sometimes referred to in accounts of the history of disabled people', as Ardha Danieli and Peter Wheeler have acknowledged in 2006, but 'the significance of their actions and argument is not sufficiently recognized'.[49] Very few disability scholars have made use of the League's archive in Salford and most have relied on the League's official organ the *Blind Advocate* as well as its two hagiographical jubilee brochures for information on the organisation. Published by the League in 1949 and 1974 to mark the fiftieth and seventy-fifth anniversaries of its registration as a trade union, these brochures provide only a very selective and one-sided account of the League's history.[50]

Cultural and social historians, however, have shown a growing interest in the history of disabled people in general and blind people in particular over the last two decades.[51] As Selina Mills put it in 2013, 'Blindness and its history have become fashionable.'[52] A number of works which deal with efforts to improve the situation of people with visual impairments refer to the League in passing and broader historical studies also often mention the organisation briefly.[53] The major exception is Gordon Ashton Phillips' magisterial and excellent study, *The Blind in British Society*, published in 2004. Phillips' work devotes significant space towards the League, but focuses mainly on charitable organisations and only covers the period up to 1930.[54] Many of these general works on blindness suggest that the League's militancy and hostility towards charity was only temporary. Phillips, for example, comes to the conclusion that the organisation's 'combative phase' ended in 1905, while Madeline Rooff claims that the League had reached its objectives during the interwar years and that it was 'no longer in open conflict with other national bodies' from then on.[55] This study argues that the League's militancy was much more enduring and also provides the first published academic monograph on the organisation's history and development.

Works which are based predominantly on primary sources from the League are still rare and selective in scope. C. Kenneth Lysons produced a pioneering study in 1973 with his PhD thesis on 'The Development of Social Legislation for Blind or Deaf Persons in England 1834–1939'.[56] Lysons' research was actively supported by the League which gave him access to a wide range of primary sources and figured prominently in his work.[57] However, the first published works only appeared after the League had handed over its archive to the Working Class Movement Library in Salford. Peter Carter subsequently produced a short article on the 1920 march to London for the Library's Bulletin in 1997, and a more extensive article on the 1920 and 1936 marches appeared in *Labour History Review* in 2005.[58] In the same year BBC Radio 4 broadcast a separate program on the 1920 march, while Tony Baldwinson's 2012 study *Unacknowledged Traces* made use of the League's photo archive.[59] A critical study of the National League of the Blind of Great Britain and Ireland is therefore overdue, as the organisation did have a significant impact on the lives of blind people in the United Kingdom. While this book does not match the monumental scope of the official 1116-page history of the National Federation of the Blind in the United States, it will hopefully prove to be useful for anyone interested in the history of disabled people or social movements in general and inspire further research.[60]

1

New Union or Poor People's Movement? Building the National League of the Blind

One of the most striking features of the League is its longevity. As a radical poor people's movement founded in the last decade of the nineteenth century, the League's odds of surviving as an independent organisation for more than a hundred years had been slim. By their very definition poor people's movements are unstable and the League was no exception. Yet the organisation was able to overcome sectional differences, internal power struggles and programmatic disputes as well as an almost constant scarcity of resources to emerge with a stable, sustainable and effective structure in the mid-1930s. By that time the League had managed to see off all its major rivals and could legitimately claim to be the most representative voice of sightless workers in Great Britain and Northern Ireland. Members of the League were given seats on committees dealing with the welfare of blind people, employers accepted the organisation as a collective bargaining partner, and the TUC as well as the Labour Party had made the League's key political demands their own.

The price of these impressive achievements was centralisation and a complete dependence on the trade union movement. During the first four decades of its existence the League changed from a lively and relatively loose federation of branches into a centralised organisation dominated by the Executive Council and the Central Office in London. This process was not achieved without resistance from the grassroots, but mirrored the development of the wider trade union movement in Great Britain. While the League was able to significantly amplify its influence through its affiliation with the TUC, its trade union status also created problems and confusion. This chapter will analyse why the League decided to become and remain a registered trade union and how this status contributed to its longevity.

Creating a history

Foundation narratives can contribute to an organisation's survival by providing cohesion and meaning. Pinpointing the start of a movement is essential for creating a narrative of steady progress which promises to eventually culminate in the fulfilment of the movement's demands or goals. Commemorating those who created the movement and highlighting their vision and sacrifices offers an opportunity to emphasise the values on which it is founded and can encourage as well as inspire members. The Labour Movement systematically began to use the so-called Tolpuddle Martyrs for these purposes in the early 1930s. The six men from Dorset were arrested and sentenced in 1834 to transportation for seven years for administering an illegal oath when forming their Friendly Society of Agricultural Labourers in Tolpuddle. Following a wave of criticism and protest the six individuals were pardoned two years later, but the memory of the injustice they had suffered remained alive within the Labour Movement. In 1932, however, the TUC lifted the commemoration onto a whole new level when it began to develop plans for marking the upcoming centenary of their convictions. Among other things a play was produced, a book published and a memorial created in Tolpuddle in the form of six cottages for retired agricultural workers, each named after one of the martyrs. The TUC also unveiled a plaque, held a demonstration, created a museum in the central hall in Tolpuddle and started an annual festival. All this served to inspire a movement in crisis and provide it with a new focus and sense of purpose. The example of the six men and the trade union values they supposedly stood for were celebrated along with the progress made by the Labour Movement since 1834.[1] To this day the Tolpuddle Martyrs are portrayed as 'key to the formation of modern trades' unionism' and they have become 'some of the most celebrated names in the trade union martyrology'.[2]

At the same time the TUC elevated the six men from Dorset 'to a representative standing in the movement's history', the National League of the Blind developed its own foundation myth which likewise centred on martyrs, pioneers, collective struggle and sacrifice.[3] The League's founders became 'old warriors who, mostly sightless but farsighted, pointed and led the way in showing how organisation could benefit those whom they sought to serve'.[4] Members of the League were warned to never 'ever underestimate the trials and tribulations of the pioneers, who were often victimised', and their sacrifices were presented as both the foundation upon which subsequent generations were able to build as well as a debt which needed to be repaid through the continuation of their work.[5]

It took a while before the League felt the need to write its own history. The first suggestion to write and print a history of the organisation was made by the Edinburgh branch in 1927 but unanimously rejected by the Executive Council who found that 'owing to the cost and labour entailed [...] no useful purpose would be served by launching on such a scheme'.[6] Only a few years later, however, the Executive Council changed its mind and decided to produce a handbook 'to present in a convenient and concise form the progress in Blind Welfare Services during the last fifty years in Great Britain, with particular reference to the influence exercised by the Nation League of the Blind'.[7] An appeal to all members to provide 'reliable information regarding the activities of the League since its inception' was issued in June 1931 and the handbook was finished in the following year.[8] The League's efforts to construct a celebratory narrative of its history therefore only slightly preceded the TUC's decision in 1932 to commemorate the centenary the Tolpuddle Martyrs' convictions. Both efforts were inspired by a sense of crisis, although the League's problems were more of an internal nature, as will be shown later on.

It would take another seventeen years after the *Handbook* before the League published a new account of its history and mission.[9] By convention the League had started to celebrate its moment of birth from when it first registered as a trade union and a *Golden Jubilee Brochure* was published in 1949 to mark the fiftieth anniversary of this event.[10] Edited by the League's General Secretary T. H. Smith and with a foreword from the TUC's General Secretary Vincent Tewson, the brochure offered an official and concise treatment of the League's history.[11] Although the Golden Jubilee celebrations focused on the year 1899, Smith decided to start the League's foundation narrative with a meeting of a small group of blind workers in South London in 1891.[12] Their attempt to organise was described as 'a weak and ill-conceived effort which speedily collapsed', but it allowed him to link the League's inception to the 'new trade unionism' of that period and the iconic London Dock Strike of August 1889 which came to symbolise it.[13] Stressing that 'blind people were not immune' to the forces which fuelled the growth of non-craft trade unions from the 1880s onwards, Smith suggested that it was not a coincidence that 'the first attempt at organisation among blind workers occurred in South London, the centre of the dockers' historic struggle, and just two years after its victorious conclusion'.[14] Writing in 1949, Smith conveniently ignored the fact that the dockers' success was short-lived. In London their union was practically defeated by the end of 1890 and the Dock, Wharf, Riverside and General Labourers' Union only survived in strength around the Bristol Channel. Concessions gained by other trade unions of non-skilled workers during that period were likewise quickly lost again as employers started to fight back immediately after the strike of the dockers.[15] Nevertheless, Smith claimed that the workers in the London docks had 'demonstrated that unskilled labour could be organised and held together by militant leadership; that it could be marshalled to fight its own battles and fight them successfully'.[16] The support that Ben Tillett, the leader of the dockers, gave to the League from 1920 onwards probably helped to maintain the myth that the London Dock Strike of 1889 provided the spark for the League's creation. Given the legendary status this conflict had within the Labour movement by 1949, the League was eager to embrace this invented tradition.[17]

According to the *Golden Jubilee Brochure*, the other major factor contributing to the creation of the League was the report of the Royal Commission on the Blind, the Deaf and Dumb in 1889, the same year that the London Dock Strike took place.[18] In contrast to the somewhat questionable impact of the latter, the influence the Royal Commission had on mobilising the blind community is obvious. Established in 1885 the Royal Commission revealed the poor conditions in which many blind people lived and suggested steps to address this problem. Its recommendations regarding the education of blind people were implemented with the passing of the Elementary Education (Blind and Deaf Children) Act of 1893, but its proposals to provide industrial training and workshops for blind people in every major city were not carried out.

The Act of 1893 set a precedent for state action on behalf of the visually impaired and thereby provided an incentive for future agitation. In the same year a small conference of blind people, mostly from Manchester and London, met and issued a manifesto entitled 'A Blind Person's Charter', thereby linking their nascent movement to the agitation of the Chartists half a century earlier. The document criticised the existing charitable organisations as inefficient and corrupt, denounced the workshops for the blind as 'sweating dens' and demanded that the state should take direct responsibility for both the employment and the adequate remuneration of blind workers.[19] Branches in London, Manchester, Oldham, Cardiff and other cities were formed and loosely united in the following year under the title National League of the Blind of Great Britain and Ireland in order to promote the aims listed in the Blind Person's Charter.[20]

The branches corresponded with each other but were not integrated into an organisational structure and many of them quickly ran into problems. In an effort to avoid the collapse of the League in their region the Northern England branches united under the authority of an Executive Committee at a conference in Manchester in November 1897 and elected Ben Purse as their General Secretary.[21] A Dublin branch was founded in 1898 which also affiliated with the Northern Section.[22] The London branch had apparently collapsed by that time. In September 1898 Purse announced in the League's organ, the *Blind Advocate*, that he had received 'definite information' about 'strenuous efforts' being undertaken to reorganise the 'late London branch' of the League.[23] These efforts apparently took place in the Limehouse and Poplar area in East London and the first activities of the Limehouse branch under the leadership of W. H. Rooke were reported in the *Blind Advocate* in December 1898. Among other things Rooke organised a public meeting at Limehouse Town Hall which was presided over by the trade unionist William Charles Steadman, who was also a member of the London County Council and the newly elected Liberal MP for Stepney. Ben Purse also gave a speech at that meeting but was only referred to as 'a blind man' from Manchester.[24]

Nevertheless, the contact between the Northern and the London section was already closer by that time than the League's *Golden Jubilee Brochure* suggests, and Rooke was elected to the new Administrative Council of the Northern section in January 1899.[25] Although the London section appointed William Banham as its own secretary in 1899, the signs were set for a merger of the two sections.[26] A national Code of Rules was drafted and the League registered as a trade union in December 1899. The foundations for the subsequent election of a representative Executive Council were laid at a conference at Derby on Easter Monday 1900. Banham was appointed as the League's General Secretary while Purse was elected National Organiser in 1901. By the time of the 1902 Trades Union Congress in London the League had also affiliated to the TUC and successfully moved its first resolution in favour of state aid during that Congress.[27]

The League's foundation narrative presents the creation of the organisation as a new beginning and hails it as 'a trade union of a new kind'.[28] This was a misrepresentation as other organisations of blind workers had already been created well before 1891.[29] A Union of Blind Basket-Makers was founded several years before the creation of the League and had branches in different cities.[30] An organisation by the name of the United Kingdom Association of the Blind claimed to have 'various branches [...] throughout the country' in December 1884 although its centre seemed to have been in Sunderland.[31] The Association petitioned the Royal Commission on the Condition of the Blind, Deaf and Dumb for the privilege to submit evidence through delegates and its President George Walter was indeed interviewed on 3 February 1887. Walker, a blind man who taught at the Blind Institute at Sunderland, had to admit that the local branch was 'almost out of existence' by that time, but the Association's petition had nevertheless been signed by 657 blind persons over the age of 16.[32] The Royal Commission also received a separate memorial from an organisation of blind workers in Huddersfield.[33] In Hull, Peter Miller founded the Industrious Blind Association before becoming instrumental in creating the National League of the Blind. Miller also chaired the organisation's first two National Conferences and was very actively involved in the League's early agitation.[34]

The League's most direct predecessor was, however, the British Blind Association in Scotland.[35] The first recorded meeting of the Association seemed to have taken place in October 1870 when the Glasgow, Kilmarnock and Paisley branches met 'to consider the best means to be taken to forward the objects for which they are associated'.[36] An Executive Committee was appointed 'to carry on the business of the central society'. The body was supposed to meet at least once every month and it was also decided to print 30,000 copies of a pamphlet explaining the objects of the Association.[37] Branches in other cities, towns and regions followed. The Association lobbied Parliament 'for a measure providing for the education and industrial training of the blind, and the employment of the able-bodied' and even claimed credit for the establishing of the Royal Commission.[38]

Like the League later on, the British Blind Association was formed for the somewhat broad 'purpose of securing the rights of the class which it was intended to benefit' and had its strongholds in the charitable institutions for the sightless.[39] In contrast to the institutions in England which mainly provided temporary training for blind people and discharged them after they had completed their apprenticeship, Scottish institutions also had a workshop component which offered employment for adult blind individuals living outside the institution.[40] The British Blind Association formed around these workshops and it is likely that the workers of the Edinburgh, Glasgow, Dundee and Aberdeen institutions which submitted a memorial to the Royal Commission under the name of the 'Industrial Blind of Scotland' belonged to it, although its name does not appear in the document.[41]

The British Blind Association's most vibrant and long-lasting branch was Aberdeen. The city survived the depression of the 1880s relatively well, partly due to its expanding fishing industry, and saw a re-emergence of trade unions for unskilled workers during this decade which received strong backing from the local Trades Council.[42] The Secretary of the local branch of the British Blind Association was John Keir, a blind man who also served for some time as the Association's President and later became President of the Aberdeen United Trades Council.[43] Keir and his colleagues celebrated trade union values as the annual social gathering of the Aberdeen branch in December 1887 showed. The Chairman of the meeting saw the thriving state of the branch as a sign of 'a sound and resolute manhood' and told 'the workers' that the community was 'glad to see that the blind in Aberdeen were standing shoulder to shoulder, using their own powers, relying upon themselves, addressing themselves to the difficulties that lay in their path'.[44]

John Keir also attended the 1889 Trades Union Congress in Dundee as a delegate of the Aberdeen Trades Council and took this opportunity to move the first Congress resolution in favour of state aid for the blind, thirteen years before the League's first Congress resolution.[45] In his speech Keir argued that 'men who had discharged their duty to themselves and families for many years, and who by no fault of their own were deprived of their sight, were entitled to receive State aid', and the resolution was unanimously adopted.[46] In March 1890 Keir represented Aberdeen at the British Blind Association's conference in Edinburgh. The event also featured delegates from the Scottish capital, Glasgow and Dundee and was held to inject the voice of the Association into the debate around the Elementary Education (Blind and Deaf Children) Act the government was preparing at that time.[47] In his conference speech Keir branded the practice of keeping blind children 'for exhibition in institutions in order to make the stream of charity flow' and demanded that they should be 'educated along with ordinary children at Board Schools'.[48] A resolution to this effect was passed, and also one expressing the wish that the technical and industrial training of the blind 'should be aided by the Educational Department' as recommended by the Royal Commission in its report. The final resolution demanded that 'all blind persons who from any other causes are incapacitated or prevented from earning a sufficient livelihood for themselves should receive State aid, and any such assistance should come direct to the individuals'.[49] The National League of the Blind would later make the same demands.

Given the fact that blind workers in Scotland were already well ahead of the League it is hardly surprising the latter struggled to establish itself north of the border and the first Scottish branch was only started in 1906. Already in December of that same year the Aberdeen branch of the British Blind Association decided to reconstitute itself as a branch of the National League of the Blind and the older organisation ceased to exist.[50] The League's foundation narrative does not mention its predecessor and portrays the London Dock Strike of 1889 and the publication of the Royal Commission's report as the sparks which brought the League into existence. Both events took place in the same year and epitomised the League's dual approach of collective action from below and social reform from the top. In addition, the two events were also suitably dramatic to appeal to a campaigning organisation in search of an invented tradition.

Developing an identity

Another similarity between the League and the British Blind Association was that they both functioned as organisations of blind workers as well as pressure groups for all blind people. The ultimate goal of both organisations was to represent the voice of the blind community on every level of society and to promote their interests beyond the narrow confines of the workshops and institutions which formed their power bases. The British Blind Association had hoped to build 'an organisation that would be able not merely to protect the interests of the blind throughout the whole country, but to advance them in a very decided way'.[51] In a similar fashion, the League presented itself as the sole voice of all visually impaired people in the United Kingdom and tried to organise them under its banner. Banham's somewhat hyperbolic claim in 1901 that 'this League speaks on behalf of thirty-six thousand of the blind of the United Kingdom' reflected this aspiration and was repeated in various forms throughout the years.[52]

Membership of the League was reserved for the visually impaired of either sex until the 1960s when the organisation also opened its ranks to the physically disabled.[53] A minimum membership age of sixteen was introduced in 1905 and new Rules adopted in 1915 made it clear that partially sighted people were also eligible for membership.[54] Individuals holding 'authoritative official positions in charitable institutions for the blind' were banned from joining in the early 1920s, but otherwise no restrictions in terms of class, gender or employment status were introduced.[55]

Hostility towards the voluntary sector was a central tenet of the League's identity and the exclusion of charity officials reflected this. Pride in being a self-advocacy group was at least as important. 'We are <u>of</u> the blind; we are the blind. All others are <u>for</u> the blind [emphasis in the original],' the League's Scottish Organiser proudly proclaimed at a trade union meeting in 1923.[56] This naturally limited the role sighted people were able to play in the League. Two sighted people were elected as trustees to administer the League's financial transactions as directed by the Executive Council.[57] Other sighted people willing to become actively involved in the League's affairs could become associates against the payment of an annual subscription.[58] The Northern section of the League had banned associates from becoming branch secretaries in November 1898, but this ban was apparently lifted after the merger with the London section in 1900.[59] Associates could be admitted by a branch and from 1905 onwards also by the Executive Council.[60] They had 'the right to attend and take part in the business of the meetings of the League' until 1924 when it was made clear that associates were not permitted 'to vote on any question relating to a strike or lock out'. From 1929 onwards, they were not allowed to vote at all in branch meetings.[61]

Although official positions within the League had always been restricted to members, the 1924 Rules stated specifically that associates were 'not eligible for election to Executive Council or the office of President'.[62] Despite this clarification some branches apparently made no distinction between members and associates. The League's Executive acknowledged the existence of sighted branch secretaries in 1928 and some associates were issued ballot papers in 1931.[63] After receiving legal advice that associates were not members of the League, the Executive was forced to remind branches in 1932 that they were 'not eligible for any office, national or local'.[64] The level of protest this decision triggered showed the extent to which many branches relied on sighted officials, especially for the positions of secretary or treasurer. At least twelve branches and one District Council asked the Executive to revert to the previous practice as they considered the new ruling 'impracticable'.[65] However, they were informed that this would be 'distinctly illegal' and while branches were allowed to accept the help of sighted persons the latter were strictly forbidden from occupying official positions at branch or district level.[66] A compromise was only reached in October 1934 when branches were allowed to appoint a sighted 'Assistant Secretary' to conduct the correspondence and also assist the branch secretary in other matters.[67]

The League's willingness to accept new members based on a shared disability rather than their employment status repeatedly created confusion after the organisation registered as a trade union in 1899. Attempts from inside the League to restrict membership to those who were part of the workforce were blocked. When the employees of Glasgow Blind Asylum voted to create a branch solely for workers in 1924, for example, the Executive Council vetoed the initiative.[68] Instead, the Executive urged all branches 'to make a persistent effort to organise all blind people in their respective areas'.[69] In a similar fashion the League's Executive also rejected the idea of an upper age limit for members of the League in 1937.[70] Ben Purse, who had done more than anyone else to create the League, eventually became the sharpest critic of this policy and argued in 1947 that 'the recruitment of unemployable blind people [...] cannot be justified on normal Trades Union practice'.[71] He disputed that the League was able to speak for the blind community as a whole, or even just for the working blind and argued that its claim to do so was 'much resented by many blind individuals and by independent organisations of the blind such as the National Federation of the Blind, the Yorkshire Blind Workers Association, the Association of Certified Blind Masseurs and Groups of Blind Workers in London and Leicester'.[72]

The League's nature looked equally confusing from the outside. The Charity Organisation Society (COS) investigated it in 1906 and came to the conclusion that it was 'a kind of trade organisation with a benevolent branch, consisting entirely of blind <u>workers</u> [emphasis in the original]'.[73] After the First World War the King's Bench Division of the High Court of Justice stressed the League's dual character even more. Despite vigorous protest from the League, the Lord Chief Justice of England ruled in *Barber v. Chudley* in December 1922 that the organisation was a charitable organisation as well as a trade union.[74] Other trade unions often expressed doubt whether the League was a genuine trade union and the TUC was frequently contacted to confirm that it was indeed an affiliated organisation.[75] The Secretary of the Mansfield, Sutton & District Co-operative Society was not alone in expressing surprise about this fact in 1940, since his Committee had 'in the past made grants to this organization [*sic*] in the belief that it was a charitable organization [*sic*] and not solely a Trade Union'.[76] Only a few years earlier the Ministry of Health came to a different conclusion and called the League 'a Political organisation of a Trade Union character'.[77]

The League, in other words, was of a multi-faceted nature, and Purse's claim that its founders had not contemplated the inclusion of individuals unable to perform work is clearly incorrect.[78] In fact, the League's earliest surviving statement of aims focused on community building and integration rather than industrial issues. Published by the Northern Section of the League in November 1897 it listed the promotion of 'brotherly love and unity amongst the blind in the United Kingdom' as the organisation's primary aim, followed by securing 'direct State Aid as against the present inadequate voluntary system'. Improving the working conditions in 'all public institutions and workshops for the blind' by bringing them under the purview of the Factories' Acts was next in the list, while the fourth point demanded 'the vote by Ballot in all national affairs for the blind'. The final two points aimed at integrating blind people by removing both 'the hindrance to the employment of the capable blind in the Trade Union and other workshops' as well as 'the objections raised by Friendly Societies and Assurance Companies to the blind being admitted members' and also by improving 'the moral, social, and political condition of the blind in the United Kingdom'.[79]

Trade union status was clearly not necessary to achieve these aims and why the League decided to register as one only two years later is a difficult question to answer. The League's most important political demand was for direct state aid, and the idea that the state should have a direct, exclusive and unmediated relationship with each sightless person was a radical idea in late Victorian times. 'Our policy was most bitterly opposed by most of the officials of Blind Institutions and ridiculed by many of them', the League's leadership later recalled: 'Some of them called us revolutionaries, some Socialists, whilst others detected symptoms of madness in the advocacy of such extravagant proposals.'[80] In fact, the concept of direct state aid was so radical that it had to be explained frequently to the League's own rank-and-file members.[81] The leading figures of the League also had a realistic attitude regarding the time and effort necessary to convince those outside of the organisation to support this goal. 'Many years must elapse, I fear', a member of the League wrote in April 1899, 'before Parliament will be persuaded to do anything effective for the blind, and many large sums of money be spent in agitation and propaganda.'[82] What were needed for the struggle were a stable and tested organisational template as well as strong allies. The trade union movement offered both, and its commitment to socialism as a long-term goal likewise made it a natural partner for the League which regarded an activist state as the solution to all problems blind people faced in British society. Following the earlier lead of the Social Democratic Federation (SDF), the Independent Labour Party (ILP) had started to proclaim a 'right to work' in 1895. The demand that the state should provide either work or full maintenance for the unemployed mirrored that of the League for sheltered employment or pensions for all blind people and both programmes also included an element of industrial training for those employed in declining trades. Both the SDF and the ILP worked with the trade unions and the London Trades Councils in their 'right to work' campaign and trade union status offered the League a chance to integrate its programme into the growing demand for state action to solve the twin problems of poverty and unemployment.[83]

In addition, the League and the trade union movement also shared a commitment to mass action. As the *Blind Advocate* put it in April 1899:

> It is from the mass of the blind themselves, and from that alone, that such a solid phalanx can be created as shall rouse from their apathy even the well-intentioned and influential laymen and parliamentarians to action on anything like right and effective lines.[84]

In true Socialist tradition, solidarity and unity were presented as necessary conditions for influence and success:

> Were even a tithe of the blind of the country to loyally cast in their lot with the League, a force would at once be established which would command recognition and respect, and which [...] would prove practically irresistible in our interests, and realise some at least of our aspirations sooner than the most sanguine of us could dare to anticipate.[85]

To play a role in the trade union movement, however, the League had to formally become a trade union organisation. Earlier activists like John Keir had been able to exert influence through local Trades Councils and Keir did submit his 1889 Dundee resolution as a Trades Council delegate. However, this avenue was blocked by the decision of the 1895 Congress to exclude Trades Councils from being affiliated with the TUC.[86] From then on only delegates representing affiliated trade unions had the right to submit resolutions to Congress which made it necessary for the League to aspire to this status in order to be able to insert its policies into the TUC's agenda.

Trade union status had the additional advantage of opening up the workshops for blind people for the creation of a nationwide network of branches. Workshops were the ideal recruiting grounds since it was here that a relatively high number of blind wage earners with a common identity and legitimate set of grievances congregated every day. Industrial training was, together with religious education, one of the

two pillars of the voluntarist effort in Great Britain since the founding of the Liverpool School for the Indigent Blind in 1791. Workshops
were therefore an integral part of charitable institutions and blind people spent most of their waking hours in them. The goal was not only
to provide additional income for the institution and keep blind people
occupied, but also to teach them a trade and industrial habits which
would enable them to become self-sufficient after leaving the school.
These aims were, however, rarely met. The number of trades blind people were able to learn was severely limited, many of them were outdated
and few offered any prospect of economic independence.[87] The shortcomings of the industrial training provided by the schools for blind
people was revealed by the 1851 Census which showed that at least
eighty per cent of the blind population over twenty years of age in
England and Wales was without employment. Subsequent reports by
the Charity Organisation Society and the Royal Commission confirmed
these findings.[88]

Independent workshops were developed as an answer to this problem. The first enterprise of this kind was set up by Elizabeth Gilbert,
the blind daughter of the future bishop of Chichester, who was supported by William Hanks Levy, a blind man teaching at the London
Society for Teaching the Blind to Read. Gilbert founded the Association
for Promoting the General Welfare of the Blind in 1854 which helped
blind home workers engaged in producing baskets, mats or brushes to
sell their wares. In 1857 the Association also opened a workshop in
London although it continued its support of home workers and only
two years later it supported no less than nineteen different trades.[89] Similar facilities were founded in other cities, most of them independently
of the Association for Promoting the General Welfare of the Blind, while
some of the existing schools for blind people also set up workshops for
sightless adults.[90]

In ideological terms the workshops were an unqualified success. By
providing supervised and regulated employment they allowed individuals to live up to Victorian ideals of self-help and respectability within
the wider framework of charity. Work was more than a way to earn a
living; it was an indication of moral fibre and, if performed successfully, a reflection of an individual's worth. In economic terms, however,
workshops often struggled due to the low productivity of their employees and the long time it took to train them. Lack of skills or ambitions
amongst management, inflexible administrative arrangements, competition from prison labour or other institutions and limited financial
reserves also added to the workshops' problems. Wages were usually

low and fluctuated over time. As an incentive to maintain productivity, workshops paid piecework rates rather than daily wages with the result that the vast majority of blind workers earned significantly less than sighted workers in similar positions.[91] Working and pay conditions also varied considerably as workshops responded to local markets and continued to rely on financial support from local benefactors. All workshops for blind people were comparatively small and there were not nearly enough places to accommodate all those who sought employment in them. Their small size also made them vulnerable to the usual variations in demand for their products and the income of workshop employees also fluctuated as a result.

All of these problems, the League argued, could be solved by transferring the workshops into national or municipal ownership. If the workshops were supervised by a State Department and backed by the financial power of the state, they would be able to pay their employees 'a real living wage'.[92] The term would later become 'minimum living wage' and then the 'municipal minimum wage', but the concept remained the same: 'an amount which, despite variations in the money market will be capable of providing for all the prime necessity of existence, such as proper food, clothing, decent housing accommodation', with enough money to spare to provide for the worker's retirement.[93]

This demand provided a focal point for the political mobilisation of workshop employees. To give them an incentive to actually join the League, the organisation also catered for the more immediate needs of its members and fulfilled some of the traditional functions of trade unions and mutual aid societies.[94] In fact, until the First World War the League's Annual Reports focused predominantly on the organisation's ability to provide relief for members in distress without submitting them 'to the humiliation of the inquisitorial methods usually adopted by the busy-bodies who take a hand in managing the affairs of some of the societies for helping the blind'.[95] Industrial questions were hardly mentioned before the First World War. Only in 1915 did the League's Rules begin to list 'regulating the relationship between workers and employers' as the organisation's primary aim and even then it was argued that 'organising the blind with a view of obtaining direct State Aid for the blind' was a way of achieving this objective.[96]

The League also retained a focus on those who were not employed or employable. In addition to the creation of national and municipal workshops it also demanded 'the establishment of Technical Schools for the capable blind who can be made industrially self-supporting' as well as pensions 'for the incapable, aged, and infirm blind [...] adequate to keep them in a proper and human manner'.[97] Reacting to the

rising unemployment rate in the 1920s the goal of enabling 'the physically and mentally fit blind' to produce their own food was added in
1924.[98] By the end of the Second World War, however, this aim had
been dropped again.

Alongside its political, social and industrial agenda the League also
campaigned for the prevention of blindness. The first issue of the *Blind
Advocate* opened with an article on 'those sources of disease which go to
produce blindness' and the League's 1925 Manifesto likewise began with
a paragraph on 'Prevention of Blindness'.[99] The most important pre-
ventable cause of sight loss was *ophthalmia neonatorum*, a disease which
caused blindness in new-born children unless it was treated quickly.
Ben Purse in particular campaigned vigorously to educate people about
this disease and to make its registration compulsory in order to allow a
rapid medical response. After the president of the Local Government
Board authorised local authorities to make *ophthalmia neonatorum* a
notifiable disease in 1909, the League informed its members and supporters how their local council should be approached to make use of
this power.[100] Other campaigns targeted industrial accidents or poor
workplace conditions as causes of sight loss.[101]

Building a centralised structure

The League's diverse geographical roots in Scotland, London and Northern England as well as its multifaceted identity and broad agenda made
the creation of an effective organisational structure very difficult. For
many years the organisation experienced serious internal tensions until
a centralised structure was instituted in the 1930s.

At first the League was apparently governed by an executive meeting to which all branches were entitled to send delegates.[102] By summer
1898, however, it had become clear that a more formal structure was
necessary and two models were debated. Peter Miller, the Honorary
Secretary and Treasurer of the Hull branch, proposed the creation of a
National Governing Body. Miller suggested that one hundred members
of this body would be elected for life while the rest would be elected
annually for one year. Each branch would have at least one representative and be entitled to another for every fifty members. The Governing
Body's one hundred permanent members would choose the thirteen
members of the Executive Committee from their ranks and also elect
the branch secretaries and treasurers. Perhaps tellingly for the precarious economic position of many League members at this time, it was
stated explicitly that permanent members would not lose their seat on

the National Governing Body should they be forced to apply for parish relief or enter a workhouse.[103]

Ben Purse agreed that drastic changes in the League's constitution were necessary in order to provide 'a thoroughly legal basis' for its operations.[104] However, he argued that the proposed National Governing Body would be too large and he was also sharply critical of the idea that a privileged hundred should have life membership. 'There are many of us who could never consent to be nominated for such positions', Purse argued 'because we feel that our movement, from its very conception, is a keen uncompromising war against class privilege and class domination.'[105] Instead, Purse's proposal of a nine-man-strong 'Administrative Council' was adopted by a conference in Manchester in January 1899.[106]

The adoption and registration of the League's first national Code of Rules in 1899 finally created a relatively simple three-tier structure consisting of local branches, District Councils and an Executive Council. Each branch elected a Branch Committee which initially consisted of a Secretary, Chairman and three other branch members.[107] The Executive Council at the top consisted of a President, General Secretary and five other members. District Councils could be formed in areas with several branches to coordinate their work.[108] After the First World War, however, their creation had to be approved by the Executive Council.[109] All officers of the League were elected annually by ballot, including the members of the Executive Council. The first revised Rules stated that the Executive Council should meet at least once every quarter, but this was reduced to twice a year in 1905.[110] The 1905 Rules also added a Treasurer to both the Branch Committees and the Executive Council which reflected the organisation's ongoing expansion and rising income.[111] Another new feature was the provision that the Rules could only be revised every three years.[112] Until 1905 the League's annual elections had offered an opportunity to submit amendments of the Rules, and the new procedure added a degree of stability and continuity to the League's constitution.[113] From 1946 onwards, the Rules were even valid for five years.[114]

At first the League also held annual conferences to which branches with up to fifty members were allowed to send one delegate while larger branches were entitled to send more.[115] From 1905 onwards these conference were called at the discretion of the Executive Council, and in 1915 the League switched to a system of regular triennial conferences to be held at Whitsun.[116] In between Executive Council meetings business was conducted by a Management Committee.[117] The first Code of Rules was silent on the Management Committee's composition, but the 1905 Rules stated that it would consist 'of one member (approved by the Executive Council) from each branch in London'.[118] This provision probably goes a long way in explaining the dissatisfaction in the North with how the League was governed and a more representative system was gradually introduced. The Executive Council was expanded to seven members in 1915 and the United Kingdom divided into a corresponding number of areas in 1924. From then on each area elected one member of the Executive Council by ballot, thereby making it truly representative.[119] Elections were held annually until 1952, when the term of office was extended to three years.[120] From 1924 onwards the Executive Council had to meet at least four times a year. It was also allowed to call Special Meetings or correspond in writing about pressing issues in between regular meetings.[121] The Management Committee was abolished but recreated in a different form in March 1933 when the Executive set up an Emergency Committee to deal with pressing business.[122]

The Code of Rules placed the 'government of the League' into the hands of the Executive Council, but attempts to enforce its authority often triggered resistance, especially from branches in the North of England. In 1902 a Northern Federation was founded within the League which effectively claimed autonomy for the branches in the organisation's old heartland.[123] Twelve years later the League's Lancashire, Yorkshire and Cheshire branches met in Manchester to express their discontent over the way the League was governed. The delegates were critical that the League officials allegedly tended to regularly violate the organisation's Rules and argued that they only had 'discretionary power on points where the Rules are silent'.[124] Resolutions were adopted which demanded annual conferences to act as the League's 'supreme body' with the power to elect the Executive Council. Although a motion which threatened a breakaway group was rejected by the conference the delegates from the three counties agreed to meet at least annually and appointed a sub-committee to prepare the next conference.[125]

The conflict between the Northern England branches and the Executive Council continued after the First World War. The League's Manchester branch, for example, was dissolved by the Executive and reconstituted in 1920.[126] Such authoritarian action did breed resentment. In 1923 the Bradford branch demanded that the Executive Council should be dissolved and replaced 'by men of decision and democratic ideas'.[127] In the following year the North-Western District Council began its long conflict with the Executive which ultimately resulted in the District Council's de-facto expulsion from the League in December

1927.[128] By the late 1920s many branches in the North of England were openly hostile towards the League's Executive. Huddersfield, for example, accused the leaders of the League of corruption in 1929, while the Warrington and Bolton branches both labelled the Executive incompetent. Warrington even expressed the opinion that the Executive was 'unable to administer the affairs of the League' and threatened to ignore its decisions. In return the Executive decided unanimously to ignore any further correspondence from the two branches until they withdrew their accusations and threats.[129] A letter from the Birkenhead branch attacked the League's General Secretary in such strong terms that the Executive decided to seek legal advice in Spring 1930 and by the end of that year it had formed a subcommittee 'to examine and reply to the charges' made by different Northern England branches against the Executive and Central Office.[130] The 1931 Triennial Conference in Leeds only increased the rift within the League. J. Whittam, the Executive Council member for the North-Western District, unsuccessfully tried to remove the President and General Secretary from office after the conference and the Norwich and Edinburgh branches likewise demanded their resignation.[131] Bolton called for the entire Executive and all officials to step down in order to make room for people 'who will command the respect of the whole of the movement' while the South London branch only called for the General Secretary to be replaced.[132] Some of the delegates in Leeds formed a 'Special Committee' and requested to see the Executive after the conference, but the League's President successfully blocked this move which again triggered criticism from a number of branches.[133] Chaired by James Grierson, the Special Committee apparently turned to circulating in writing among the branches its criticism of the League's General Secretary and by 1932 Wolverhampton branch could speak with some justification of the 'warfare that is going on between Head Office and certain branches and councils'.[134] The conflict continued even after Grierson was elected President of the League in early 1933.[135]

The Northern England branches were not the only ones which had problems with the League's Executive Council, but the conflict between the two seemed to have been especially intense.[136] The fact that the Rules placed the 'government of the League' in the hands of the Executive was interpreted by the latter as a mandate to decide any point not specifically regulated by the Rules.[137] Backed up by a statement from the League's solicitors the Executive even claimed the power to reject resolutions passed by the League's own conferences.[138] The subordination of the conference under the Executive violated cherished traditions of British trade unionism which had its strongholds in Northern England

and triggered accusations of dictatorial behaviour. It was only in 1946 that the League's Rules were altered to state that the 'interpretation and development of League policy shall be invested in the Triennial Conference'.[139]

Up until then ballots were the main way through which the branches were able to influence the administration and policy of the League. Ballot papers were printed and sent out by, as well as returned to, the League's Central Office. However, Central Office clearly struggled with this task. The result of the 1932 election of the Executive Committee and other League officials had to be voided after many branches severely criticised the way the ballot had been conducted. The newly elected Executive at first refused to stand down but was eventually forced to hold a Round Table Conference in October 1932 and agree to new elections in 1933.[140] To avoid another disaster the new ballot was placed completely into the hands of the League's solicitors and the League would continue this expensive practice until 1936 when it tried to convince the TUC to conduct its elections.[141] When the TUC refused a firm of accountants was instructed instead.[142]

The ballot for the revision of the League's Rules in 1931 was an even greater disaster and triggered an internal conflict which forced the League to operate under its 1929 Rules until after the Second World War.[143] The problems also briefly left it without an Executive Council between March and June 1934.[144] Numerous ballots were held and legal advice was sought during the 1930s with the result that the search for a new Code of Rules which was acceptable to both its members and the Registrar of Friendly Societies became a significant financial burden for the League.

The internal conflict about democracy and transparency was accompanied by disputes over the control and distribution of the League's income. If anything, this fight was contested even harder. 'For nearly 12 years the League has been split into several sections threatening one an [sic] another with legal proceedings on more than one occasion', two blind trade unionists summarised the situation in October 1933. 'The origin of these dissentions is in the main strong disagreement as to the method to be adopted in allocating the subscriptions received from Trades Unions, Co-ops and kindred organizations [sic].'[145]

Initially the branches had to send all membership contributions to the Central Office at the start of each month. Funds required to keep the branch going had to be raised locally until 1924 when the branches were allowed to keep one-third of the membership contributions.[146] Central Office received additional income through legacies and the so-called 'Collectors' it employed. Because the latter received 75 per cent commission they attracted considerable criticism and were eventually replaced with full-time salaried Organisers who acted as fundraisers in their respective districts.[147] The money raised by the Organisers also went to the Central Office and requests by branches to receive a share of the funds collected in their respective districts were denied by the Executive.[148]

The 1920 Blind Persons Act further strengthened the Executive's control over the organisation's income. The start of the First World War in 1914 had led to the expansion and growing professionalisation of the charitable sector in Great Britain and charitable organisations began to pioneer a number of new fund-raising techniques. As people were asked to give for a wide range of causes, concern over mismanagement and fraud grew. To safeguard the reputation of the sector, a number of established charities began to press for government regulations which eventually led to the passing of the War Charities Act in 1916. The Act required charitable organisations to register with local authorities in order to be allowed to appeal to the public for funds. The granting of a registration certificate was subject to certain conditions, such as the existence of a governing body which met regularly or legitimate book-keeping.[149]

Section 3 of the Blind Persons Act of 1920 brought organisations trying to raise funds for blind people under the provisions of the War Charities Act of 1916 and made it mandatory for them to register as a charity first. As will be shown in Chapter 3, the League argued in vain that it was not a charity but a trade union organisation and therefore not affected by this provision. The *Barber v. Chudley* decision in December 1922 finally confirmed that – at least in the eyes of the law – being a trade union and a charity was not mutually exclusive and that the League therefore had to register in order to publicly appeal for funds. The League refused to comply and tried to minimise the danger of further prosecution and the substantial expenses this entailed by restricting all of its fundraising efforts to trade unions or kindred organisations of the labour movement.[150] The Executive appealed to all branches and District Councils 'to desist from collecting money' and entered into negotiations with the Ministry of Health which eventually accepted in 1924 that the League would not have to register as a charity as long as it restricted its fundraising efforts to labour movement organisations.[151] The agreement benefited the Executive which was the organisation's main contact point with the labour movement and increased its control over the League's finances. Before 1924 the Executive Council had already invited the League's Districts to sign up to a 'centralisation of finance scheme', but only Scotland had accepted this offer up to that point. Once the consequences of the High Court decision became clear, however, other Districts also petitioned the Executive to come under the centralisation scheme.[152]

In order to be accepted into the scheme District Councils and branches had to agree to forward all their income to the Executive which would then redistribute the funds.[153] When the North-Western District Council refused these terms a conflict erupted which illustrates the problems the branches in the North of England had with the Executive Council. The North-Western District Council applied to come under the centralisation scheme in January 1924 but failed to formally agree to its terms.[154] Despite its failure to do so, the District Council began to pressure the Executive to apply the scheme to the North-Western Area, but it quickly became clear that the District Council retained some of its income.[155] In response, the Executive instructed the Organiser for the North-Western District 'to make an earnest effort to obtain this money and forward it to the Central Office' as well as 'to explain and push the policy of the Executive Council' vis-à-vis the branches in his area.[156] In addition the Executive also tried to bypass the District Council by organising conferences for all branches in the North West interested in coming under the centralisation scheme.[157] The North-Western District Council continued to express its intention to opt into the scheme, but requested permission to keep its income from workshop levies which amounted to around £200 per year. This was rejected by the Executive as 'creating a dangerous precedent which might lead to future complications'.[158] The conflict continued to smoulder and in November 1927 the District Council finally issued an ultimatum. Unless the Executive would agree by the following month that the District Council could keep all income from workshop collections, private donations or other such sources, the latter would 'launch a new organisation for the area'.[159]

By that time the Scottish, North-Eastern, London and Midland District Councils had all accepted the centralisation scheme. The Executive was unwilling to grant the North-Western Council special conditions, especially since only 39 per cent of the members in the North West had supported the District Council's resolutions.[160] The Executive confirmed its previous decisions and announced that the North-Western District Council and the branches which supported it had broken away from the League.[161] As a result the Executive refused to accept contributions from the respective branches or pay benefits to their members. The League's General Secretary Henderson also informed the Trades Councils in the region of the North-Western District Council's secession, although the latter protested vehemently that it had not broken away and sought legal advice as well as the help of the TUC's General Council.[162] A three-hour meeting between the two parties in the office of the League's solicitors on 1 February 1928 did not settle the dispute.[163] The Executive set up a new District Council for the North West which duly applied for participation in the centralisation scheme 'as laid down by Central Office'.[164] The request was unanimously approved and the new District Council was quickly given the funds to which the North-Western area was entitled to under the scheme.[165]

The delegates of the League's National Conference in 1928 tried in vain to bring the Executive to meet with the old North-Western District Council. A conference resolution passed to this effect was rejected by the Executive with the argument that the old District Council first had to rescind its ultimatum from November 1927.[166] The suggestion of the Scottish District Council to set up an impartial tribunal to investigate the dispute and come to a settlement which would be binding for both parties was likewise rejected by the Executive as a violation of the Rules.[167] The old District Council carried on until the League's General Secretary informed the clerk of Lancashire County in April 1932 that only the Secretary of the new District Council was authorised to speak for the League. This made the split in the League public, weakened its authority in the North West and triggered further unrest within the organisation.[168] Nevertheless, a motion at the Executive meeting in June to recognise the old North-Western District Council 'in order to prevent the recurrence of such humiliating incidents' was successfully ruled out of order by the League's President.[169] Efforts to reunite the two District Councils were only resumed with the arrival of a new President in early 1933 and were finally brought to a successful conclusion in early 1934.[170]

The North-Western District Council was not the only critic of the centralisation scheme. Because it made these bodies completely financially dependent on grants from the Executive, some District Councils decided to take matters into their own hands. The Executive learned with some disapproval in 1929 that the North-Eastern District Council had introduced a scheme in which the Organiser for the District raised funds in cooperation with the local branches. When the Organiser was reminded that he worked for the Central Office and that the centralisation scheme was still in force the North-Eastern District decided to opt out of the scheme in early 1930.[171] The Scottish District Council was likewise concerned about its future role and passed a resolution calling 'on all branches to oppose strongly any attempt to undermine its authority whatever may occur in the general machinery of the League'.[172] Midland

District Council eventually decided to employ its own Organiser and offered to transfer to the Executive only ten per cent of the net profit raised by its new employee.[173] This prompted the Executive to take legal advice and remind all branches in June 1930 that District Councils or groups of branches were not allowed to raise funds. Those who ignored this ban would face disciplinary action.[174]

To calm the growing discontent the Executive Council had already agreed in June 1929 to develop a more acceptable scheme for the allocation of resources. The first proposal was rejected by a majority of branches in early 1930, but time was working for the Executive.[175] It dealt with requests for financial aid on a case-by-case basis and used this power to bring District Councils and branches in line. The North-Eastern District Council, for example, only received a grant in September 1930 after it had decided to come back under the centralisation scheme and end all of its fundraising efforts.[176] Proposals to give branches the power to raise funds were emphatically rejected by the Executive and branches or District Councils which violated the centralisation scheme were categorically denied financial assistance from the centre.[177] Bradford branch reacted by trying to form 'a Minority Movement of the branches in the West Riding area' in late 1931 with the purpose of collecting funds from local trade union organisations, but this move apparently had little success.[178]

In late October 1931 the Executive's Finance Committee finally came up with a new allocation scheme. After deducting all expenses of Central Office the Executive would receive 10 per cent of the League's net surplus income. Branches would divide 15 per cent equally among themselves, while 75 per cent of the League net surplus would be distributed to the branches on a membership basis. Legacies were not to be divided but retained by the Executive. District Councils would receive no income under this scheme. Branches who accepted the new allocation scheme were not to appeal for or retain donations from trade unions, Cooperative societies, Labour Parties or other labour movement organisations.[179] The scheme was submitted to a branch vote but the response was meagre. Although the League had eighty-eight branches in 1931 only thirty-nine voted on the new scheme. Twenty branches expressed support for it while nineteen voted against it. This was hardly a convincing victory but the Executive decided to press on. The new scheme was to come into operation at the start of 1932 and branches were given until mid-September 1932 to contract-in.[180] Once again the reaction was sluggish and the deadline had to be extended to get a significant number of branches to respond. Those who did declare their position overwhelmingly supported the new scheme. Of the sixty-seven branches which responded by December 1932, fifty-four accepted it while only thirteen opposed it.[181] With that the scheme was officially adopted, although some branches decided to remain outside of it in order to keep donations they received locally.[182]

The adoption of the new allocation scheme did not end the debate on how the League's financial situation could be improved or how the available funds should be distributed. Above all, the new scheme left District Councils financially dependent on their affiliated branches and the Executive. After repeated protests from various District Councils and branches the Executive provided emergency funding for the Councils in July 1934 and promised to review the matter.[183] This was done at a special Executive Council meeting in February 1935 and yet another allocation scheme was drafted in June. Any surplus funds raised by the Organisers would be allocated on a national basis with the Central Office receiving 10 per cent, the District Councils 50 per cent and the branches 40 per cent. Organisers were now explicitly encouraged to fully cooperate with District Councils and branches to raise as much money as possible.[184] The proposal was approved by a majority of branches in the summer of 1935 and came into effect in the following year. Participation in the scheme was voluntary, but only branches and District Councils which had opted in were entitled to receive any funds. By the end of 1935 branches in the North West area therefore protested with some justification against 'being compelled to accept the scheme'.[185] However, the Executive was now firmly in control of the League's finances.[186]

The system of rebates endured until 1991 when the League introduced a central accountancy system. Branch expenses were now covered by Central Office. Once again, not everyone was comfortable with the new system which strengthened the position of the Executive. 'This was somewhat difficult to get through but we did manage it', the League's former President Gareth Davies later acknowledged.[187] In the first year only twelve branches signed up for the new scheme. A further thirty branches opted in after changes were made in the following year, leaving only twelve branches to continue operating their own finances in 1993. The new system was more efficient and, for example, allowed Central Office to invest surplus funds to earn interest.[188] In the face of declining income and membership numbers such considerations were important to ensure the League's survival. The Executive acknowledged that many members found such reforms 'unpalatable to swallow' but insisted that they were necessary.[189] At the same time it also pointed out that the League's problems were not unique and that 'quite a number of smaller unions have had to take the unthought [*sic*] of step of merging with another union'.[190] On 8 February 2000, the League would become one of them when it joined forces with ISTC.

Conclusion

The League's drive towards centralisation mirrored a broader trend within the British trade union movement after the First World War. The end of the brief post-war economic boom in April 1920 also marked the end of the period of revolutionary militancy which had accompanied it. As trade union power began to wane and membership numbers started to fall, many trade unions tried to consolidate their positions by creating increasingly effective centralised structures.[191]

The League followed this trend in the 1920s partly to further emphasise its trade union identity. The organisation had been founded in the 1890s with the aim of becoming the voice of all blind people in Great Britain and Ireland. This mission was also expressed in the 'Song of the National League', its official anthem, which was sung at the end of national conferences.[192] Written in the year the League registered as a trade union the lyrics of the song make no reference to workers or trade unionism, but celebrate brotherly love, unity and success.[193] To achieve its aim of organising the entire blind community the League deliberately kept membership fees low. After all, a large number of blind people lived in poverty at that time and high fees would have prohibited them from joining the organisation. To finance its various activities the League therefore had to resort to raising additional funds and the ways in which it did this strongly resembled the fundraising techniques of the charitable organisations it so despised. The League publicly appealed for donations or subscriptions and also organised dances, bazaars, whist drives or other such activities. In the run-up to Christmas 1911 it even sold boxes of toys through the mail which had been given to the organisation by 'a number of generous Toy Manufacturers'.[194] However, most of the League's income before 1921 came from collections and the proceeds of the Annual Concert which was held each December. In 1905 the League derived over £391 from this source while donations from trade unions amounted to only twenty-seven shillings. Its total annual income for 1905 was slightly over £566, so it is not surprising that the General Secretary considered the Annual Concert of that year a 'phenomenal success'.[195] But this was just the beginning. In the following year the proceeds from the concert and collections alone amounted to over £546.[196] This rose to over £780 in 1907 and reached a new record high of over £1,977 in 1912.[197]

However, income from donations and the Annual Concert began to drop with the start of the First World War as the general public now favoured charitable causes connected to the war effort. By 1916 income from 'Concert, Collections and Donations' had fallen to £1,645 13*s.* 8½*d.* and the League now decided to approach the trade union movement for what it called 'systematic financial support'.[198] Until then only a handful of unions had donated money to the League and the sums involved had been, as already mentioned, comparatively small, but the League was aware that trade union support could be more dependable and regular than donations from the general public. The Amalgamated Society of Carpenters and Joiners had started in 1902 to ask its members 'for a levy of one penny per annum for the National League of the Blind', and it was such support that the League was now after.[199] At the Congress in September 1916 the League's newly appointed Financial Organiser R. D. Smith appealed to the TUC to support the League with a donation of 1*d.* 'per member per annum of the membership of the affiliated unions'. This, Smith argued, was better than giving money to the National Institute which had also approached the TUC for financial support in 1916. It would give the League

a sufficient sum of money, not to give away in charity, but to pay for the organisation of the blind into a decent Trade Union society, and thus help to bring into being a society which would be able adequately to voice the claims of the blind.[200]

Congress emphatically supported this call for self-representation over charity and by the end of 1916 the League had already received over £757 from 'Trade Union Levies and Grants'.[201] More importantly, a wide range of trade unions now donated funds to the League. Income from this source was still lower than the donations received from the general public, but the year nevertheless marked a crucial watershed in the League's history. With competition for public donations becoming fiercer because of the war effort, the League drifted closer to the trade union movement to secure its financial future. The League's subsequent annual balance sheets unfortunately fail to specify how much of its income came from other trade unions, but revenue from 'collections' (which included trade union grants) began to rise again from 1917 onwards. In 1920 the League collected over £4,281 and a special donors' booklet from that year shows that many trade unions gave generously. The largest single trade union donation came from the Amalgamated Society of Carpenters and Joiners which transferred £350.[202]

When the Blind Persons Act came into effect in 1921, however, the impact on the League's finances was dramatic. It now had to restrict its fundraising activities solely to other Labour Movement organisations and income from collections dropped by nearly 60 per cent in 1921 compared to the year before.[203] Despite growing financial support from TUC affiliated organisations since 1916, the general public had still been the largest donor. Nevertheless, the League was unwilling to register as a charity in order to be allowed to resume its normal fundraising activities. Fewer resources and the lingering threat of further litigation were the spark behind the Executive's attempt to gain greater control over the League's finances. The financial dependence on trade union donations also provided a strong incentive for the League to stress this side of its identity. As will be shown in Chapter 3, the League vigorously defended its position as the sole trade union for blind people after 1920, even though the Executive finally decided in the early 1930s to register as a charity. It was not a coincidence that it simultaneously decided to commission the first official history of the League which emphasised the organisation's historical connection with the trade union movement. Registration as a charity only strengthened the trend towards centralisation. From now on all branches were required by law to submit annual balance sheets to the Central Office and all public fundraising efforts had to be pre-approved by the Executive in writing. The latter also had to accept full responsibility for branch and District Council compliance with the law, which provided an additional incentive to keep a close eye on their activities.[204]

Once the centralisation of finances started in 1924 it also affected other areas. As already mentioned, an 'Information Bureau' was created in the League's Central Office in the following year. Headed by the President it had the task of providing up-to-date data on the situation of blind people in Britain for the League's political campaigns.[205] Based on its privileged access to information, in the second half of the 1920s the Executive successfully established the right to preview – and if necessary alter – all pamphlets and placards produced by branches and District Councils and in July 1933 an up-to-date central register of the names and addresses of all League members commenced in Central Office.[206] By the mid-1930s the League had changed from a federation of branches into a centralised organisation. The Blind Persons Act of 1920 had been a major catalyst in this process and it is this landmark legislation to which this book will turn in the following chapter.

Case Study A: Ben Purse

Figure 1.1 'Ben Purse'. Photograph of Ben Purse, reprinted in the National League of the Blind and Disabled's *Golden Jubilee Brochure* © National League of the Blind and Disabled

Leadership is a crucial element in the success or failure of social movements. Small organisations such as the National League of the Blind with limited tangible resources depend on the energy, expertise and standing of dedicated individuals to survive and flourish. On the other hand, charismatic figures can become a problem if their leadership is challenged and they decide to withdraw. This problematic twofold nature of leadership is amply illustrated by the case of Benjamin ('Ben') Ormond Purse.

In the words of the organisation's *Golden Jubilee Brochure*, Purse was the 'Principle Architect of the National League of the Blind'.[207] The son of a general labourer, Purse was born in Salford on 29 August 1874. His eyesight started to deteriorate while he was still a child and he was eventually sent to Henshaw's Institution for the Blind in Manchester at the age of thirteen.[208] Later on he attended lectures at the Bristol Literary and Philosophical Society where he met and developed a life-long friendship with Ernest Bevin.[209] A trained and certified piano tuner, he eventually set up a struggling business in Manchester. By his own account he first became interested in the social and industrial conditions of blind people in 1893, the year the Elementary Education (Blind and Deaf Children) Act was passed. The National League of the Blind was launched in the same year and Purse was one of a 'few enthusiasts' who later helped to save the branches in the north of England from collapsing by uniting them under an Executive Council in November 1897.[210] He was elected General Secretary of that Council and held the post for the next two years. Using his own funds Purse started the *Blind Advocate* in September 1898 as a monthly journal and edited it for a year.

In March 1899 Purse ran for election to the Board of Guardians in Broughton near Manchester but finished last.[211] Two years later he became the League's National Organiser, a paid full-time position, which he held until 1916. During this period Purse participated in a number of activities and campaigns. He gave speeches and lectures, attended an international conference of blind welfare workers, lobbied municipal authorities for travel concessions, gave witness before the Royal Commission on the Poor Laws and Relief of Distress, successfully campaigned for the compulsory notification of *ophthalmia neonatorum* and served on the government's Advisory Committee on the Welfare of the Blind for England and Wales.[212] By 1914 he was praised in the House of Commons as 'a blind man who has done more than any other single person for the benefit of the blind'.[213]

Between 1905 and 1916 and again from 1918 to 1920, Purse was also the League's President. Despite the League's pronounced hostility towards the voluntary sector he accepted an invitation to join the National Employment Committee for the Blind during that period.

Founded in 1905 to promote blind workshops and their products, the Committee consisted 'of the leading officials of the most important institution [for blind people] in the Country'.[214] In 1916 Purse resigned as the League's National Organiser and accepted an invitation by Sir Arthur Pearson to join the staff of the National Institute for the Blind.[215] Both men had served together on the Hayes Fisher Committee since May 1914 and therefore knew each other well.[216] Although partly motivated by the higher salary the Institute was able to pay him, the move also signalled Purse's growing disenchantment with the tactics and aims of the trade union he had helped to build.[217] Shortly after joining the National Institute, Purse wrote a letter to the League offering it a regular annual grant of £500 from his new employer. In return the League was asked to refrain from soliciting donations from the trade union movement. The National Institute was planning to also approach the TUC for financial support and Purse argued that 'it would seriously inconvenience the Trade Organisations to be troubled with two appeals on behalf of the Blind'.[218] The proposal significantly undermined Purse's standing within the League of which he was still President. He suffered a further defeat in the following year when his resolution that 'the League must agree to co-operate with any or all existing institutions and organisations that appeared to be desirous of securing improved social and economic conditions for the blind' was narrowly defeated at the League's annual conference in 1917.[219] Purse eventually resigned from his post as President of the League on 10 May 1920. He left the organisation at the end of the following year to create the National Union of the Professional and Industrial Blind of Great Britain and Ireland (NUPIB), which was renamed the National Association of Blind Workers (NABW) in March 1933.[220]

The schism had a profound impact on the League. As a result of his long service as National Organiser, Purse was extremely well connected and it 'was rare to find a blind person whom Purse did not know', as one observer put it later.[221] His 'encyclopaedic knowledge of industrial conditions and insatiable interest in economics and statistics' made him an effective advocate of all blind people in employment and very difficult to replace.[222] Even worse, Purse now turned his considerable talents against the League which he thought had 'fallen into the hands of extremists and irreconcilables who are determined, apparently, to exact everything from the state and the municipalities and to require nothing from their members in the shape of concrete service to the community'.[223] Purse had also been the League's living archive and much of what is known about the organisation's early years is based on information he provided.[224]

Purse had a distinguished career at the National Institute for the Blind. After serving as director of the After-Care Department (later renamed Personal Services Department) for four years he superintended the administration of relief, training and general employment until 1943 when he became head of the Institute's welfare services.[225] In 1942 Purse also became the first blind person to be elected a vice-president of Henshaw's Institution. A serious illness forced him to resign his position as Honorary Secretary of the NABW and editor of its journal, *Tribune*, in the same year and he also gave up his seat on the Government's Advisory Committee on the Care and Supervision of the Blind.[226] When he retired from the National Institute for the Blind in 1944, its chairman Sir Beachcroft Towse VC presented him with a gift of £500 subscribed by blind workers throughout Britain. He was also awarded an OBE in recognition of his services for blind people.[227]

Despite his retirement and ill health Purse accompanied the Institute's deputation to the Minister of National Insurance as a 'Welfare Advisor' in November 1947. With a deputation from the League also present, the Institute's Secretary General used the occasion to pay tribute to 'all the good work done by Mr. Ben Purse' under the two Blind Persons Acts.[228] Although the minutes note that the 'meeting was pleased to approve this tribute', it must have cost the League's leadership some effort to remain silent in this situation. They never forgave Purse for breaking with the organisation and its principles. A suggestion to invite Purse to the League's Golden Jubilee celebration in 1949 was voted down by the organisation's National Executive and the *Blind Advocate* reminded its readers that Purse had 'tried to split the League in 1921' and actively worked against it afterwards.[229]

Purse held an MA degree and authored and edited a number of pamphlets, articles and books, including a volume of his own poems.[230] He was a keen cricket player in his youth and served as secretary, treasurer and eventually chairman of the old Henshaw's Cricket Club at various times.[231] He survived his wife, whom he had married in 1899, and two children and died at Wembdon, Bridgwater, on 31 March 1950.[232] A memorial service for him at Holy Trinity Church, Marylebone, on 17 April 1950 was attended by the Secretary of State for Foreign Affairs as well as representatives from the Ministries of Health and Labour, the Labour Party and charitable organisations such as the National Institute for the Blind and the Royal Blind School at Edinburgh.[233] Purse's life mirrored the League's own difficult journey from radicalism to respectability and some of the beliefs which caused him to split from the League were later adapted by his old organisation. The fact that the League survived the departure of its best known leader is also worth noting. By the 1920s it had, like many other trade unions too, developed a bureaucratic structure which made it less dependent on charismatic individuals like Purse and the knowledge and contacts he had accumulated.

2
'Justice not Charity': Framing the Message

'We are living in a period in which it would seem that every class in the community is seeking, by combined action, to press upon the nation a recognition of the claims for which they stand,' the President of the National League of the Blind wrote in 1908.[1] In order to successfully compete with these other causes and bring Parliament to pass a bill which provided direct state aid for blind people outside of the framework of charity, the League had to frame its demands in a way which resonated with the British public.[2] That it would be able to do so was by no means assured. There can be no question that the plight of blind people attracted considerable public sympathy and that they were widely regarded as 'deserving poor'. However, this sympathy was expressed in the form of charity. Voluntary institutions for the visually impaired were well established by the early twentieth century and usually highly regarded. The League was determined to change that and to convince the public that the state needed to take sole responsibility for the welfare of blind people in Great Britain.

'Justice' became the keyword in the League's campaign. Direct state aid for blind people was not portrayed as a paternalistic favour for a disadvantaged group. Rather than degrading its recipients, the League argued, direct state aid would allow blind people to become free, independent and useful members of society. As a sighted associate and committee member of the Warrington branch put it, the League fought for 'justice and liberty. That liberty which economic conditions determine, and that justice which is supposed to be the birth-right of the British!'[3] It was not their disability but society which prevented blind people from living productive lives and only the state was able to change that through legislation. 'Hampered as we are by the physical defect imposed by nature sometimes but much more frequently by the social

46

sins of the community', a member of the League explained in 1899, 'we are unable to fight the social and economic battle on an equal footing with our sighted fellow-workers.'[4] The organised blind therefore demanded 'legislation to provide fairly-remunerative work in the place of present charity, to secure for us a decent sustenance rather than the semi-starvation which is common to our great majority'.[5] Saving blind people from poverty was equivalent to granting them full participation in society. 'It is the material necessities of life we need', another member of the League asserted in 1920: 'The right of Citizenship, not pauperism and beggary, the right to live, and the right to work for that living.'[6] The League's vision was not to just replace the source of funding for the existing system, as Phillips has argued, but to achieve social citizenship for all blind people.[7] Entitlement to state-funded services and welfare measures signalled inclusion in society and participation on the basis of equality. Charity, in contrast, indicated marginalisation and the League continued to make this connection until the arrival of the comprehensive welfare state in the 1940s. *'The object of our policy'*, it wrote in a joint statement with the Labour Party in 1935, *'is to enable the blind to stand on their own feet, to be independent, to be citizens as their sighted colleagues are citizens and to get rid of the atmosphere of charity which is often so well-meaning and often so disastrous to self-respect.'*[8]

Any attempt by blind people to achieve this noble goal on their own was bound to fail, as the League frequently tried to illustrate through the stories of individuals. In 1909, for example, the *Blind Advocate* carried a story about W. P. Davies, the owner of a little dry goods store in Stoke Newington, London. Davies was described as a

> poor being deprived of God's greatest blessing, the gift of sight, cheerfully fighting the battle of life and ekeing [*sic*] out a mere existence. Lonely, without human consolation, and yet gloriously triumphant in his independent, but alas, futile effort to live a manly life. Surely such courage demands admiration. Surely it is a convincing proof, a living testimony, of the capability of the blind.[9]

The League was arguing that all that was needed for blind people to fulfil their potential, achieve equality and make a useful contribution to society was a helping hand from the state.

In an effort to gain broad support for its demands members of the League emphasised the permeability of the seemingly fixed border between sighted and blind people. Sighted people could become blind at any point in their lives. As Ben Purse stressed in his statement to the Royal Commission on the Poor Laws and Relief of Distress in 1906, 40 per cent of all blind people had lost their sight after their thirty-fifth birthday.[10] In a later pamphlet, the League became even more explicit. Playing on Rudyard Kipling's warning of hubris in the poem 'Recessional', 'Lest You Forget!' offered a stark warning to all sighted people that indifference to the plight of the blind community could come back to haunt them: 'The slightest accident, and often the simplest, will deprive people of their sight, yet how many view the problem of Blindness from the standpoint: "If I were Blind?" '[11] Blind people had done their part for society and justice now demanded reciprocity:

> Many have lost their sight in assisting to build up the wealth of the nation, blinded by accident. Many thousands have lost their sight in middle age, after giving of their best to the nation in wealth production. Why should they not be cared for? Why should they have to depend on alms?[12]

Charity was framed as the binary opposite of justice and 'Justice not Charity' eventually became the League's main slogan.[13] Voluntary organisations were portrayed as 'inefficient, unequal to the task, and uneconomic', accused of patronising blind people and of diverting too much money donated to help them into the pockets of paid charity officials.[14] Voluntary organisations provided only local solutions to what the League regarded as a national problem and were limited in their outlook as well as their financial abilities.[15] Because the voluntary sector could not offer enough workshop places, many blind people had to beg in the streets or rely on Poor Law support. Ben Purse argued in a speech in Birkenhead in August 1898 that

> If the state provided work for the blind, the people of the country would not be so heavily taxed, for at present they had to pay rates to keep the blind in the unions, and then they had to put their hands in their pockets in the street.[16]

The League's journal ran a regular column 'The Bitter Cry of the Blind!', a reference to the classic 1883 study of extreme poverty in London which inspired numerous similar inquiries in other British cities. In this column the editor of the *Blind Advocate* again and again contrasted the small number of blind people who had found paid employment in workshops or institutions with the large number of 'blind persons pauperised through the poverty resulting from affliction'.[17]

An unnamed delegate of the League who stated its case to the *Manchester Guardian* in August 1919 described the failures of the voluntary sector in very personal terms. The interviewee was portrayed by the newspaper as well informed and articulate. He was also depicted as a family man and caring father who refused to employ his eldest child as a guide because this would deprive it of playtime. Forced into basket making at a young age by a lack of opportunities, he claimed that he worked for thirteen consecutive hours each day at piece rates to make a meagre living and avoid falling onto the Poor Law.[18] The League argued tirelessly that only direct state aid in the form of national or municipal workshops which paid a living wage, the provision of industrial training or payment of pensions for those incapable of work could provide a lasting solution to such waste of human potential. This view was propagated in the League's own journal, books, pamphlets and leaflets, in public testimonies and through demonstrations and rallies. It would eventually culminate in the 1920 march to London which achieved an almost mythical status within the League and was credited for the passing of the Blind Persons Act in the same year.

Lobbying for legislative action

The League constructed its demand for direct state aid as a logical progression from the Elementary Education (Blind and Deaf Children) Act of 1893. Many leaders of voluntary organisations shared this sentiment and also pressured the government to assume greater financial responsibility for the employment of blind workers in a realistic assessment of their own limited financial possibilities.[19] Other groups and individuals, such as the Irish Nationalist MPs, Archbishop Walsh of Dublin and the London School Board were likewise sympathetic.[20] The 1893 Act had made the Local Education Authorities rather than the Poor Law Authorities responsible for the education of blind and deaf children and required them to develop special schools for that purpose or grant-aid schools in the voluntary sector.[21] In the eyes of the League, the precedent set by the Act had 'once and for all time, completely annihilated the so-called basic principle of non-interference, the cherished idol of the anti-progressive'.[22] A Blind Persons Act providing blind people with paid employment was portrayed as the logical next step. Ben Purse argued in 1899 that

The Government has already partly recognised its responsibilities in matters of education, but this is not nearly sufficient. We contend that, having given us a sound elementary education, it is also as just and much more necessary that the State should provide us with suitable employment, in order that the education we have received may be utilised and sustained for our own and the general good. This, then, is what we mean when we plead for Direct State Aid.[23]

The League's efforts were mainly channelled through its allies within the trade union and labour movement in Great Britain. Keir Hardie, the founder of the Independent Labour Party and first chairman of the Labour Representation Committee, presented a petition on behalf of the League to the House of Commons in May 1901 and the League's General Secretary William Banham also provided him with notes for his speech for this occasion.[24] Among other things, Banham stressed that state aid was only a 'matter of justice, since the organised community is responsible morally for the afflicted citizens it produces'. The majority of blind people were 'anxious for work' but were only offered the workhouse, although government departments as well as the armed forces had a demand for the goods blind people could produce. There was therefore an 'opportunity of making the blind valuable members of society instead of paupers'.[25] Society, according to Banham, produced disabled people and turned them into paupers instead of supporting their realistic ambition to become useful and productive citizens. The only way blind people were able to arouse public sympathy was by exhibiting their affliction in the street, although this was 'the worst possible torture' they could be subjected to.[26] Nevertheless, this was exactly what the League would repeatedly do in an effort to generate public support for its demands and raise funds for its campaign.[27]

Street processions and public rallies were a part of the League's protest repertoire almost since its inception. As early as February 1899 Ben Purse had informed the League's branches that arrangements were 'being made for the prosecution of a vigorous outdoor campaign during the coming summer months'.[28] Such events were regarded as an important way of attracting public interest and thereby also support for the League's demands. As Conservative MP Sir Henry Bemrose put it at a meeting in Derby in May 1899, 'if the public would only look into the subject of the destitute blind, their interest and sympathy would at once be kindled'.[29] Politicians like Bemrose, as well as other dignitaries, often attended League meetings and thereby helped to create publicity, but the League also knew of other ways of getting attention. On Easter Sunday 1899, for example, members of the Hull branch proceeded through the main streets of the city 'in a large wagonette, preceded by the Jubilee

Christian Concertina Band' before holding a public meeting, followed by a concert in the evening.[30] The demonstration was repeated in June the same year when the members of the League marched in procession from St George's Hall in Story Street to Wycliffe Church in Anlaby Road. The Christian Temperance Silver Band marched at the head of the procession and the ' "Hallelujah Chorus" and other selections were rendered en route'. An open-air mass meeting of working men was held in the evening.[31]

Once the League became affiliated to the TUC, trade unions began to provide more organised support. A parade to Trafalgar Square on 27 April 1902 was also attended by 'members of the Gasworkers, Navvies, Coalporters, General Labourers, London Carmen's Trade Union, the Phoenix Pioneers, [...] St Clements Danes Volunteers Society, Order of Oddfellows, and a host of others' and therefore attracted substantial press coverage.[32] Not all reports were positive, however. The *Daily Mail*, for example, portrayed the event as a tragicomic gathering of demoralised and emasculated beggars, 'a motley gathering of men wearing huge sashes, some in khaki, and others in grotesque garb, rattling the coppers in collection boxes' who were 'led by women and children' to Nelson's Column where they 'turned their sightless eyes to the sunshine, or stood in the attitude of hopeless dejection common to the poor blind'.[33] However, it was just the beginning and the League's organisers were still learning. Numerous other demonstrations followed, the most important of which took place on 11 July 1909 when three contingents of marchers converged on Trafalgar Square from different directions.[34] The event was organised by a joint committee of the League's London branches and huge emphasis was placed on an orderly appearance.[35] Once again the demonstration was 'loyally supported by all sections of Trade Unionists and liberal thought, while branches of the Socialist movement assisted to make a success of the meeting, each and all recognising a common duty to their fellow men and appealing for justice and fraternity'.[36]

The event again attracted substantial press coverage and the *Blind Advocate* proudly listed the titles of thirty newspapers which had covered it.[37] The demonstration had been called to support the Blind Aid Bill which William Charles Steadman, now MP for Central Finsbury, had introduced in the Commons on 7 May 1906, but the bill failed to make it onto the statute books.[38] It did not have the support of the voluntary sector and Purse now pressed the latter for a policy of cooperation with the League to achieve legislation which suited both parties. Purse was also a member of the National Employment Committee for the Blind, set up by representatives of the voluntary sector and he suggested this approach at a meeting of the Committee in July 1906. He also tried to win Keir Hardie's support for it, although Purse admitted to Hardie that it would be difficult 'to induce my own organisation to accept this course'.[39] This assessment proved to be correct as it took until late 1910 before the TUC's Parliamentary Committee was able to arrange the start of negotiations between the representatives of the charitable institutions and the National League of the Blind.[40]

Despite these talks the League introduced another Bill in the House of Commons on 30 March 1911, with the help of trade unionist and Labour MP Charles William Bowerman.[41] However, the League's hostility towards the voluntary agencies proved to be an insurmountable obstacle to its campaign and a deputation to the Home Secretary in February 1912 was told that it should first make its peace with the National Employment Committee, which was conducting its own campaign for new legislation.[42] A first step in this direction was taken in May when the TUC's Parliamentary Committee arranged a cross-party meeting of MPs at the League's request. At the suggestion of Ben Purse a special committee consisting of four Liberal, two Labour and two Conservative MPs was formed to help draft a Bill which would be acceptable to all sides. This was finally achieved in the following year and the League's members accepted the compromise Bill in a ballot in the summer of 1913.[43] Before the Bill was introduced the House of Commons passed a Resolution which declared that

> the present system of voluntary effort in aid of Blind People of this Country does not adequately meet their necessities and that the state should make provision whereby capable Blind People might be made industrially self-supporting and the incapable and infirm maintained in a proper and humane manner.[44]

The Bill itself was introduced in May 1914, withdrawn and re-introduced on 2 July 1914. By that time, however, the government had already set up a Committee 'to consider the whole question' before legislative action would be taken.[45]

Despite the protestation of Herbert Lewis in the Commons, creating a Committee did not expedite the legislative process.[46] Set up in May 1914 and chaired by Conservative MP Hayes Fisher, it consisted of Members of Parliament as well as representatives of various government departments, charitable organisations and Ben Purse as the representative of the National League of the Blind. When it finally issued its report in

August 1917, it emphasised the need for state action and recommended, among other things, the creation of a special government department to control and coordinate the work of charitable organisations, as well as an Advisory Committee of seven experts to aid its work. The report stated the urgent need for 3,000 new workshop places and made recommendations regarding the education as well as professional and industrial training of blind people. Further measures for the prevention of blindness were proposed and a recommendation made to give preference to blind institutions in certain government contracts. The Hayes Fisher Committee also offered a definition of blindness, recommended a complete census of blind people, the enfranchisement of those who were in receipt of Poor Law relief, an increase in pensions for blind individuals and an extension of the latter to all those who were 'incapable'.[47]

Many in the League were disappointed with the report and the prominent role it continued to assign to charitable organisations. Ben Purse also described the demands made by the Departmental Committee, of which he had been a member, as 'exceedingly modest' and criticised the Treasury's reaction that the implementation of the proposals would have to wait until peace had been declared.[48]

The League therefore resumed its campaign for a Blind Aid Bill once the First World War came to an end. Resolutions demanding legislation were passed at the Labour Party Conferences of 1918 and 1919. Trade unions forwarded resolutions drafted by the League to the government and the Trades Union Congress of 1919 also supported a Blind Aid Bill. A demonstration was held at Trafalgar Square in July 1918 and a national conference was held at Clerkenwell, London, at the end of July 1919. After the conference Ben Purse led a sizeable delegation to the House of Commons on 1 August. When the representatives of the League sent for their respective MPs, an impromptu meeting between the Members of Parliament and the delegation from the League was organised. Stephen Walsh, a trade union leader, former Parliamentary Secretary to the Local Government Board and first chairman of the Advisory Committee, took the chair. Walsh argued that much more government involvement was needed 'if they wanted to encourage the blind to become self-respecting citizens' and it was agreed to form a permanent committee to keep the issue on the agenda and exert pressure on the government.[49]

Mixing conventional lobbying with 'unconstitutional but intelligent action' a group of blind volunteers in the galleries disrupted a statement by the Pension Minister Laming Worthington-Evans in the chamber of the House of Commons while the meeting between the MPs and the delegation took place in a committee room.[50] The initial assumption was that the protestors were ex-servicemen as one of them shouted that he had lost his sight in the service of his country, although, as the *Manchester Guardian* commented, at least one 'blind interrupter in the Distinguished Strangers' Gallery was obviously of too mature an age to be a recently discharged soldier'.[51]

The League also organised a large demonstration in Hyde Park on 17 August 1919 which was supported by various trade unions, Cooperative and Friendly societies, socialist groups and the Federation of Discharged and Demobilised Soldiers and Sailors.[52] Similar demonstrations were held in numerous other cities and towns and resolutions were passed demanding 'such legislation as will secure to the blind increased educational facilities to the young, employment to the employable and the aged and infirm, pensions adequate to maintain them in a human manner'.[53] Responding to a question by the Liberal MP Arthur Murray the new Minister of Health Christopher Addison conceded in the Commons that he was 'aware of the activities of the National League of the Blind' and that he had received 'numerous resolutions'.[54]

Labour politicians also began again to introduce Private Member Bills in Parliament. Stephen Walsh presented a 'Blind (Education, Employment and Maintenance) Bill' in the Commons on 25 November 1919 which closely resembled the Bill introduced in July 1914.[55] When it failed to secure a second reading it was reintroduced by fellow trade union veteran Ben Tillett on 13 February 1920.[56] Although his biographer, Jonathan Schneer, has presented this as one of Tillett's few successes during a period in which he was handicapped by poor health, the controversial leader of the Dockers' Union had a largely formal role in the proceedings.[57] It is likely that he was asked to reintroduce the 'Blind (Education, Employment and Maintenance) Bill' because he was an otherwise underutilised member of Labour's 'Old Guard'. Even though the League later tried to link its history with the Dockers' Strike of 1889 it was only because of the Bill that Tillett became subsequently associated with the cause of blind welfare. People began to refer to it as 'Tillett's Bill' and, as Chapter 4 will show, he continued to support the League's initiatives in both Parliament and Congress afterwards. On his death in 1943 one trade union branch decided to honour his memory with a donation 'to a fund for the blind'.[58]

Tillett's Bill was debated in the House of Commons on 12 March 1920 and received virtually no opposition.[59] Like Walsh had already done the year before, many MPs stressed the desire of blind people to help themselves, that they were not paupers and expressed admiration for their spirit of independence. Tillett himself set the tone by proclaiming that 'the realm of the blind' was 'the kingdom of poverty'. However, he emphasised that he did not propose charity as a solution: 'This Bill is not a Bill to pauperise; it is a Bill to give efficiency, to provide machinery, to give technical instruction and to give great hope to the blind.'[60] Association with the victorious soldiers of the First World War was the ultimate way of confirming respectability and deservingness and one MP therefore expressed his desire 'to see the Victoria Cross awarded to some of those [blind men and women] who have so proudly fought against this hard fate', while also emphasising that the Bill did not attempt 'to do anything in the nature of charity'.[61] Even the Minister of Health supported the second reading of the Bill, but he also announced that the government would either reform it or introduce its own Bill on this subject.[62]

The decision for a march to London

It was probably this announcement which triggered the League's decision to organise a march to London in support of Tillett's Bill. The failure of Walsh's Bill in the House had been interpreted by the *Blind Advocate* within a wider framework of post-war betrayal and class conflict. The journal fumed in January 1920 that

> We have been promised a new world, we have been promised that this land would be made a fit place for heroes to live in, we have been promised a generous measure of State Aid for the Blind – but not to-day, some other time, next year, early in Spring, any time but the present time.

Although 'the ruling class seem to have concentrated their strength' the *Blind Advocate* found reasons to be optimistic:

> There is assuredly an awakening taking place among the workers, and as it grows, it is opening up a new vista, a new and a growing hope, a broader, a more comprehensive outlook, which is bound, in the very near future, to revolutionise Society.[63]

New tactics were needed to harness this awaking revolutionary power for the benefit of the blind community and John Orr, a delegate from Bolton, struck a chord when he suggested a march to London at conference of the League's North-West District Council in Blackburn in January 1920.[64]

The idea was not entirely new. The right to present petitions to the government was an ancient one and various marginalised groups had come to London to exercise it throughout the centuries. The unemployed of Leicester had set the template for the modern period with their march to London in 1905 and the National Union of Women's Suffrage Societies (NUWSS) added a new dimension in 1913 by organising a 'pilgrimage' from seventeen large cities to London. Starting in June the different contingents slowly converged on the capital holding meetings, distributing literature and collecting donations along the way until they met in Hyde Park on 26 July.[65] Unemployed ex-servicemen revived the tradition of marching after the First World War with a tramp from Manchester to London in September 1919.[66] Some of the delegates at the League's North-West District Council Conference in Blackburn pointed out that their march had produced very little effect, but the *Blind Advocate* insisted that a march of blind workers would be different. The perceived failure of the Manchester war veterans was blamed on a 'lack of numbers' and the fact that they had been 'leaning too much upon the slender reed of civic conventionality and respectability'. The League, in contrast, would not rely on civic dignitaries to help its marchers but on members of the labour movement in the towns along the way.[67] 'Comrades. 1920 is here', one of the radicals proclaimed on the pages of the *Blind Advocate*: 'The workers of the country are with us. We need seek no favours, cap in hand, from the old order of things.'[68]

Orr's plan was favourably considered and a committee was appointed to organise the march.[69] The final plan was similar to the 'pilgrimage' organised by the NUWSS in 1913 and had similar objectives. Three contingents of complete or partially sighted men from different cities in Britain and Ireland would converge on the capital holding mass meetings along the way and seeking a meeting with the Prime Minister after their arrival in London.[70] It is not clear whether the blind marchers were directly inspired by the suffragettes' 'pilgrimage', but the latter had received support from the trade union movement as well as the ILP in 1913. It is therefore very likely that at least some members of the League were aware of it when the 1920 march to London was discussed and prepared.

The 74 blind men of the North-Eastern contingent assembled in Leeds and consisted of marchers from that city as well as from Edinburgh, Glasgow, Paisley, Sunderland, South Shields, Newcastle, Bradford, York and other localities. The sixty-man-strong North-Western contingent started in Manchester, although the League's branch in this city refused to take part in the march and was dissolved by

Central Office as a result.[71] This contingent included men from Oldham, Warrington, Blackburn and other towns in Lancashire as well as from Ireland. The third contingent from the South West began in Newport (Monmouthshire) and numbered about 37 blind men from Plymouth, Bristol, Bath, Newport, Cardiff, Swansea, Rhondda and Pontypridd.[72]

Female members of the League were not allowed to participate in the march although women represented slightly over 11 per cent of the membership in 1920.[73] No explicit explanation for this decision was given, but the logistical problems of finding separate accommodation for them on the road as well as the marchers' self-perception as respectable workmen and the organisers' attempt to link them to the veterans of the First World War were probably the reasons.[74] Women were only allowed to see the marchers off, together with their children, a scene which might have triggered memories of the departing troops during the war.

The main purpose of the 1920 march was to gather public support for Tillett's Bill and to establish its provisions as the minimum requirements for the government's forthcoming Blind Persons Bill. By marching to London the organised blind workers hoped 'to put their case as plainly as possible before the people of the country' and exert pressure on the government.[75] The march was timed to reach the capital after Parliament's Easter recess when the government had promised to introduce its Bill.

On the road to London

Mass meetings preceded the departure of the contingents on Easter Monday, 5 April 1920. According to the *Leeds Mercury*, 'holiday makers [...] thronged the Leeds main streets' and frequently commented on the North-Eastern contingent assembling for the march. Although labelling the event a 'sad spectacle', the newspaper acknowledged that the blind marchers were very upbeat and attracted a 'large number of interested people'. After dining at a local restaurant, they walked 'whistling and singing' to Victoria Square opposite the city's Town Hall where a meeting was held. The crowd unanimously adopted a resolution which criticised the social and industrial conditions blind people were in and demanded that the government should implement Tillett's Bill to rectify these issues. The marchers were then marshalled into formation and gave three cheers. Shouting 'Are we downhearted? No!' and singing 'It's a long way to Tipperary', they went on their way to London, guided by sighted aides.[76]

If the League had hoped to gain instant support for its march the initial reaction of the press must have been disappointing. Both *The Times* and the *Leeds Mercury* called the contingent of marchers 'pathetic', although the latter acknowledged that the men themselves were 'far from sad'.[77] The *Manchester Guardian* was likewise not impressed:

> Despite their merriment it was one of the saddest sights which has been seen in the city [of Leeds], and the collecting-boxes which some of their sighted friends carried on the flanks of the procession were kept tinkling with donations from the holiday-makers whose hearts were touched.[78]

The Times painted an even more depressing picture of the departure from Manchester and was openly critical of the endeavour. The send-off in this city was preceded by a mass meeting in Stevenson Square which was attended by several hundred people. Among the speakers addressing the crowd was Ben Purse, the League's President.[79] According to *The Times* the marchers were then led by their women and children

> on the first stage of the melancholy journey, through the almost deserted streets of a city that is not only keeping a Bank Holiday but is unusually quietened by the strike of the tramwaymen. In physique, in equipment, in their preparation for the journey, most of all in their disabling blindness and in the inexperience of much walking resulting from their affliction, they seemed wholly unfit for the arduous march before them.[80]

Despite these initial negative overtones, many papers also presented the marchers in religious terms. They were frequently called 'pilgrims' and their undertaking was described as a 'pilgrimage'.[81] The National League had facilitated this religious association by starting its march on Easter Monday and a powerful claim to the title of 'pilgrims' was made by one of the marchers in Bedford on 19 April 1920. Reminding his comrades that this was the town where John Bunyan had written the *Pilgrim's Progress*, he proclaimed: 'And now, we are the pilgrims'. When the now united contingents marched past Bunyan's cottage the next day, the *Daily Herald* reported that many marchers broke ranks in order to touch its walls.[82] Indeed, marching with the people from the League became 'something in the nature of a revelation' for the *Daily Herald*'s reporter.[83]

Blind people were usually perceived as the recipients of help and charity, but this time the marchers endured hardship to help those who were even worse off. The blind marchers emphasised that they did not ask for themselves, as many of them had work, but for those who were unable to earn a living because of additional disabilities.[84] Suffering hardship for the sake of others is an essential Christian quality and the marchers were gradually transformed into heroes by most newspapers. The dominant story became one of triumph over adversity, 'of men of ardent spirits, which will enable them to triumph over physical defects; and if blindness is no hindrance to such an expedition there is little else that need be'.[85] The men became 'cheerful crusaders' and the newspaper-reading public learned about laughing, joking and singing blind men who faced the hardships of the march to London to become 'free from the necessity of appealing to charity in the streets'.[86] The fact that they felt compelled to march such a long way was proof of how serious the problems of the blind community were. 'But all these things are forgotten for the time, while they are on the march, breathing the good fresh air of the open country, and feeling the wind beating on their faces; for, after all, it is good to be alive, in England, now that April's there [sic].'[87]

These 'things' were by no means forgotten, for the hardships endured on the march were intended to underline the greater hardship suffered by many blind people on a daily basis. Those who questioned the wisdom of subjecting sightless men to such a punishing exercise were informed that 'whatever the hardships [of the march] the conditions were an improvement in those under which many of the blind had to live'.[88] According to one marcher, 'it was to the everlasting disgrace of the community that they were compelled to adopt such methods'.[89] In this way, the hardships of the march were successfully blamed on those who opposed the League's demand for direct state aid. A Councillor in Sheffield, for example, agreed that it was 'a disgrace to civilisation and Christianity that these men should have to parade themselves in the public streets to call attention to their great needs'.[90]

The march was still often described as a 'pitiable spectacle', but most newspapers also stressed that the participants, 'despite the hardships endured on the journey', were 'not only cheerful, but enthusiastic and determined'.[91] When a blind speaker at a meeting asked the chairman 'to give him the wink' if he spoke for too long, the joke was approvingly reported.[92] Before they reached London the blind marchers had become 'heroes of the first water' and 'brave men who were making this march in aid of the blind of England and Ireland'.[93] However, admiration was still mixed with pity. Observing the marchers at Sudbury near the end of their long journey, the London correspondent of the *Manchester Guardian* 'could not help feeling impressed' by their appearance. 'It was all so different from what one had expected.' Nevertheless, even this sympathetic observer found that there 'was, indeed, something pitiful' about the march and that its banner should be altered from 'Justice, not Charity' to 'Justice, not Pity'.[94]

Everywhere the marchers stopped open-air meetings were held, literature distributed and 'the usual resolutions' adopted.[95] Despite the initial announcement in the *Blind Advocate* that they would not rely on civil dignitaries, the marchers were given a welcome by the mayor and a civic reception in several towns and cities along the road.[96] However, it was usually the local Trades Council and Labour Party which organised the reception in conjunction with the Cooperative Societies. Food and cigarettes were provided and accommodation was often found in the private homes of sympathisers.[97] This arrangement made it unnecessary for the men to carry much baggage with them.[98] When the North-Western contingent's arrival at Macclesfield was delayed because the marchers had taken a detour to enjoy the hospitality of a sympathetic farmer, the Macclesfield Trades Council despatched several cars to Prestbury to pick them up and give them a lift to the borough boundary. From there the marchers walked to the market square, headed by a local band, where they held a public meeting and adopted a resolution, followed by a hot supper provided by the Cooperative Society in the Trades Hall.[99] This pattern was repeated at Congleton, their next stop, where they were also received by a band, as well as at many other locations.[100]

In financial terms the march quickly proved to be a success. The marchers had their own collection boxes and sympathisers also often solicited donations on their behalf.[101] Street collections taken in different towns sometimes produced spectacular results. At Stockport, for example, more than £65 was collected on the first day of the march. The next day, more than £47 was raised at Macclesfield. On the same day, the North-Eastern contingent collected over £90 in Barnsley. Leicester proved to be especially generous. The local reception committee collected £103 before the marchers' arrival on 14 April. During the usual meeting in the market square, which was attended by over a thousand people, another £40 was collected. Further subscriptions to the same amount and additional collections in the factories made Leicester one of the most rewarding stops in financial terms. However, the record was probably set by Northampton where about £400 was collected, which was equivalent to over £14,000 in 2013 prices.[102]

Weather conditions were somewhat less favourable, as the men experienced daily showers and often high winds from the start.[103] Aided by the police, sighted sympathisers and a few partially sighted marchers they tramped along in files of four or five with their arms linked or holding on to light sticks or ropes to stay in formation.[104] A wide variety of songs were sung, among them 'The Red Flag' and 'The International', which underlined their membership in the Labour Movement. David Lawley, the leader of the North-Eastern contingent, also wrote a special song for the occasion. 'The March of the Blind' was sung to the rousing tune of 'England Arise', Edward Carpenter's popular socialist anthem.[105] The average daily distance covered was about 12 miles and the contingents picked up more marchers in the towns along the way.[106]

The most important contingent was that from Manchester, which included the President of the Blind Workers' Demonstration Committee, James Grierson and the organising secretary, George Chamberlain.[107] Their five banners proclaimed the slogans 'We demand justice, not charity'; 'Fellow workers, we want the right hand of comradeship'; 'We demand State aid direct and complete'; 'He who would be free must strike the blow' and 'Citizens, compel the Government to duty'.[108] The Manchester contingent reached Birmingham on 10 April where it joined up with the South-Western delegation from Newport and a fresh group of marchers from the Midlands. Four days later they merged with the North-Eastern contingent in Leicester which brought their total numbers up to about 250 men.[109]

The 'widespread interest manifested in the pilgrimage' provided the League with hitherto unprecedented opportunities to present its case to the public.[110] Again and again the marchers were able to reiterate their aims and demands on the pages of various newspapers. Time and again speakers stressed that less than 3,000 of the 35,000 blind people in the United Kingdom had been given employment by charitable institutions, while a further 2,000 had found work by themselves. More than 10,000 blind people depended on the Poor Law and about 7,000 more were begging in the streets. Legislation to deal with this problem was necessary and overdue, according to the League, and the state should provide the necessary financial means to implement the proposals of Tillett's Bill.[111]

Perhaps even more important was the visual impact the marchers had on their way to London. The emotive effect of seeing contingents of blind men passing through can hardly be overestimated before the arrival of television. 'The blind we have always had with us', one newspaper wrote, 'but it needed this mass presentation of the tragedy of the sightless to bring home to the hearts of many their difficulties and their needs.'[112] The *Yorkshire Evening Post* correspondent contended that the 'sight of a blind man in his helplessness is one to touch the heart of every sympathetic person' and reported that he saw 'many a woman moved to tears' watching the procession.[113] According to the *Northampton Mercury*, the 'eyes of not only women, but men spectators welled with tears of sympathy with the blind as they moved slowly and pitifully along. [...] Who could resist that sightless appeal?'[114] The marchers were, in the words of a Derby Councillor, 'human documents trying to prove that in the past the realm of the blind had always been closely allied with the realm of poverty'.[115]

The impact of the marchers' appearance was maximised by splitting the contingents into smaller groups upon arrival in larger towns. In Sheffield, for example, three separate groups were formed after the contingent had paraded through the streets past 'thousands of men, women and children'.[116] This gave more people a chance to get close to the speakers' platforms and hear the marchers and their supporters. Sometimes, smaller groups of marchers were even detailed to towns not directly located on the blind men's route to London. After arriving at Stoke-on-Trent, for example, the men were divided into two groups and led to Longton and Hanley respectively, to hold meetings there.[117] At Luton some of the marchers were sent to Dunstable for another open-air meeting. When they left Luton the main contingent marched on foot to Harpenden while another group was taken by bus to Hemel Hempstead and re-joined the main group in Watford on the next day.[118]

True to the League's message the blind marchers tried hard to distance themselves from pauperism and stressed again and again that they wanted 'simple justice and not charity'.[119] This message was emphasised in Lawley's 'The March of the Blind'. The song's lyrics portrayed the marchers as the 'Blind from mill and mine and shop and womb [...] In quest of Justice in the People's Name'.[120] Lawley himself was introduced at meetings as a former miner and frequently stressed, together with other speakers, that the aim of the blind was to become 'as self-supporting as possible'.[121] By emphasising their status as active workers the marchers demanded not only 'the same respect and treatment as the railwaymen or the miners', but also stressed that blindness could affect anyone.[122] Working people should display their solidarity with blind men and women because they might join their ranks in the future. Former servicemen were especially endangered according to Lawley. Linking blind people to the heroes of the First World War, Lawley claimed that 23,000 men had been discharged from the armed forces 'with impaired and defective eyesight' and that most of them 'were destined to become blind'.[123] Although the marchers were not former servicemen, some newspapers declared them to be 'blind ex-soldiers' or assumed that at least some of them had lost their sight during the war.[124] At other times the allusion was more subtle. The *Daily Herald*, for example, referred to the men as an 'army of the sightless' while a newspaper in Luton reported that part of the marchers' accommodation in this city 'resembled an Army baggage department'.[125] According to the *Yorkshire Weekly Post* the marchers imitated British soldiers 'in singing various national and sentimental ditties, and pantomime songs'.[126] The fact that socialist songs were at least as popular was not mentioned.

By the time the marchers approached London they had made a 'deep [...] impression on public opinion' and their confidence grew in response to the public support they experienced.[127] Prime Minister Lloyd George had already indicated before the start of the march that he could not receive a deputation of marchers immediately after their arrival in the capital as demanded by the League.[128] A meeting with Bonar Law, the Privy Seal, was offered instead, but rejected by the marchers. 'We are asking to meet the Prime Minister, and it is he whom we intend to approach, even though it involves a stay in London of 12 months', one of the leaders of the march declared, while an Irish marcher put it more bluntly: 'We want Bonar Law no more than we want the Poor Law.'[129] The marchers proclaimed that they would stay in London until Lloyd George returned from an international conference at San Remo, Italy and found time to see them.[130]

The united contingents reached Watford on 22 April 1920 where they were joined by a group of blind men from London. After a day of rest they marched on to Paddington and finally reached Trafalgar Square on 25 April 1920. It was, as the *Daily Herald* jubilantly put it, 'THE Day of the Blind; it was also a day of Labour.'[131] The blind marchers headed a large procession of London trade unionists who entered the square with their banners. Over 10,000 people listened to three platforms of speakers, amongst which were several members of Parliament as well as the Secretary of the London Labour Party, Herbert Morrison.[132] Ben Purse earned himself a quotation in the *Daily Herald* by opening his speech with: 'Ladies and gentlemen, policemen, and members of the Secret Service'.[133] In contrast to the appreciation expressed during the debate in the Commons on 12 March for the work of the voluntary agencies, the speakers denounced them in the sharpest terms.[134] Lawley, for example, accused them of exploiting the blind, labelled them 'parasitic' and asked the audience to 'wipe them out' by stopping their subscriptions.[135]

On the following day Minister of Health Christopher Addison pre-sented the government's 'Blind Persons Bill' in the Commons, the provisions of which are explained in greater detail below.[136] As the League had feared, it fell well short of what had been demanded in Tillett's Bill. On the morning of 30 April 1920, Prime Minister Lloyd George eventually received a deputation from the League at 10 Downing Street, led by the MPs William Graham and Stephen Walsh.[137] During the brief meeting, Purse and Lawley both stressed the strong support the blind marchers had received everywhere they went and repeated the League's demands. The effectiveness of permissive legislation was denied and the provisions of Tillett's Bill described as the minimum required by the blind community. Lawley again tried to link blind people to the vet-erans of the First World War by stressing that many had lost their sight while working 'during the distressing period of the war' and asserting that they had 'sacrificed' their sight in industry.[138]

The Prime Minister, in return, apologised for the fact that the post-war settlements had kept him from becoming acquainted with the exact details of the two Bills. However, he pointed out that the country's finan-cial resources were severely limited and that the League was not the only group making claims. Lloyd George defended the government's Bill as the most liberal in the world and promised to carefully consider the statements he had heard and to pass them on to his fellow ministers. In addition, he promised to help the marchers find funding for their rail journey back home and to intervene if participants of the march were victimised by their employers for having left work without permission. After emphasising that not only the eyes of the country, but also the eyes of the whole world were on the Prime Minister to see how he would react to the marchers' demands, the deputation withdrew.[139] 'It is clear that our fight is only just beginning', was the disappointed reaction of one of the members of the deputation afterwards. The League's Execu-tive Council passed a resolution expressing deep regret 'that Mr. Lloyd George was unable to make a more explicit statement' and stating its dissatisfaction with 'the attitude of the Government as expressed by the Prime Minister'.[140] In addition, it ordered the preparation and pub-lication of a new pamphlet 'showing the failure of the Government measure'.[141]

Conclusion

The government's Bill became law as the 'Blind Persons Act' on 10 September 1920.[142] It conferred a duty upon every County and County

Borough Council in England and Wales, as well as all County and certain Burgh Councils in Scotland, to promote the welfare of blind people residing in their area. However, it largely left it up to them how this would be done.[143] Local authorities were given permission to provide and maintain workshops, hostels, homes or other such places for blind people, or to give financial support to existing institutions run by charitable organisations. Local education authorities were required to provide technical education for blind people living in their area who were 'capable of receiving and being benefited by such education' and blind people now became eligible for old age pensions at the age of fifty. The Act also provided for the stricter control of charitable organisations for blind people by requiring them to register under the War Charities Act of 1916.[144] Because the Blind Persons Act gave local authorities broad discretion in how to care for blind men and women within their jurisdiction, it failed to end local disparities in the welfare, training and employment provided for them across the country.[145] The desire to provide equal conditions for all blind people in Britain had been one of the reasons why the League had pressed for the state to assume complete control and the organisation was therefore far from satisfied with the new legislation.

However, the initial disappointment quickly faded away and by 1940 the League's North-Western District Council hailed the Blind Persons Act as 'the Magna Carta of the Blind'.[146] By the end of that decade the League even argued that the Act was 'of more than national significance, and its influence in shaping international policy on the scope of social welfare is being increasingly felt as time goes on'.[147] Disability activists have more recently praised it 'not for its content, but because it set the precedent for the state to be actively involved in attempting to overcome the disadvantage faced by disabled people'.[148] In a similar fashion the march itself was described as an 'eminently successful' demonstration only sixteen years after its disappointing outcome.[149] Other members of the League praised it as 'the greatest and most far reaching propaganda effort which the blind in this Country have ever embarked upon' and a direct link between the 1920 march to the capital and the passing of the Blind Persons Bill was assumed.[150] Already in 1923 the League's Organiser for Scotland stated that 'Mr Lloyd George's Government, largely as a result of the great march to London, was compelled to pass this Bill.'[151] In a similar fashion, the League's *Handbook* argued in 1932 that the Blind Persons Act 'was brought about chiefly by the activities organised by the National League of the Blind' and that the march in 1920 created 'such public interest that the Government were compelled to recognise the demand of the organised blind'.[152] In 1997, Peter Carter, who was one of the first historians to write on the march claimed that it deserved 'full credit for firing the imagination of public and press alike and virtually forcing the hand of government' while Ó Catháin argued in 2006 that it 'proved to be of crucial importance in forcing the coalition administration of Lloyd George to concede the Blind Persons Act'.[153] As late as 2013 the League claimed on its official website that its 'successful and crucial campaign in 1920 [...] provided disabled people with the first legislation specifically for blind people'.[154]

There is little evidence to support this view, despite the fact that the march in 1920 was an embarrassment for the government. A Blind Aid Bill had been in the pipeline for a considerable time and enjoyed cross-party support in Parliament due to the fact that it was supported by both the voluntary sector and the National League.[155] Although the government had planned to drop the issue after the First World War, the constant agitation of the League and its allies made this impossible.[156] Hayes Fisher also took an active interest in seeing the recommendations of his Committee implemented and the fact that it was demanded by the voluntary sector meant that there was little opposition to it. On the contrary, the experience of the First World War had further increased the sensitivity to the plight and needs of disabled people.[157] It was the government's desire to counter Tillett's Bill with a less generous measure which led to the passing of the Blind Persons Act, not the 1920 march to London.[158] The purpose of the League's march had been to establish the provisions of Tillett's Bill as the minimum blind people could expect from the government's measure and it had clearly failed to achieve this aim.

That is not to say that the 1920 march to London had been in vain. The event had inspired the men who had been involved in it and given them the impression that the country had closed ranks with the blind community. In addition, it had created an elite group of activists within the organisations. Many of the marchers were celebrated after their return and all received a small silver badge saying 'March to London April 1920' to commemorate their participation.[159] 'Those who participated in the march to London have returned, and again settled down to their work', a member from Glasgow reported in 1920: 'They speak very highly of the kind treatment meted out to them on their journey, and although it does not seem as if much had been attained, yet it is an experience which they will never forget.'[160] In Paisley 'five heroes of the march were entertained to a substantial tea and social evening' and also received a gift of five shillings each from the working women of the community.[161] Others gave talks on their experience and a Braille account of the march was produced.[162] The Demonstration Committee which had organised the march to London also tried to maintain the momentum generated by the event. Instead of disbanding after the march it met again in Liverpool on 23 May 1920 and appointed a committee to conduct a national propaganda campaign.[163] However, the League's Executive saw this as a challenge to its authority and refused to recognise the body.[164]

What the march also achieved was to separate the League's demand for government support from the wider issue of charity and establish the notion that blind people were entitled to direct state aid as a right. As a speaker at a meeting in Luton told the marchers and supporters to the shouts of 'hear, hear' and applause, they 'were to have their rights, those rights which were theirs as their fellow-citizens'.[165] The slogan 'Justice not Charity' captured this view in a nutshell and the League remained committed to a 'Justice/Rights' frame. 'Justice, not Charity' once again became the official slogan when the League marched to London for a second time in 1936 and was also the title of a leaflet appealing for donations from other trade unions in the late 1950s.[166] The 1998 Special Edition of the *Advocate* still proclaimed 'Rights not charity' on its back cover and the League's website summarised its history with the words 'Striving for Social Justice' in 2012.[167]

Members of Parliament who discussed the various bills introduced in the House of Commons before the 1920 march to London clearly had a different perspective. They wanted to help blind people out of compassion as the debates in the House clearly show. Direct state aid paid on the basis of disability could easily be construed as charity in anything but name. Ben Purse, at least, eventually concluded after the march that it did not matter where the money came from, as will be discussed in the next chapter and others followed him down this path. In 1920, however, the League managed to convince the public that it did make a difference through which channels blind people would receive support. Ironically, the organised blind achieved this by presenting themselves and their disability to the public eye on the route to London and in the capital itself, an act which resembled the form of beggary the League wanted to see abolished once and for all, by creating an entitlement to direct state aid for all blind people. For all their radical rhetoric the blind marchers had to realise that their sensory impairment remained their most powerful weapon in the public relations battle with the government.

3
Mutually Exclusive Principles? Trade Unionism and Charity

As pointed out in Chapter 1 the League was not founded as a trade union but eventually chose to become one in 1899. Even after this its aims were never limited to regulating industrial relations and it took a while before it fully developed its identity as a trade union. The League's hostility towards charity, on the other hand, remained the one constant element in the organisation's long history and its defining characteristic. Becoming a trade union had also been a way for the League to express this hostility as trade union status and charity were deemed to be mutually exclusive. The Blind Persons Act of 1920, however, forced the members of the League to reconsider their dichotomous world view. As discussed, the Act made it mandatory for organisations dedicated to the welfare of blind people to formally register as a charity before publicly appealing for donations or subscriptions, or raising money in other ways. In addition, the Blind Persons Act also cut the League off from the decision-making process at Whitehall. The Government Advisory Committee on the Welfare of the Blind was reconstituted in April 1921 so that County and County Borough Councils, Boards of Guardians and charitable organisations could advise the Minister of Health on 'matters relating to the care and supervising of the Blind, including any questions that may be specifically referred to them by the Minister'.[1] While the first Advisory Committee had been a relatively small body of experts, the newly constituted Committee quickly developed into a large representative body which dealt with every aspect of blind welfare.[2] The League had been allowed to nominate candidates for the previous Advisory Committee, but it was no longer invited to do so in 1921 because it was not a registered charity.[3] In other words, the Blind Persons Act marginalised the League politically and threatened its financial survival by assuming that non-governmental work for blind people could only occur within the framework of charity. Registration as a charitable organisation provided an obvious solution to both problems, but potentially endangered the League's standing within the trade union movement. The problems which resulted from this dilemma are the topic of this chapter.

The National Union of the Professional and Industrial Blind of Great Britain and Ireland (NUPIB)

The dangers created by the Blind Persons Act of 1920 were not immediately apparent, especially since the Charity Commission informed the League that 'it did not come within the Act'.[4] Nevertheless, the League's Executive decided to ballot its members on whether the organisation should register as a charity. The result revealed a majority of 2,130 to 1,430 votes against registration in January 1921 and the Executive accepted the decision.[5] But the Blind Persons Act quickly triggered an internal debate on whether it would be best to use its provisions to secure concrete benefits for the blind community in Great Britain, or whether it was necessary to press for new and more comprehensive legislation. The debate would eventually cause Ben Purse and his supporters to leave the League in late 1921.

Purse later claimed that he was initially critical of 'what appeared to be the very meagre provisions set forth' in the 1920 Blind Persons Act.[6] However, it did not take him long to reconsider this position. Against the predominant view held within the League, Purse began to dispute the need for new legislation and argued that there was 'nothing of material importance that is required for the well-being of the blind community which cannot be secured under the present enactment'.[7] In addition, Purse also abandoned the League's central demand that the maintenance of blind people should be the exclusive responsibility of the state. He praised the 1920 Blind Persons Act for 'wisely' preserving the charitable organisations and creating a 'three-fold partnership, viz., the cooperation of the State, the County and County Borough Authorities, and the voluntary agencies' whose activities were 'mutually helpful' and 'complementary'.[8] From the League's point of view, this was heresy.

Purse later claimed that his change of heart was the result of a reluctant learning process while administering with 'much foreboding then and not a little suspicion' the provisions of the 1920 Blind Persons Act.[9] The short time span between the passing of the Act and his departure from the League in late 1921 makes this explanation unconvincing. As already pointed out, Purse had been involved with the voluntary sector for many years and accepted a paid position at the National Institute for the Blind in 1916. This made him a 'Charity Official', the League's favourite bogey man and he made it immediately clear where his loyalty lay. Only a month after joining the National Institute Purse gave his backing to a plan which would have committed the TUC to supporting voluntary over state aid and effectively marginalised the League within the trade union movement.

The President of the National Institute and founder of St Dunstan's, Sir Arthur Pearson, approached the Parliamentary Committee of the TUC in May 1916 with the suggestion to create a training and placement scheme for 200 newly-blinded workers per year. Modelled after St Dunstan's, which successfully provided similar services for those blinded in the First World War, the scheme was to be financed by a monthly levy of one penny per trade union member. Pearson acknowledged that the League demanded state aid for all blind people but argued 'that the Institute could not wait until the State thought fit to act'.[10] Purse was part of the deputation which presented the scheme to the TUC's Parliamentary Committee and when questioned on his relationship with the League the Committee was informed that Purse was 'no longer connected with the National League of the Blind'. In reality Purse had only resigned as the League's Organiser and was still the organisation's President.[11]

For well over a decade the TUC had adopted the League's resolutions demanding state aid for blind people. Embracing Pearson's plan would have meant a complete reversal of the TUC's policy, and the League's Executive worked hard to block it.[12] Even worse, Pearson and Purse envisioned the TUC's financial support for the National Institute's scheme to be exclusive. The League was asked to refrain from further financial appeals to other trade unions in exchange for a regular grant from the National Institute. Accepting this proposal would have been tantamount to accepting the National Institute's status as the leading organisation for blind people in Britain and the League refused to even reply to the offer.[13] Nevertheless, Purse tried again in 1917 to formally commit the League to a policy of cooperation with the voluntary sector. The result was four years of 'continual abuse' as he later put it.[14] When the League's Rules were up for revision, Purse's critics moved to make membership in the League incompatible with holding a position in a charitable organisation. Purse responded by rallying his supporters and leaving the League with around 285 other blind people.[15]

The hostility created by this split makes it difficult to separate fact from slander. For the members of the League, charity officials were 'like the employers etc. of the blind working class', i.e. the class enemy and the fact that their own President had switched sides was hard to stomach.[16] However, Purse argued that the League's aim of securing direct state aid ran counter to working-class values. A guaranteed income for all blind people would 'inevitably destroy our initiative and undermine self-reliance without which non-seeing people as a community must ultimately degenerate into paupers and beggars'.[17] Any form of voluntary payment in cash or kind was charity, according to Purse, regardless of who provided it. Instead of focusing exclusively on their perceived right to yet more support, blind people should also consider their obligations towards a society which was already subsidising their livelihood in order to allow them a dignified existence. That obligation was to take pride in one's work and aspire to become more proficient and productive.[18] Purse told his critics:

> If we could be induced to talk and act a little more like bona fide workers, and fret and fume just a little less because all the charity does not come our way, we would be far happier people, and our status as citizens would rise proportionally.[19]

The new trade union Purse founded after leaving the League tried to organise those who shared his position. The National Union of the Professional and Industrial Blind of Great Britain and Ireland (NUPIB) was registered in December 1921 and open to all blind or partially sighted people 'capable of engaging in useful professional or industrial avocations'.[20] The League, in contrast, accepted all 'blind or partially blind persons of either sex' as members with the exception of those holding 'official positions in charitable institutions for the blind'.[21] Sighted persons could become honorary members of NUPIB but were not eligible to hold office or vote on financial matters.[22] The cooperation with 'any or all existing Institutions, Societies and Agencies for the Blind' to improve the situation of the latter was one of the core principals of Purse's new trade union. Another was the adoption of 'every legitimate means for the purpose of avoiding disputes' between NUPIB and employers and no strike action was supported unless 'conciliation and arbitration' had been tried and failed.[23] At a time when most other trade unions still pursued a policy of militant confrontation, NUPIB explicitly pursued a policy of cooperation and negotiation in the workplace.

In particular, NUPIB targeted those individuals who felt little incentive to join the League. Men and women not employed in workshops for blind people, such as telephonists or shorthand typists, could and often did join the regular trade union of their sighted co-workers rather than the League. Indeed, Purse was able to claim with some justification that the League had 'no machinery whatever for dealing with the claim of professional men and women and is not in touch, in any marked degree, with the aspirations and desires of such'.[24] In addition, Purse also thought that many industrial workers were reluctant to join the League because of its affiliation with the Labour Party and his new organisation was therefore explicitly non-partisan.[25] A NUPIB organiser presented the latter as the main difference between his organisation and the League at a meeting in Aberdeen in October 1922. He was challenged by Charles Lothian and other members of the League who successfully prevented the creation of a new NUPIB branch in the city by appealing to the need for unity and by denouncing Purse as a paid employee of the voluntary sector.[26]

NUPIB's emphasis on industrial peace and its refusal to use its resources or industrial bargaining power – however small either of it was – for political purposes makes it a pioneer of non-political trade unionism during that era. The National Union of Seamen (NUS) under Joseph Havelock Wilson had already set an important precedent for such an organisation before the First World War. In contrast to the formerly militant NUS, however, NUPIB was founded from the beginning on the principles of cooperation and moderation. Non-political trade unionism would experience its heyday in the mining industry after the General Strike of 1926.[27] The most important of these supposedly non-political trade unions was the Nottinghamshire Miners' Industrial Union, or 'Spencer Union', after its founder and President, Labour MP George Spencer. It had the active support of Havelock Wilson as well as a number of employers and successfully managed to compete with TUC affiliated organisations for a number of years.[28] The Nottinghamshire Miners' Industrial Union eventually united with the Nottinghamshire Miners' Association in September 1937, largely on Spencer's terms, to form the Nottinghamshire and District Miners' Federated Union.[29]

NUPIB likewise tried to compete with the TUC affiliated National League of the Blind and its ambition to replace the latter was expressed in its official short title 'The National Union of the Blind'. An attempt to also make this its official name was, however, blocked by the Chief Registrar of Friendly Societies on the grounds that it would lead to confusion with the League.[30] In June 1924 NUPIB formally applied to the TUC for affiliation for the first time. Claiming incorrectly that the organisation had around 1,200 members, Purse stressed in his letter to the TUC that his organisation was 'in no way connected with the National

League of the blind [*sic*]' and different in character: 'This Union is not supported by funds derived from any other Trades Union Organisations [*sic*], but is entirely self-supporting from members contributions.'[31] In other words, its members were independent and respectable – two core values of the trade union movement. The League, in contrast, was financially dependent on other trade unions after its refusal to register as a charity under the 1920 Blind Persons Act.

When approached by the TUC's General Council for a comment, the League's Executive stressed its long connection with the trade union movement and argued that there was no need for a second trade union for blind people in Great Britain. John Edward Gregory, the League's General Secretary, emphasised that NUPIB was a breakaway organisation, that Purse had left due 'to personal differences with some of our members' and that he had recently taken the employers' side in a strike at Henshaw's Institution for the Blind in Manchester, Purse's alma mater. Gregory also pointed out that NUPIB had registered as a charity for blind people while the League had refused to do so and added that it 'appears to us to be a bit incongruous for any Trade Union to declare itself a charity or for the T.U. Congress to affiliate a Society which does so'. Finally, he pointed out that NUPIB was for cooperation with the voluntary agencies while the League fought for state and municipal aid for the blind.[32] In other words, NUPIB stood for disunity, blacklegging, hand-outs and compromise. These qualities were alien to the trade union movement and NUPIB's request for affiliation was rejected by the TUC's General Council.[33]

A seasoned trade unionist himself, Purse correctly identified the League's opposition as the main reason for the failed application. In his reply to the General Council he argued that his organisation should have had the chance to comment on the League's statement and once again presented financial independence as the most important hallmark of a genuine trade union:

> Fortunately we are able to conduct successfully our negotiations with the employers because we are recognised as a bona fide Trade Union entirely supported by men who have principles and who believe in paying for the maintenance of the principles they hold.[34]

Purse was informed that his letter would be considered by the committee which had dealt with the application and he interpreted this as a sign that the matter was not yet settled. After waiting a long time for a response he submitted another request for affiliation in February

1925. Despite stressing again that NUPIB was 'a bona fide trade union entirely composed of persons who are obtaining their livelihood either by the pursuit of an industrial occupation or professional calling', the application was once again refused.[35]

Undeterred but clearly exasperated, Purse launched another attempt in May 1926 after Walter Citrine had become the TUC's new General Secretary. This time he explicitly contrasted NUPIB's financial as well as political independence with the situation of the National League of the Blind. Purse conceded that NUPIB had been founded by former members of the League, but stressed that they wished 'to be allied with the Trade Union movement through Congress because of the objects and purposes for which we are organised'. The possibility of a merger with the League was categorically rejected.[36] Citrine consulted the League's head office on the request, but the latter reaffirmed its opposition to NUPIB's application and stressed that there is 'still room for only one organisation of the Blind in this country. This League is still out for unity.'[37] Sensing an opportunity, Citrine asked the League to discuss the possibility of amalgamation with NUPIB and reminded it that the TUC encouraged such mergers 'between Unions catering for similar classes of workers'.[38] The League's Executive Council shrewdly responded to this appeal for class unity by sending Citrine excerpts from the *Tribune*, NUPIB's official organ, which revealed Purse's own reluctance to reunite the two organisations. In addition, the articles also emphasised NUPIB's non-partisan character and willingness to cooperate with the voluntary sector.[39] The League pointed out that such a stance was incompatible with TUC policy as the League's opposition to the 'Voluntary System' had been 'constantly endorsed year after year by the T.U.C.'[40]

The rift, however, was about more than policies. The two organisations represented different visions of what trade unions should be about. The League, which was affiliated to the Labour Party as well as the TUC and militant in outlook, represented one alternative, NUPIB with its cooperative and non-partisan approach represented the other. The latter must have actually appealed more to Citrine who worked hard after the General Strike of 1926 to promote cooperation between trade unions and employers.[41] However, his efforts to reconcile these two visions of trade unionism remained futile. Both the League and NUPIB rejected the General Council's offer to chair a conference between the two organisations in order to discuss the possibility of amalgamation.[42] Purse, however, used the opportunity for a final desperate plea for recognition.[43] Sensing how important unity was for the General Council, he repeated a previous pledge that NUPIB would be loyal to the

TUC's constitution, 'never on any occasion' discuss its differences with the League either 'in Congress or before the public generally' and 'use the good offices of the Dispute Committee' should the need arise.[44]

It was, however, in vain. Being already on the inside, the League successfully managed to keep its rival at bay and prevent its affiliation to the TUC. Closely linked with this struggle was the League's campaign to have the Birmingham branch of NUPIB disaffiliated from the local Trades Council.[45] Birmingham was the only Trades Council to recognise a branch of NUPIB and the campaign to destroy this foothold was led by the League's Midland Organiser J. Perry, who repeatedly stressed that NUPIB was a registered charity while the League was a genuine trade union: 'We give no tea parties, but, spend our funds in promoting legislation for the blind, paying strike and victimisation allowances; and our Organisers are persistently pressing Charity Managers and Local Authorities for improved treatment of the Blind.'[46] Even worse, NUPIB was also denounced as an 'employers [*sic*] organisation' which had committed 'unpardonable crimes against the working class Blind'. In case their fellow trade unionists in Birmingham missed the significance of this statement, the League reminded them that the Miners Federation and other trade unions were 'confronted with a similar struggle at the present time'.[47] By linking the dispute with NUPIB with the fight against the Spencer Union, the League invested it with added significance for the wider trade union movement.

The relentless campaign showed results. In a letter to Citrine in July 1927, the Honorary Secretary of NUPIB's Birmingham branch complained about the effect the League's hostility had on his organisation, but nevertheless stressed his willingness to cooperate peacefully with it in the city. 'Where it is possible to work with them, we will do so, and where we differ we would prefer that it should be without anger on either side.'[48] Referring to the League's campaign against NUPIB he protested that 'no tangible evidence has been forthcoming that we are not Trade Unionists and not desirous of becoming affiliated to the Trade Union Congress, or that the Union has not done its best to uplift the Blind Workers in so far as is humanly possible'.[49] It was, in effect, an admission of defeat.

NUPIB continued to be active for some time. One of its members ran for Parliament on a Labour Party ticket in 1931 and its Brighton branch troubled the League to such a degree that it felt compelled to organise a campaign against it in the same year.[50] A proposal from the Secretary of the Swiss Cottage Old Pupils Association in 1932 to merge his organisation with NUPIB and the National League of the Blind was rejected by Purse and in March 1933 NUPIB changed its title to the National Association of Blind Workers (NABW).[51] After a last attempt to affiliate one of its branches with a Trades Council was blocked by the League in July 1945 the NABW eventually decided to 'get rid of the trade union label' and formally dissolved itself on 14 September 1946.[52] The remaining members of the NABW were offered the option to join a new organisation which developed out of the cooperation between Ben Purse and John Wilson at the National Institute for the Blind. Wilson, who later described Purse as his 'particular mentor', had joined the Institute as Assistant Secretary in June 1941 and later set up the 'Worcester Study Group' for blind academics and professionals. Founded in 1866, Worcester College was at that time still the only avenue for blind children with academic aspirations.[53] After a meeting between the Worcester Study Group and the NABW, the National Federation of the Blind was founded in 1946 which again registered as a charity.[54] The National Federation continued to attack the League along the lines outlined by Purse earlier and portrayed it as a radical, politically one-sided and dogmatic organisation which had little to give to professional and self-employed blind people.[55] Eventually, however, the hostility between the two organisations ebbed away. When the National Federation started to invite the League in the 1960s to send observers to its Annual Conference, or to cooperate 'on any resolution on which it would seem that joint action would be more effective', these approaches were still ignored or declined.[56] By the 1970s, however, both organisations began working together.

Becoming a charity

The fact that NUPIB had registered as a charity was a major weapon in the League's fight against it. 'As a charity Trade Union [...] oh, what shame it will bring to a name, honoured by struggles it won', a leading member of the League had rhymed in 1922.[57] How important this issue was for many trade unionists became evident when the League itself was eventually forced to register as a charity. After its members had initially rejected such a step in early 1921 the League's leadership had warned in a circular that 'the police in the various districts of our branches will become active when our decision becomes known to the authorities' and that breaking the law carried a heavy penalty.[58] In August 1922 two members of the League were indeed convicted in Tower Bridge Police Court for holding a street collection on behalf of the National League of the Blind. The proceedings against them had been initiated with the consent of the Charity Commission as the law required. Contrary to what it had stated in 1920 the Commission now expressed the view that the League was indeed an unregistered charity in violation of the Blind Persons Act and the War Charities Act. The King's Bench Division of the High Court of Justice agreed in *Barber v. Chudley* when it upheld the convictions of the two League members in December 1922. Speaking for the Court the Lord Chief Justice of England stated that the League could be both a trade union and a charity at the same time and declared that he could not imagine 'that any great mischief' was going to overtake the League as a result of this decision.[59] He was wrong.

Many blind people in Britain lived in poverty and the League had always kept membership fees low to enable everyone to join the organisation. As a result it depended on financial donations from outside, but this became a risky endeavour after the High Court's decision. Even collections in workshops for blind people were now deemed to be in breach of the law.[60] The *Barber v. Chudley* decision triggered requests from several branches to hold another ballot vote on the question of registration, but the League's Executive Council narrowly decided against it.[61] Instead, it was decided to restrict future fundraising appeals to other labour movement organisations in order to minimise the danger of further prosecution and the Ministry of Health accepted in 1924 that the League would be allowed to do that without registering as a charity.[62]

In 1932, however, two officials of the League once again found themselves in court for violating the Blind Persons and War Charities Acts. After the failure of Ramsay MacDonald's Labour administration in 1931 and the subsequent formation of a National Government dominated by the Conservative Party, the British state began a crackdown against real or perceived Communist organisations. The League got caught up in this development and the prosecution of the two members shows the degree of paranoia which had gripped the authorities in the early 1930s. It also illustrates the heavy-handed way in which the law was used to deal with supposed subversives at that time.

Edward Fuller, the secretary of the League's Haslingden branch in Lancashire, triggered the case in 1932 by unwisely providing the British Legion and the Conservative Club in his home town with leaflets advertising the League. The document listed the various ways in which the League had improved the lives of blind people through its activities and contained an appeal to join the organisation. Sighted people were informed that they could become honorary members for a minimum annual subscription of one shilling.[63] The Conservative Club interpreted this as an appeal for donations and passed the leaflets and accompanying letter on to the police who, after making 'discreet enquiries', quickly concluded that Fuller was a Communist.[64] James Kilgallen, the League's District Chairman, who was also mentioned in the leaflet, was found to be an unemployed man of 'Communistic tendencies' as well as an agitator. Kilgallen had once organised a strike of blind workers at the Accrington and District Institution for the Blind against the payment of non-union wages and was laid off as a result.[65] The nature of the League triggered some confusion as no one seemed to know anything about it, but the police eventually concluded that it was 'controlled entirely by the Communist Party' and collecting funds on its behalf.[66]

The Chief Constable of Lancashire contacted the Charity Commission in London which confirmed that the League was not registered with them. Although the Commission was far from convinced that a conviction could be secured, it nevertheless gave its consent to the prosecution of Fuller and Kilgallen.[67] The League's barrister argued that Fuller and Kilgallen had only tried to increase branch membership, but both were found guilty in Haslingden Magistrate Court in March 1933 and fined for soliciting subscriptions from the public.[68] The League's appeal was dismissed at Preston Quarter Sessions in the following month and the convictions upheld.[69]

In reaction to the decision the League sought legal advice and was informed that it would be liable to prosecution, including prison sentences, even if it continued to restrict its financial appeals to other trade unions, Cooperative Societies or other labour movement organisations.[70] Faced with the prospect of a dramatically reduced income stream the League's Executive contacted the branches in May 1933 and asked them to vote on the matter of registration as a charity. It was stressed that registration would not lead to a change in fundraising policy, while a decision against it would mean a trebling of membership contributions as well as drastically reduced services.[71] The result was a vote of 36 branches to 16 in favour of registration. The Executive quickly initiated the necessary steps and the League became a registered charity on 1 January 1934.[72]

Today's non-governmental organisations often have two or more legal entities, but many members of the League were distinctly uneasy about the organisation's new dual status in 1933.[73] The League's North-Eastern District Council sharply condemned the decision to register as a charity on 29 July 1933 and the extent of the discontent became fully apparent at a special National Conference in York three weeks later which had been called after the branch vote to debate the matter.[74]

A resolution moved by the Newcastle branch which condemned the branch vote as 'irregular and illegal' and ordered the Executive Committee 'to take no steps to carry out the results of that vote' until all members had a chance to consider the alternatives was ruled out of order by the Standing Orders Committee of the conference. The delegates refused to endorse this decision and the Newcastle resolution was narrowly carried with a vote of 32 to 31.[75] The Bradford branch, which had expressed the view that registration as a charity 'would mean suicide to the organisation' withdrew its equally critical resolution in response.[76] The conference was then adjourned to give the Executive a chance to meet with the rebels and listen to their suggestions. However, the delegates from Bradford and Newcastle demanded that the Executive Committee first withdrew the application for registration as a charity.[77] On the following day the League's President declared on behalf of the Executive that the conference had no authority to overturn the result of the branch vote, a somewhat dubious claim which was nevertheless accepted by the majority of delegates. Nevertheless, the dissenters forced a debate on the question of de-certification and the conference unanimously agreed that the League's Executive should consider this step.[78]

The League's General Secretary Alec Henderson later explained to Walter Citrine that they had decided to register as a charity in order to avoid the threat of further prosecution and that they only did so under protest. The decision would have no impact on the League's policies nor affect the scope of its activities. Expressing the strong desire to remain affiliated to the TUC, Henderson stressed that the League's members felt 'that their safeguard for the future is their continued affiliation to Congress'.[79] The General Council accepted this explanation with surprising ease and allowed the League to remain an affiliated association.[80] The rank-and-file trade unionists both inside as well as outside of the League were not so easily swayed.

The Amalgamated Union of British Blind (AUBB)

From October 1933 onwards the TUC's General Council started to receive a growing stream of enquires and complaints about the League's decision to register as a charity. The Leeds branch of the League simply enquired whether it was possible for the organisation to remain affiliated to the TUC under these circumstances.[81] The members of the League in Stockport decided to split from the organisation and formed the Stockport Blind Union.[82] In Hull, members of the local League branch were so enraged by what they considered 'a backward action' which removed them 'from the useful sphere of a Trade Union' that they formed the Amalgamated Union of British Blind. Faced with a deputation from this new trade union, the General Secretary of Hull and District Trades Council likewise wanted to know from Citrine whether the League would be allowed to remain affiliated with the TUC after registering as a charity.[83] The Trades Councils in Newcastle and York were also approached by newly formed AUBB branches in their cities and the latter unanimously passed a resolution asking the General Council to receive a deputation from this new union, or to at least accept a statement from it outlining the reasons why it wanted to affiliate with the TUC.[84] Further AUBB branches were also formed in Leicester and Middlesbrough.[85]

In contrast to NUPIB in the 1920s the AUBB enjoyed broad support, especially among Trades Councils in the North East of England.[86] Purse's organisation had been formed in 1921 on a policy of cooperation with the voluntary sector. The AUBB, in contrast, was created to avoid what some blind workers considered the stigma of belonging to a registered charity. As a result, many sighted trade unionists considered them worthy of support. This time, however, the TUC had a binding policy on breakaway organisations in order to combat what was clearly a growing phenomenon in the second half of the 1920s. A wave of supposedly non-political trade unions had been formed after the General Strike of 1926 and a second wave of trade unions hostile to the TUC had been formed under Communist leadership after that Party had switched to a policy of confrontation with the labour movement in 1928.[87] In response to this twin development the 1929 Congress in Belfast had 'emphatically' condemned 'the formation of breakaway unions under any circumstances' as well as pledged 'all possible assistance to any affiliated union affected by a breakaway of its members' and prohibited the General Council from affiliating any such organisation.[88]

In addition, the TUC's General Council was now trying to rein in the local Trades Councils and assert its authority over them. The creation of the Trades Council Joint Consultative Committee in 1924 and of an Annual Conference of Trades Councils in the following year had heralded the General Council's attempt to gain more control over these often unruly local bodies.[89] However, the General Council's Assistant Secretary Vincent Tewson had still argued in June 1927 that 'Trades Councils as Trades Councils are not affiliated to the British Trades Union Congress, and as a consequence the Trades Union Congress General Council has no disciplinary or executive powers over Trades Councils.'[90]

In fact, Citrine had given the Birmingham Trades Council free hand in solving the dispute between the branches of the League and NUPIB in the city.[91] In 1933, however, Citrine used the new crisis to forcefully assert the TUC's authority over the Trades Councils and promote his vision of the General Council as 'a general staff' of the trade union movement.[92]

Although it was not clear to the participants at that time, the General Council's conflict with the Trades Councils over the AUBB became a kind of dress rehearsal for the subsequent conflict over the so-called 'Black Circulars'. Issued in October 1934, TUC Circular 16 banned Trades Councils from admitting delegates who were associated with Communist or Fascist parties or their organisations and declared that those who disobeyed the ban would 'be removed from the list of Trades Councils recognised by Congress'.[93] As will be shown, Citrine and his staff had already used this threat successfully in the dispute over the AUBB and the two struggles should be seen in conjunction as they redefined the roles of Trades Councils within the wider trade union movement and strengthened the position of the TUC's General Council.

The General Council's decision to allow the League to remain affiliated with the TUC triggered opposition from several Trades Councils. The General Secretary of Hull Trades Council informed Citrine that his members were 'much concerned about the introduction of Charity into the accepted business of a Trade Union' and demanded to know whether this had set a precedent.[94] This was not a simple dispute over formalities but a question of principles. The blind workers who had formed the AUBB were described as 'very thorough Trade Unionists' and 'Concientious [*sic*] Objectors' who had Hull Trades Council's 'full support, in their objections, to the Charity clause'.[95] With noticeable disbelief, York and District Trades Council also asked for confirmation of the General Council's decision. Informing Citrine that the League's York branch had already dissolved itself and that its members had joined the AUBB, it argued that these men were 'the representatives of the Blind who can rightly claim to be affiliated to the T.U.C.' and that they deserved a chance to argue their case for recognition.[96] Newcastle and District Trades Council made the same request and reported, to the alarm of Citrine, that some Trades Councils in Yorkshire had already accepted requests from AUBB branches for affiliation.[97] Middlesbrough Trades and Labour Council conceded the importance of discouraging breakaways within the trade union movement but stated that its own members were sympathetic to the AUBB's desire to distance itself from charity.[98]

Citrine and his staff tried hard to explain why the League had to register as a charity. The General Council reminded the Trades Councils of the need for unity and that their organisations 'as bodies composed of representatives of affiliated unions' were also bound by 1929 Congress Resolution.[99] Their opponents were, however, unimpressed and argued that the League's decision to register as a charity was more than a meaningless formal act to protect itself from further litigation. The Trades Councils argued that the League had actually developed a charity mindset by relying too much on outside financial support. Such a mentality was unbecoming of a true trade union as well as unnecessary. 'The people who constitute the A.U.B.B.', their supporters stressed, were 'prepared to pay contributions of 6d. for men, 4d. for women, and 2d. for unemployed, in order to establish an organisation to look after the interests of its members.'[100] Such commitment was indicative of a true trade union mentality and the Secretary of Bradford Trades Council claimed that 'the employed and employable blind' were joining the new trade union 'whilst the unemployable blind and those more or less dependent on charity are sticking to the League'.[101]

Ben Purse had made a similar argument in the 1920s, but his NUPIB had only attracted the support of one Trades Council. The AUBB was much more successful, partly because the men behind it often had impeccable labour movement credentials. R. W. Hanlon, the AUBB's first President, for example, had been in the League for 25 years and a member of its Executive Committee for four. When the AUBB began to form, he stood as a Labour candidate endorsed by his local Trades Council in the municipal election in Newcastle.[102] F. Warburton, the sighted Honorary Secretary of the Leeds branch, had worked for over three decades in the labour movement and had held several positions, amongst them President of the Trades Council in Leeds.[103] Like Purse before them, the leaders of the AUBB argued that the wages and welfare payments in Great Britain were now high enough to allow their trade union to become self-supporting and that there was 'no real need for a Trade Union catering for the Blind to register as a Charity or make appeals to Trades Unions [*sic*]'.[104]

The Federation of Trades Councils in Yorkshire accepted this view and argued that 'the A.U.B.B. has remained true to the principles of Trade Unionism, whilst the National League of the Blind is content to rely upon charity and appeals to organisations like the Haslingden Conservative Club for its support'.[105] The AUBB received substantial backing in Yorkshire, which was also the most important stronghold of the Spencer Union, and the Federation supported Trades Councils which affiliated local AUBB branches with a resolution criticising both the National League and the TUC.[106]

Despite the General Council's best efforts the Trades Councils were not ready to withdraw their support from an organisation which they considered a more genuine trade union than the League. As the General Secretary of Newcastle and District Trades Council put it: 'The general view is that this is not a breakaway union, but that the National League of the Blind have ceased to be a recognised union by forsaken [*sic*] trade union principles and becoming dependent on charity.'[107] While Citrine wanted the Trades Councils to follow the General Council's lead, the Trades Councils believed that it should be the other way around. York and District Trades Council argued that since Trades Councils were allowed to accept branches of unaffiliated trade unions in the hope that they would later seek recognition by the TUC, it was 'logical to assume that the converse will hold true', i.e. that the TUC would affiliate the AUBB if enough Trades Councils had recognised the new union.[108]

This was not an attitude the TUC's General Council was willing to tolerate. For a while both Citrine and the League's Executive Committee struggled to get reliable information about the scale of the rebellion.[109] Once they came to the conclusion that it was limited to the North East and only included a few hundred former members and a handful of Trades Councils, the General Council moved to bring the rebels back into line.[110] The Trades Councils were given a final warning, but York and District Council in particular persisted in its demand that the AUBB should be given a chance to tell its side of the story.[111] While still attacking the League's decision to register as a charity, York began to shift the emphasis to the behaviour of the League's Executive Committee at the Special Conference and its decision to ignore the narrowly adopted Newcastle resolution.[112] This subtle change of focus helped the Trades Council to gather more support. Local branches of the Amalgamated Society of Woodworkers, the National Union of Railwaymen, the Railway Clerks' Association of Great Britain and Ireland as well as the Yorkshire Federated Trades Councils all passed resolutions condemning the League's decision to register as a charity in spite of the Newcastle resolution adopted at the Special Conference.[113] The York branch of the AUBB also produced a circular which asked trade unions to stop donating money to the League as such financial assistance was no longer necessary and not in 'the best interests of Trade Unionism and of the Blind themselves'.[114] Bradford and Hull likewise refused to disaffiliate the local branches of the AUBB. Hull even denied affiliation to the local branch of the League because it had registered as a charity, while Middlesbrough openly threatened to recognise the new trade union.[115]

On the initiative of the General Council the Trades Councils' Joint Consultative Committee responded by threatening to remove the rebels from the list of recognised Trades Councils.[116] At the same time the General Council announced that it was willing to help reconcile the differences between the AUBB and the League. This mixture of pressure and conciliation finally produced results. York, which was also threatened by expulsion from the Lancashire and Yorkshire Federation of Trade Unions, 'reluctantly' agreed to disaffiliate its AUBB branch, although it took them four months and further pressure from the General Council to actually carry out that promise.[117] Like York, Bradford also wanted to know more about how the General Council would try to bring the two organisations back together and therefore decided to defer the question of disaffiliation for three months.[118] The General Council reacted by suspending its recognition of Bradford Trades Council, a move which placed its 'existence in real jeopardy' as the Secretary of the TUC's Organisation Department helpfully pointed out to them. Since the non-recognition of breakaway unions was one of the 'fundamental principles of the British Trade Union Movement' he reaffirmed that no compromise on this issue was possible.[119] The Secretary of Bradford Trades Council tried to convince the societies affiliated with his organisation to support the AUBB when the issue would be discussed at the next Congress, but his Council nevertheless decided to disaffiliate the AUBB branch in July 1934.[120] Hull also had to give in under heavy pressure from the TUC but deferred the re-affiliation of the local branch of the League so that the latter eventually asked Citrine for help.[121] Middlesbrough was warned that it would be 'removed from the register of Trades Councils recognised by the Trades Union Congress' should it decide to affiliate a branch of the AUBB.[122]

The AUBB eventually had no choice but to reunite with the League, although the League's Executive initially rejected the General Council's offer to preside over amalgamation talks with the AUBB. However, the Executive was overruled by the League's Triennial Conference in September 1934 which ordered it to approach all other trades unions of blind people 'with the object of achieving the amalgamation of such bodies with the League'.[123] The General Council quickly organised talks between the two parties, which were presided over by William Kean, the chairman of the General Council and also attended by Assistant Secretary Vincent Tewson.[124] They managed to reach an agreement that the AUBB would reunite with the League and that a membership ballot organised and administered by the General Council would determine whether the reunited organisation would or would not remain registered as a charity.

The path to unity was not without difficulties. The League triggered a crisis when it initially insisted on registering its new Rules before the ballot could take place.[125] Because of the problems discussed in Chapter 1 the League was still operating under its Code of Rules from 1929 and many members were eager to see the new Rules registered. Under pressure from the TUC and after a very narrow branch vote the Executive finally decided to postpone the registration of the new Code of Rules in December 1935.[126] The AUBB also started to present additional demands to the League after the membership ballot in April 1935 had produced a clear majority for registration as a charity.[127] One request was to allow AUBB branches to retain their identity after reunification with the League, a point on which AUBB members in Hull were especially keen.[128] Tewson and Kean called yet another meeting and persuaded both sides to agree that the General Council would determine the terms of the fusion.[129] The Hull branch, however, categorically refused to merge with the local branch of the League and threatened to rather form a new trade union than lose its autonomy.[130] When Tewson pointed out that such an organisation would again be treated as a breakaway organisation, the branch secretary replied they had no need for the TUC's support because they had the public on their side: 'as far as blind persons are concerned they have the public support out of sympathy, a thing which a sighted union how-ever [sic] deserving never gets from the public'.[131]

The AUBB's Leeds branch also reconstituted itself as a separate branch of the League after the membership ballot. Its sighted secretary complained to Tewson that the League treated the AUBB members 'in the traditional spirit of conquered peoples' although the latter 'were the active Branch in Leeds and were also Numerically [sic] the strongest'.[132] The League's Executive Council refused to recognise the separate branch and once again called on the General Council to mediate.[133] The blind workers in Leeds eventually managed to reunite their branches without the help of the General Council, but Hull proved to be a more difficult case.[134] Since the two branches were unable to reach an agreement they charged Kean and Tewson with working out the terms for reunification at a joint meeting in February 1936.[135] The TUC's proposal was eventually accepted and the subsequent fusion of the two branches in Hull completed the reunification process.[136]

The reunification ballot also caused the long-forgotten Stockport Blind Union to contact the General Council and apply for affiliation to the TUC.[137] Both the League and the General Council had been apparently unaware of its existence which is an indication of how poorly-developed the bureaucracies of both organisations still were at the time. However, it, too, was quickly brought into line and organised a membership ballot on whether it should reunite with the League.[138] When the League's Scottish Organiser discovered the existence of an Ulster League of the Blind a few months later the Executive instructed him to enlist the help of the Belfast Trades Council to merge it with the League's branch in Northern Ireland.[139] Affiliation with the TUC clearly enhanced the League's ability to absorb rival trade union organisations. However, this ability had its limits. Following the instructions of the 1934 Triennial Conference the Executive had also approached Purse's trade union with the suggestion of merging the two organisations. The National Association of Blind Workers rejected the proposal as 'impracticable and inadvisable' although it 'expressed the hope that cordial relations would always exist between the two societies'.[140] The Irish National League of the Blind, which had also been approached, likewise declined the offer but expressed its willingness to cooperate with the British organisation at all times.[141] Since neither organisation was susceptible to pressure from the TUC or its organisations the League's Executive simply noted their responses. Negotiations with the Belfast and Northern Ireland Unemployed Blind Persons Movement in 1937 also proved difficult. The Unemployed Movement was apparently concerned that its specific interests would not get enough attention if it merged with the League and it was finally allowed to maintain its identity by converting itself into a separate Belfast branch of the League.[142]

Conclusion

The League's fight with NUPIB and the AUBB show how emotionally charged the issue of charity was for the trade union movement. In a history not short of internal conflicts, the disputes with these two organisations were clearly the most threatening for the League.[143] Both NUPIB and the AUBB had attractive messages. Many sighted trade unionists and even the TUC's General Council made it repeatedly clear that they had 'much sympathy' with their efforts to make their respective organisation self-supporting.[144] Ben Purse's desire to create an efficient as well as responsible trade union which used the established voluntary framework of British industry to maximise benefits for its members was also well in line with the policies pursued by Walter Citrine and other trade union leaders during the interwar period. Purse's NUPIB only accepted for membership blind people who were capable of performing work, while the League's ranks were also open to what contemporaries called the 'unemployable blind'. The leaders of the AUBB likewise claimed that the active and productive part of the blind community had joined their side while the rest had remained with the League. Nevertheless, the League managed to fend off its rivals mainly because it had been established first and was already firmly entrenched when the new organisations challenged its position.

The timing of these two crises indicates that they were not just about abstract ideals. NUPIB was founded shortly after Great Britain had slipped into economic recession and trade union power started to erode. As already pointed out in Chapter 1, many trade unions reacted to this development by trying to consolidate their positions and developing centralised bureaucracies in the 1920s and 1930s. This created a number of relatively well-paid and secure jobs within these administrations which were worth fighting over.[145] The creation of both NUPIB and the AUBB must be seen in this context.

Ben Purse's NUPIB did not adopt the League's radicalism. Instead, its cooperative approach to workplace relations promised more stability for the higher earners within the blind community. This group, to which Purse also belonged since accepting a job at the National Institute for the Blind in 1916, had the most to lose in a confrontation with employers. Purse's departure from the League was also an attempt to retain his eroding status as a trade union leader, which was under threat due to his decision to join the National Institute for the Blind. Although he had at one time been a paid officer of the League, Purse began to criticise his old organisation for maintaining an expensive payroll financed by trade union donations. He was especially critical of the League's four regional Organisers who each received an annual salary of £250 and whose 'entire business' he claimed was 'to appeal to Trade Unions for funds. We do not consider that this parasitical attitude should be countenanced by a responsible body of Trade Unionists.'[146]

The breakaway of the AUBB likewise took place in difficult economic times and grew out of tensions over how to administer and allocate the League's income. As already explained in the first chapter, a number of League branches were quite critical of the attempt to centralise the League's finances, especially since this process threatened to drastically reduce the power of the District Councils. The AUBB goal to become financially self-supporting and rely mainly on membership contributions would have shifted the balance of power in the organisation back to the grassroots. The fusion agreement between the AUBB and the League eventually came up with a compromise. The League remained a registered charity and therefore also retained its ability to appeal for donations and subscriptions. At the same time branches were empowered to raise their membership contributions to up to sixpence per week, thereby providing them with more funds to spend.[147] Nevertheless, the issue of finances continued to arise. A motion at the Executive Council meeting in December 1936 to deregister as a charity and become financially self-supporting was only narrowly defeated, for example, and no less than three resolutions submitted to the Triennial Conference in May 1937 demanded to jettison the new status.[148]

The TUC's General Council emerged as more powerful from this controversy. Not only did both the AUBB and the League allow the General Council to dictate the terms of reunification, but by insisting on the letter of the 1929 Belfast Resolution condemning breakaway unions, Citrine and his colleagues further strengthened their position as arbitrators of TUC policies. As Tewson lectured the recalcitrant Honorary Secretary of the AUBB's Hull branch, the General Council considered itself to be in a 'unique position' within the trade union movement and therefore able to cast a more balanced judgement than the activists on the ground.[149] The rebellious Trades Council highlighted in vain the paradox in the General Council's argument that those who had left the League because of the Executive's supposedly dictatorial behaviour should rejoin the organisation and strive to change it from within. In a similar fashion the General Council also ignored suggestions for how to work around the wording of the 1929 Belfast Resolution in order to give the AUBB at least a hearing.[150] Eventually the rebels had to concede that they were unable to exist without official recognition from the TUC and gave in.

The experience would be repeated again shortly afterwards over the question of cooperation with the Communists. Some of the Trades Councils resisting the so-called 'Black Circular' of October 1934 were the same which had fought the case of the AUBB and they suffered the same form of disciplinary action. Bradford was banned from sending a delegate to the Trades Council Annual Conference in May 1935 for refusing to implement Circular 16 and only gave in 'under protest' when it was once again threatened with being struck off the recognised list.[151] In Leeds, two union branches disaffiliated from the local Trades Council when it accepted the Circular, while Middlesbrough also formally accepted the Circular but failed to act upon it.[152] Despite such opposition the TUC was able to force its view on the Trades Councils and assume control over their activities and even membership in the process. This crucial redefinition of their role and position within the trade union movement started with the dispute over the AUBB's break away from the League. When it ended the Trades Councils were reduced to being nothing more than 'direct instruments of the policies of the national leaders of the movement', as Alan Clinton has put it.[153]

As this and the previous chapter have shown, the League's affiliation with the TUC did not just provide it with fundraising opportunities which were crucial for its survival. Membership in the trade union movement also provided it with mass support for demonstrations, access to the political establishment and protection against rival organisations. The League's affiliation with the Labour Party was, however, a much more mixed blessing, as the next chapter will demonstrate.

Case Study B: The *Blind Advocate* and the *Horizon*

Figure 3.1 'Blind Advocate Covers'. A selection of *Blind Advocate* cover pages © National League of the Blind and Disabled

Despite being a poor people's movement the National League of the Blind managed to publish two regular journals. Neither the ink journal the *Blind Advocate* nor the Braille journal *Horizon* was started by the League, but the organisation assumed control of them once they were established.

The *Blind Advocate* was launched as a monthly journal by Ben Purse who used a legacy of £60 left to him to finance the venture.[154] The first issue appeared on 1 September 1898 under Purse's editorship with the subtitle 'Organ of the National League for [*sic*] the Blind of Great Britain and Ireland'. Already in November ownership was transferred to the Northern section of the League which also assumed 'responsibility of all liabilities in connection with the same'.[155] These proved to be considerable. Sales figures were low and the *Blind Advocate* incurred a loss of £10 7*s*. 3½*d*. in the second quarter of 1899.[156] The twelfth issue did not appear and the journal ceased publication altogether after September 1899.[157] The *Blind Advocate* was re-launched in February 1901 in a new series and was now advertised as the 'Official Organ of the National League of the Blind of Great Britain and Ireland'. The motto 'Speak to the People that they go Forward' was added to the header shortly afterwards and the League's General Secretaries now served ex officio as the journal's editors.[158]

The organisation's leadership regularly stressed the importance of the *Blind Advocate* as a propaganda outlet, but the journal also tried to build a common identity between the League's members and impress upon them that they were part of a worldwide and active community. It regularly informed readers about protest activities, rallies and deputations as well as social outings, dances and other leisure activities in the various branches. A proposal was also considered to carry advertisements for marriage partners but it was not adopted.[159] Obituaries were a regular feature, as were news reports about the situation and activities of blind people in other countries or medical breakthroughs. The journal also helped to explain changes in the law and how they affected the League's members. In short, it tried to convey to its readers that they had agency and were in charge of their own fate. From time to time the *Blind Advocate* also featured opinion pieces, for example on the question of whether blind people should intermarry.

Having an official regular ink publication was undeniably useful but also a constant drain on the League's resources. Even in the first issue of the *Blind Advocate* the leaders of the Dublin branch attributed its publication to 'superhuman effort' and 'a small money prize' was offered to any blind person able to 'suggest the most practical method of obtaining an increased circulation'.[160] An 'Advocate and Finance Committee' was formed in May 1899 and the League's members and branch Secretaries were constantly urged to sell more copies.[161] Appearance, price, size and content of the paper varied over time as editors tried to make it more attractive. In 1899, for example, the *Blind Advocate* started to print serial stories and the price (and with it the size) of the publication was cut in half between 1901 and 1903.[162] Nevertheless, the *Blind Advocate* continued to make 'substantial losses'. In 1907, for example, it produced a deficit of £24, but the League's Executive kept arguing that the journal's propaganda value made it imperative to continue with its publication.[163]

The League's other journal also appeared on a monthly basis but was published in Braille. The *Horizon* was created in the summer of 1922 and the first issue appeared in August. In the beginning it was not officially connected to the League and while the League's Executive approved of the publication it refused to accept financial responsibility for it. Instead, the venture was run by the Horizon Publishing Association which was chaired by James A. Clydesdale. Charles G. Lothian, David B. Lawley and James Grierson were also among the Board of Directors, which meant that some of the League's leading figures were behind the project. The reasons for keeping a distance from the League seemed to have been financial. The *Horizon* was marketed as an educational endeavour and members of the League were urged to approach 'their respective Home Teaching Committees or Public Library Committees with a view to persuading them to subscribe' to it.[164] It was hoped that by not officially affiliating the new Braille journal to the League, even those hostile to the League might be persuaded to buy it.[165] Such hopes of financial success were, however, short-lived. In January 1924 the Horizon Publishing Association approached the League for financial support but was turned down.[166] However, two years later the League decided to buy four pages in each edition and it eventually also helped the paper with a grant of £15.[167] By 1928 the Horizon Publishing Association was making an annual loss of £75 (or 8*d*. per copy) and in June it offered to hand the magazine over to the League. A majority of the Executive opposed the offer in the light of the financial burden this would impose on the organisation and also rejected the suggestion to assume temporary responsibility for the magazine for a trial period of six months.[168] After the General Secretary had made enquiries into the cost of publishing the *Horizon*, however, the Executive reversed its decision at its next meeting in September 1928 and decided unanimously to make it the League's official Braille publication.[169] The circulation was reduced from 189 to 133 copies to cut the deficit as each copy cost more to produce than it brought in revenue. Donations to a specially set up *Horizon* fund more than covered the League's initial losses.[170] In the following years circulation figures seemed to have fluctuated between 100 and 150 copies per month.[171]

The fluctuation for the *Blind Advocate* was even higher. When Henderson became editor in 1927 just over 1,000 copies were printed each month. He managed to increase this to over 2,000 and some issues had a circulation of 4,000 copies. By 1933, however, sales figures were back to the level of 1927 and the financial situation of the *Blind Advocate* was desperate.[172] Responding to criticism from members the paper was reorganised in 1934. The League's organisers were ordered to provide monthly reports about activities in their respective area, a panel of contributors was created which volunteered to submit articles on a regular basis and a special 'correspondence column together with space for questions concerned with the work of the League and blind welfare in general' was introduced.[173]

The hope that these changes would make the journal more interesting as well as profitable was, however, not fulfilled. The League's Triennial Conference of 1943 noted 'with considerable dissatisfaction the present content of the League [*sic*] journals' and urged 'the Executive to take immediate action with a view of making them a more effective medium for depicting the work and policy of the movement'.[174] The paper itself acknowledged in March 1944 that there had been 'much criticism in recent years of the kind of news appearing in these columns' but pointed out that it depended on members for providing more interesting material.[175] The results of the Executive's deliberations were presented at the next Triennial Conference in 1946 but found little favour with the delegates. The conference even discussed a temporary halt to publication of the *Blind Advocate* and eventually referred the problem of the journals back to the Executive for further consideration. The League's branches were also requested to submit suggestions for how to improve the *Blind Advocate* and the *Horizon*.[176]

Financial problems made it necessary to double the price of the *Blind Advocate* to 2*d*. per copy at the start of 1948 and to switch from a monthly to a quarterly publication schedule.[177] In the same year the National League of the Blind of Ireland agreed to contribute £50 per year towards the publication cost of the *Horizon* on the condition that the Braille journal would also cover news from Ireland.[178] Although the *Horizon* was never designed to make a profit, the League eventually became unable to bear the high costs of producing a Braille journal on a monthly basis. By March 1963 the League made a loss of 1*s*. 4*d*. for every copy sold, while complimentary copies of the *Horizon* created a deficit of 2*s*. 4*d*. As a result the League switched to a bi-monthly schedule in January 1964 and also increased the sales price of the journal.[179] It was not to be enough. When administration costs for the sale of the two journals started to significantly exceed income from sales the League decided to stop charging its members for the *Blind Advocate* and made the *Horizon* free for anyone.[180]

In the early years an attempt was made to generate income through advertising. Ben Purse promoted his piano tuning business and Peter Miller, the Secretary and Treasurer of the Hull branch, his Wholesale and Retail Company. Other advertisements targeted blind or partially sighted people, such as the Hull Brothers who were Ophthalmic and Refractive Opticians, or the Blind Tea Agency. Companies who catered for a general market, such as Witchell's Food, Burgon's Tea or Merrills' Penny Custard Powder, as well as local shops like Somerville Bros. in Manchester also advertised in the *Blind Advocate*.[181] British Widow's Assurance Co. Ltd. promoted its services in 1909 by claiming that it was 'especially adapted to the Blind', as its Premium Cards no longer had to be marked.[182]

Advertising in the *Blind Advocate* eventually ended before the First World War, although it is not clear why. When the Blindmans Tea Agency inquired about advertising rates in 1935, for example, the Executive simply decided to not reply to the letter.[183] Advertising only reappeared in the 75th anniversary issue in January 1974 but was restricted to workshops and their products. The editor explained that the advertisements provided 'a clear picture of the developments respecting new occupations for blind and severely disabled workers', so their purpose might have gone beyond generating income for the journal.[184] When the *Advocate* finally began to actively solicit advertisements as a form of revenue it was already too late.[185] The scarcity of advertisements for mass-market consumer goods and services in the 1980s and 1990s underlined the economic marginalisation of blind and disabled people in contemporary British society. Neither the circulation figures of the *Blind Advocate* nor the purchasing power of its readership was high enough to attract business which did not specifically cater for blind or disabled customers or trade unionists.[186] The only advertisements in the later issues of the *Blind Advocate* were for products such as Possum Controls' Moon Writer or the Binatone Speakeasy, as well as services such as NatWest's Braille Department or Unity Financial Services.[187]

The hope that the *Blind Advocate* would be read by a substantial number of people outside of the League remained unfulfilled despite repeated appeals to make it 'more interesting to the public, and thereby endeavour to increase its sales'.[188] The *Horizon* also came under fire at times. In 1937, for example, the journal faced criticism that it merely reproduced already published articles from other journals and periodicals in Braille rather than 'acting as an expression of League and T.U. [trade union] opinion generally'.[189] When T. H. Smith became editor in 1948 he admitted that the main function of the League's publications was to foster the cohesion of the organisation 'by bringing home the national character, and national importance of our Society'.[190] By focusing on these aspects they became even less attractive to readers who were not members of the League, but even the latter continued to express their dissatisfaction from time to time. In 1963, for example, the Portsmouth branch claimed that some of the articles published in the *Horizon* were 'just utter tripe to blind people at present'.[191] The General Secretary rejected such criticism as unhelpful and reminded members that it was up to them to provide more interesting articles for publication in the League's journals.[192] However, the Executive even had to remind the League's organisers of their duty to provide regular reports for the two publications.[193]

The final phase began in the 1980s when donations from trade unions to the League fell sharply. The League's membership also continued to decline due to an increase in redundancies in the sheltered work-shop programme.[194] In an effort to reverse the fortunes of the *Blind Advocate* the journal was given a final and radical overhaul in 1982. The layout was changed to resemble a regular newspaper, more photos were included, and the title was changed to *The Advocate: Journal of the National League of the Blind and Disabled*. Financial problems neverthe-less prevented the publication of the third quarter issues of the *Advocate* and the *Horizon* in 1988 and the General Secretary announced that the League would have to start charging 'a realistic and economic price for the production' at least for the *Advocate*.[195] Only three issues appeared in 1992 and that number dropped to two issues in the following year. The last regular copy of the *Advocate* seems to have been published in September 1993. A final copy appeared in autumn 1996 with financial help from the 'Friends of the National League of the Blind and Dis-abled', a charitable organisation created to raise funds for the League.[196] In June 1994 the League's General Secretary informed the members that the *Advocate* and *Horizon* had ceased production due to 'financial con-straints and difficulties' and that 'alternatives will have to be found to keep our sisters and brothers in the Trade Union Movement, along with our friends and associates, informed of our activities'.[197] There is little evidence that they were successful in doing so. The effort to create an ink journal with a broad appeal had ultimately failed. Sales figures remained too low and interest even within the League was not strong enough to make the *Advocate* economically viable. Rather than being 'a luxury', as the General Secretary called them in December 1988, the League's journals were a constant financial millstone around its neck.[198]

4
The Limits of Radicalism: Politics and Protest in the 1920s and 1930s

The 1920 march to London marked a temporary high point in the radicalism of blind people. The momentum of the campaign faded after the passing of the Blind Persons Act and the end of the post-war boom in late 1920 also reduced the trade union movement's readiness for militant action. When the League asked the 1920 Congress in Portsmouth to declare 'itself in favour of a down tools action in order to compel the Government to pass legislation the character of which has been repeatedly demanded by the organised workers of the Kingdom' the delegates showed no enthusiasm for the resolution. The League's case was not helped by the fact that the resolution was moved by a representative of the Workers' Union because its own delegate Gregory was absent and Congress quickly closed the debate without voting on it.[1]

Gregory must have been aware that his absence would doom the League's resolution and he might have actually decided to not be present in order to achieve this result. With the British economy struggling to reconvert to peacetime conditions and Labour establishing itself as the main political alternative to the Conservative Party, a substantial number of people within the League opted for working within the established framework instead of challenging it. Purse's departure and the creation of the National Union of the Professional and Industrial Blind of Great Britain and Ireland was only the most extreme expression of this trend.[2] Those who stayed with the League and sought to amend the 1920 Blind Persons Act also switched to a strategy of political rather than direct action.

The failure of the parliamentary strategy

On 6 May 1920 the League's Executive had already met with representatives of the TUC's Parliamentary Committee to discuss the

government Bill and future strategy.[3] At the same time the League's traditional focus on national legislation was criticised in the *Blind Advocate*
and it was suggested that it would be easier and 'more advantageous
to all concerned' to concentrate efforts on the local authorities which
had been given new and substantial permissive powers under the Blind
Persons Act.[4]

Eventually the League decided to do both. In 1921 its delegate
requested and received backing for a new and more moderate strategy
from the Congress in Cardiff. Together with the TUC's newly formed
General Council the League would try to amend and strengthen the
Blind Persons Act along the lines suggested in Tillett's failed Bill. At the
same time Congress called upon all Trades Councils and their affiliated
organisations to pressure local authorities to 'extract from the Blind Persons Act the maximum of benefits that can be had'.[5] In introducing the
resolution James A. Clydesdale told the delegates that they had a vested
interest in securing a decent living for blind people because 'if blind
men can live on miserable wages, they will begin to think that you can
do the same'. Clydesdale also argued that the resolution only ratified
and confirmed a long-standing position of Congress.[6] In other words,
there was nothing radical about it.

The formation of the first Labour administration in January 1924
seemed to offer the League the long sought-after chance for new legislation even though Ramsay MacDonald only led a minority government.
The question was debated by the Executive Council immediately after
the General Election and the decision was reached that the League's
President, Secretary and another member of the Executive should travel
to London immediately and attempt to meet with MacDonald. Their
task was to convince the new Prime Minister to include an amendment of the Blind Persons Act in the government's agenda and to lobby
as many MPs as possible to support this endeavour. The proposal to
invite Labour Party and Trades Councils delegates to a conference in
London in support of the desired new legislation and to instruct each
League branch to organise a demonstration in its area on a given day
was, however, narrowly defeated. Instead the Executive Council voted
unanimously for a more traditional approach. A demonstration would
be held at the House of Commons whose participants would then seek
interviews with their respective MPs in the lobby of the House. In addition the League would ask trade unions, Trades Councils, Labour Parties
and other Labour organisations to send resolutions in favour of amend-
ing the Blind Persons Act to the Ministry of Health.[7] A proposal by the
North-West District Council to support the demonstration at Parliament

with an 'intensive' nationwide propaganda campaign was rejected by the Executive.[8]

The League's efforts were successful in that a Bill was introduced by Thomas Henderson in the House of Commons in 1924. Supported by Ben Tillett and others it received cross-partisan support and the Parliamentary Secretary to the Ministry of Health asked the House to pass the Bill unanimously on its second reading.[9] It proposed to lower the qualifying age for non-contributory old age pensions to 30 years and introduce what became known as the municipal minimum wage. Wages of blind workshop employees would be at least equal to the average standard rate local authorities paid unskilled labourers in their area.[10] Shortly after the debate, however, the Lord Privy Seal John Robert Clynes responded to a question from Thomas Henderson in the House of Commons that the government was now considering a measure 'of a somewhat more limited scope'.[11] The League reacted by sending a deputation to the Minister of Health James Wheatley in July 1924 to protest against these plans.[12] Wheatley was a leading member of the ILP, one of the League's traditional allies, but he defended the autonomy of local authorities and warned that 'progress could not be more rapid than the progress of public opinion as reflected in the local authorities'.[13] He assured the deputation that 'if he remained in office long enough he would look into all the pleas put before him and see what could be done' but the government fell only four months later.[14]

In opposition Labour showed far less concern for the autonomy of local authorities or the state of public finances. After the League's Executive had invited and received suggestions from League members on how to amend the Blind Persons Act, it drafted a new Bill with the help of a barrister which was introduced by Labour MP Robert Young in the Commons in 1925. The Bill would have forced local authorities to provide employment for all blind people who were able and willing to work. If such work could not be provided local authorities were required to pay the applicant a minimum weekly unemployment allowance of twenty-five shillings. Effectively the Bill tried to establish a right to work or full maintenance for blind people, a demand socialist organisations and the Labour Party had already voiced before the First World War and which had become the main slogan of the unemployment movement in Britain during the interwar years. In an effort to speed up the creation of enough public workshop places the Bill also empowered local authorities to take over private institutions 'by agreement with the managers and subscribers thereof', thereby reversing the pattern of the 1920 Blind Persons Act which allowed local authorities to outsource their responsibility to promote the welfare of blind people.[15]

The members of the League's Executive correctly anticipated resistance against the Bill and spent the four days before the vote on its second reading lobbying various Members of Parliament. Branches were invited to send representatives at their own expense to the House of Commons on 5 May to support the Executive in its efforts.[16] The Bill was second on the order paper on 8 May 1925 and its opponents deliberately delayed the discussion of the preceding Bill to obstruct it. When Young was finally able to move the second reading of the League's Bill the resistance in the House was led by Captain Ian Fraser, Conservative Member for St Pancras North. Fraser had lost his sight in battle during the First World War and was chairman of St Dunstan's, a charity for blind ex-servicemen whose work Young had explicitly praised in his speech.[17] Nevertheless, Fraser criticised the Bill as a party measure as it 'included the principle, which the mover must have known in advance would be inacceptable [*sic*] to the majority of members, of municipalizing all the enterprises and institutions which cared for the blind'.[18] Kingsley Wood, then Parliamentary Secretary of the Ministry of Health, defended the work of the voluntary sector. He was critical that Young had not conferred with members of the other parties or any of the local authorities and called the proposed allowance for unemployed blind people 'extraordinary and peculiar'.[19] The Bill was talked out and thereby denied a second reading.

Taking the hint the League's Executive considered dropping the contentious issue of municipalisation and a circular was issued to all branches asking them to debate this option on both local and district level. Following that, delegates from the League's various District Councils met at Manchester in late October 1925 to determine the content of the next Bill which was to be presented in the House of Commons by Frank Lee, Labour MP for North East Derbyshire, in December of that year.[20] The Bill was similar to the previous one and continued to adhere to the principal of municipal control. The weekly allowance for blind people aged 21 or older was raised to twenty-seven shillings and sixpence while blind people between the ages of 16 and 21 would receive only fifteen shillings per week. The Bill also empowered the Minister of Health to review local schemes for blind people and demand changes to them. The Minister could also require local authorities 'to provide instruction, training or employment in any handicraft, trade or calling which he may specify'. Finally, the Bill also banned piecework in municipal institutions.[21] Once again it failed to get a second reading in the

Commons. It was reintroduced without any changes two years later, but again without success.[22]

The limited success of the local strategy

Repeated failure in Parliament led to a new focus on the local strategy. Following the resolution adopted by the Congress in Cardiff in 1921 the National Joint Council of Labour asked its Secretary Arthur Henderson to investigate how the Blind Persons Act was applied in practice.[23] Henderson, who was also Secretary of the Labour Party, subsequently issued a circular to all Trades Councils in which he explained the duties and powers local authorities had under the new Act, requested information as to the extent to which these powers were actually used and reminded them of their obligation to force local authorities to provide generous schemes for blind people in their area.[24] The information provided by the Trades Councils was then used by the Joint Research Department for a pamphlet which highlighted the shortcomings of the Blind Persons Act, but apart from that little else was apparently done.[25]

This changed in 1927 when the Congress in Edinburgh passed a resolution moved by Charles Lothian which re-emphasised the TUC's commitment to 'use every constitutional means to bring pressure to bear upon every County and County Borough Council to more fully exercise their powers' under the Blind Persons Act. Even after the Act had gone onto the Statute Book most local authorities continued to assist blind people under the Poor Law or outsourced the task by giving grants to voluntary associations. Employment opportunities remained few and only a handful of councils assumed control of workshops for the blind in their respective area, as the League had wished.[26] As Ben Tillett pointed out in his supporting speech, even local authorities with a Labour majority usually failed to make full use of the statutory powers given to them under the Blind Persons Act.[27] The Edinburgh resolution specifically demanded that local authorities pay a weekly allowance to all unemployed blind people in their area, a payment Lothian described as 'a compensation for blindness for those people who are unsuited to enter professional or industrial careers'.[28] Finally, the resolution committed the TUC to supporting the League's campaign for a Blind Persons Amendment Act.[29] Following the 1927 Edinburgh Congress, Walter Citrine urged all Trades Councils in a circular to implement the resolution and to remind their representatives on local government bodies of the powers granted to them in 1920.[30] A similar circular was sent to the clerks of all County and County Borough Councils, who were also approached by the League's District Councils and local branches.[31] These concerted efforts were aided by the passing of the Local Government Act of 1929, which urged local authorities to assist blind persons through means other than Poor Law relief.[32]

Judging by the complaints in Parliament about the growing financial burden the welfare of blind people represented for local authorities, the campaign had some success.[33] Outside of Parliament Ben Purse was once again the most vocal critic and condemned the attempt

> to play off one local authority against another in a nation wide [*sic*] effort to force up rates of augmentation [of workshop wages] and domiciliary assistance. A concession secured from one local authority is immediately used as a weapon against the next, and publicly elected authorities with little knowledge of blindness or sheltered employment have been powerless to withstand the demands of the League's local pressure groups.[34]

The campaign was especially successful in London and the industrialised areas of the country, but its impact in rural areas was very limited.[35]

The formation of the second Labour minority government in June 1929 raised hopes that the League's preferred course of action, i.e. national legislation, could address this problem and create equal opportunities and support for blind people all across Britain. In November 1929 Thomas Groves introduced a new Bill in the Commons. It reflected the burden of government as it was significantly less generous than previous proposals and almost identical with the 1925 Bill.[36] Nevertheless, the Bill again failed to get a second reading. The League tried to keep up the pressure on the government by, for example, circulating a petition in 1930 demanding new legislation among trade unions, Cooperative Societies and other labour movement organisations.[37] However, Parliament soon became too occupied with the effects of the domestic political and global economic crisis to contemplate another amendment bill to the Blind Persons Act of 1920.

The crisis of the Labour Party

The economic crisis started with the collapse of the American stock market in late October 1929. Its impact on Britain was less disastrous than on Germany or the United States, for example, and the British economy had already begun to recover in late 1932. However, unemployment remained high in areas where the old staple industries such as coal, steel, textiles or shipbuilding had dominated.[38] The psychological impact of the slump was also significant as many people anticipated the imminent death of capitalism and possibly also the collapse of civilisation.[39]

The debate about how to respond to a shrinking economy and rising welfare bill triggered a political crisis which weakened the League's most important allies. Trade unionism had its strongholds in the old industrial areas which were especially hard hit by the downturn and the Labour government fell in August 1931 over the proposed cuts to unemployment benefits. Prime Minister MacDonald formed a new National Government with the Conservatives and sections of the Liberal Party and took leading Labour politicians like Philip Snowden and James H. Thomas with him. His old party suffered a crushing defeat in the subsequent General Election, for which it had been thoroughly unprepared. Dominated by the Conservative Party the National Government promised and delivered stability and the electorate kept it in office until it was replaced by an even broader wartime coalition in 1940. There were, of course, occasional flares of sometimes violent protest during the 1930s, but the overall impact of the Communists and also the Fascists in Britain remained insignificant.[40] Nevertheless, Communist attempts to mobilise the unemployed in the streets frequently led to violent clashes with the police and discredited traditional forms of street protest. Although the League had successfully used protest marches and rallies until 1920 it rarely did so afterwards and hardly ever during the height of the economic crisis. When it took to the streets the effect was minimal. The London and Home Counties District Council, for example, organised a demonstration in Trafalgar Square on 29 June 1930. Although the event was well prepared for, with a conference of local Trades Councils and Labour Party Committees in April, it made no impact and even the *Blind Advocate* failed to report on its outcome.[41]

The break away of a number of branches between 1933 and 1936 further weakened the League's potential for direct action and probably strengthened the Executive's resolve to work within the established constitutional framework. An attempt to get a member of the League elected to Parliament after the First World War had failed and it would never again sponsor a candidate of its own in a General Election.[42] When the Labour Party chose a member of the rival NUPIB in 1930 to contest one of the London seats in the next General Election the League's Executive Committee refused to support the protest of its West London branch against this decision.[43] Instead the League began to intensify its cooperation with the Labour Party in an effort to influence Labour's policy at the source.

After the split in 1931 and its subsequent electoral defeat, the Labour Party stepped up its cooperation with the TUC and began to formulate new policies together with the trade unions.[44] The League used this opportunity to develop a programme with the Labour Party which was to be implemented once the latter returned to power. It was approved by the Labour Party conference of 1934 and, after further amendments had been made at the League's request, published as *The Blind Persons Charter*.[45] The title was a reference to the League's founding document and its publication was indeed another watershed moment in the organisation's history. The programme called for improved medical services for children as well as greater opportunities and improved facilities for the education, training and employment of blind people. It demanded the abolition of piecework in favour of a weekly wage and allowances for non-working individuals equal to the pensions received by those who had lost their sight while serving in armed conflict. Local authorities were to be made directly responsible for the welfare of all blind individuals and assume 25 per cent of the cost, with the national government providing the remaining 75 per cent.[46]

Rather than vilifying charitable organisations the *Charter* made its case in the same language which would later be used to justify the comprehensive welfare state. It argued that 'the provisions of a primary social service cannot be left indefinitely to flag-days, subscriptions and donations, legacies and other money-raising efforts of private charity, supplemented by public grants' and called the existing system 'on the whole haphazard, cumbersome and inefficient'.[47] The final paragraph phrased the League's long-standing objections against charity in positive terms and bold letters: '*The object of our policy is to enable the blind to stand on their own feet, to be independent, to be citizens as their sighted colleagues are citizens, and to get rid of the atmosphere of charity which is often so well-meaning and often so disastrous to self-respect.*'[48]

The *Charter* undoubtedly represented a major success for the League, which had used Labour's crisis and subsequent move to the left to make its maximum demands official Labour Party policy. Without a Labour majority in the House of Commons, however, this success was of little use and the prospects of a new Labour government continued to look dim. Although the Party slowly recovered after the disastrous defeat in 1931 and regained some ground in local elections as well as by-elections, the 1935 General Election revealed how far it still was from winning an overall majority in Parliament.[49] As a result the League began to look back to what, in hindsight, increasingly looked like its greatest success.

Debating the merits of confrontation

Repeated failure to have the Blind Persons Act amended in Parliament and Labour's poor electoral prospects eventually shifted the League's attention to other forms of political participation in the 1930s. Institutional representation had always been difficult for the League as it normally entailed cooperating with charitable organisations. The question was again intensely debated at the conference at York in 1933 and the League now decided to seek representation on all relevant decision-making or advisory bodies in order to be able to influence policies at the source. The Executive advised all branches 'to take steps to secure representation on the Union of County Associations' and 'to apply to the Boards of Management of local institutions, Blind Persons Act Committees and any other local bodies responsible for the welfare of the blind, for representation for the League'. In addition, the Executive would also seek representation on the Union of County Associations for the Blind.[50] This willingness to work with the voluntary sector as well as the state, rather than against them, represented a new departure for the League. As will be shown in Chapter 5, it would eventually produce results during the Second World War.

In addition, the League also reverted to street politics. Grass-roots support for a new march to London gradually increased within the organisation and several District Councils and local branches wrote to the League's Executive Committee suggesting such a step. As the first march to London was credited with getting the Blind Persons Act passed in 1920, the assumption that a repetition of this endeavour could also bring about the desired amendment to this Act was not unreasonable. The government's hasty retreat after the spontaneous public protests against the newly created Unemployment Assistance Board in January and February 1935 also suggested that mass action could yield immediate and significant results.[51]

The League's Executive Council first debated this question in June 1935 when letters from District Councils and local branches suggesting another march to London were read. The proposal split the Executive. A General Election was looming on the horizon and the last attempt to amend the Blind Persons Act in Parliament had been in late 1929. The Committee therefore decided by a narrow margin to defer a decision until the next meeting in September. In the meanwhile it would contact the League's branches on the matter as well as assess the chances of a change in government after the next General Election. The General Secretary was given the task to draft another Amendment Bill and submit it to the Labour Party for presentation in the House of Commons. The attempt by a group which had formed around Tom Parker to commit the Executive immediately to organising a march, or at least to express the view that it would be 'desirable', was narrowly defeated.[52]

A survey among the branches revealed strong support for a new march to London. Of the 41 branches which replied 32 supported the initiative, five opposed it and four suggested deferring the march. At the Executive's next meeting the issue was therefore unanimously handed over to a sub-committee which presented its recommendations two months later.[53] The march was to begin around 1 May 1936 and again feature three contingents, starting in Manchester, Leeds and Cardiff. The total number of marchers should not exceed 250 people and they were to be on the road for approximately three weeks. The recommendations were adopted, but it was also unanimously agreed to submit the project to the Labour Party, the TUC and Cooperative Movement and request their support before making further arrangements. A March Committee was formed which included a representative from the AUBB as the latter was in the process of merging with the League. The Committee was to start its work as soon as the League received a reply from the three organisations.[54] The Parliamentary strategy was, however, not abandoned. The Executive also decided unanimously to ask the Prime Minister to receive a deputation from the League at the earliest feasible date. The deputation, supported by representatives from all parties if possible, would try to get a promise that the Blind Persons Act would be amended by the government.[55] While building up political pressure with its preparations for the march to London, the League also continued to work within the established constitutional framework.

The National Council of Labour, which coordinated the work of the TUC, Labour Party and Cooperative Movement, decided in early 1936 to support the League's plan. This made it the only march to London during the 1930s which had the active backing of the whole Labour Movement.[56] After receiving the positive response the League's General Secretary called a meeting of the March Committee for 16 February 1936.[57] Shortly before that meeting the government learned about the project from James A. Clydesdale. Born in Glasgow in 1879, Clydesdale lost his sight in an accident at the age of eight and was subsequently educated and trained as a basket-maker at the Royal Glasgow Asylum for the Blind. He helped to found the League's Glasgow branch in 1907 and quickly became its Secretary. Only two years later he also joined the League's Executive Committee. After being elected paid Organiser for the North East District Clydesdale moved to Newcastle in February

1919. He would serve as Organiser until 1951, a record for the League. In addition, Clydesdale was also active in the ILP which he joined in 1909. He was elected Councillor for Stephenson Ward in Newcastle in 1922 and continued to hold this position until he became an Alderman in 1946. During this period Clydesdale led the Labour Group on the City Council for many years and was also nominated by the Labour Party as Parliamentary Candidate for the Central Division of Newcastle in 1933.[58] His quest for office was more successful on the local level and he served as Sheriff of Newcastle before becoming Lord Mayor in 1945. It seems as if Clydesdale did not always prioritise his duties as Organiser of the League over his other commitments. He was given notice by the League in December 1928 but successfully pleaded with the Executive to keep his job.[59] He was censored by the Executive in 1933 and again in 1934 for neglecting his duties and was again threatened with suspension in 1937.[60]

Clydesdale was no stranger to radical action. He organised his first protest action while still a pupil at the Royal Glasgow Asylum when he convinced his peers to go on strike in reaction to the poor quality and insufficient quantity of food they received. In December 1918 he led the League's successful industrial action against the Royal Glasgow Asylum, which attracted widespread regional support. Like Ben Purse before him, however, Clydesdale came to appreciate the value of cooperation through his service on numerous committees and political bodies. He was, for example, the first member of the League to be given a seat on a Blind Persons Act Committee and also served on the important Advisory Committee on the Welfare of the Blind, first as a representative of the League and then from 1931 to 1948 as a nominee of the Minister of Health.[61] It was in this capacity that he voluntarily approached C. R. Kerwood of the Ministry of Health in February 1936 and informed him about the League's plan to organise another march to London. The aim of the march was, according to Clydesdale, to urge the government to implement the programme laid out in *The Blind Persons Charter*. 'He told me that he had done all he could to persuade them not to do so, but was overruled, and in fact has himself to be in charge of one of the contingents', Kerwood reported on 15 February 1936. Asked by Kerwood if he saw any chance of stopping the march, Clydesdale said he was afraid not, but promised to keep him confidentially informed of developments.[62]

Clydesdale was not the only leading member of the League who opposed the project. When the March Committee met the next day, Whittam tried to reverse the decision for the march. At his request letters from the Bolton and Haslingden branches were read which asked the Committee to consider cancelling the project. Whittam, who had advocated the cautious approach in the meeting in June 1935, then moved that the March Committee should ask the Executive to recommend abandoning the march and continue with the strategy of organising 'national and local demonstrations to bring pressure to bear upon local authorities and the Government to secure amendments to the Blind Persons Act 1920 in keeping with recent decisions of the Executive'.[63] When Grierson, another veteran of the 1920 march, ruled that Whittam's motion was in order Tom Parker successfully challenged the decision.[64] The March Committee then continued to plan the march. Each District Council was to form its own Area Sub-Committee and was assigned a provisional quota of marchers.[65] The band of the Glasgow Institution was invited to lead the marchers and the League's Chairman and General Secretary were instructed to draft a national appeal in the form of a circular. The latter was also ordered to approach the *Daily Herald*, the BBC and the film industry with a view of gaining as much publicity as possible. Finally, it was resolved to ask the Executive for the necessary funds to cover the initial expenses of the march.[66]

Whittam's reluctance to march again was, as his motion shows, not inspired by a principle objection to street protest. Yet a march of three contingents to London was bound to trigger comparisons with the numerous Hunger Marches organised by the National Unemployment Workers' Movement (NUWM) during the interwar period. The NUWM was a Communist-led organisation and the government had tried in vain to prevent these demonstrations. It would also try to stop the blind marchers from coming to the capital.

Four days after the meeting of the March Committee, the Conservative Minister of Health Sir Kingsley Wood discussed this issue with his advisors. While his cabinet colleagues had usually refused to receive deputations from the Hunger Marchers in the 1930s, Kingsley Wood initially hesitated to follow the same policy with regard to the League. 'If we are unsuccessful in stopping the march', one of his advisors reported, 'the reception of a deputation may be the easiest way of getting rid of them, so he does not want to make it a point of honour that they should not be received.'[67] It was agreed that the Ministry of Health should attempt, with Clydesdale's help, to prevent the march from taking place and Kingsley Wood expressed his willingness to receive a deputation from the League before it began.

To pacify the League, the Minister of Health also considered lowering the minimum qualifying age for blind pensions. Although the League did not explicitly demand such a step, it would, in the words of the Minister, 'redeem an old promise [by Stanley Baldwin] and cost very little money'.[68] It also had the backing of the Advisory Committee on the Welfare of the Blind which had already recommended such a step in 1929 and again in 1935.[69] Ian Fraser had written to Kingsley Wood in February 1936 with the offer to introduce a Bill to this effect in the House of Commons. The matter was again discussed by the Advisory Committee on 22 April and a meeting of the Council of the National Institute the following day. Fraser subsequently wrote another letter to the Minister of Health in which he pressed for the lowering of the qualifying age for a blind pension and also met with Kingsley Wood in the Commons in May.[70] However, it was the League's planned march which caused the Minister of Health to act. To get the necessary approval of the Treasury a memorandum for the Chancellor was drafted on Kingsley Wood's orders.[71] It mentioned that there was 'a considerable body of opposition' to the march within the League and that the 'suggestion is being conveyed indirectly to the League that their objects would be better met by the appointment of a deputation to be seen by the Minister in the ordinary way'.[72] The memorandum calculated the cost of lowering the minimum qualifying age for drawing a blind pension with the League's maximum demands as listed in its programme and in *The Blind Persons Charter*. The object was clearly to suggest to the Chancellor that lowering the pension age might prevent the march from taking place and avoid more costly concessions to the League.[73]

When the League's Executive met again in March 1936 General Secretary Henderson submitted letters from several branches concerning the march, but President Grierson who ex officio chaired the meeting ruled them out of order. When Whittam challenged this ruling he was defeated by two votes to five. Whittam also lost his seat on the March Committee, which was reconstituted on the initiative of McAlpine and Parker.[74] Against Whittam's lone dissent, £500 was placed at the Committee's disposal to cover the initial expenses of the preparation for the march. However, he successfully reminded the Executive Council that it had agreed in December to send a deputation to Prime Minister Stanley Baldwin.[75]

Whittam was not alone in opposing the march. Arguing that it would be too expensive and that 'the blind of to-day have not the case they had in 1920' the League's North West District Council refused to take part in it.[76] Henderson and McAlpine attended the District Council's next meeting in April 1936 in an effort to reverse the decision but were unsuccessful.[77] At the same time Clydesdale continued to brief Kerwood in the Ministry of Health. After the League's Executive Council meeting Clydesdale was informed that it had been decided to apply 'at once to the Prime Minister' and incorrectly assumed that the march had at least been postponed until then. He suggested that the Prime Minister's secretary should refer the League to the Ministry of Health so that the matter 'may finally get to the place where it ought to be'.[78] Four days later he stressed again that although the League's General Secretary had been instructed to ask the Prime Minister to receive a deputation, he was 'almost certain that they do not expect to be received by him and their expectations would be realised if the Prime Minister is substituted by the Minister of Health'.[79] Clydesdale warned Kerwood that ignoring the request might increase support for the march within the League, but also conveyed the impression that the project could still be prevented if 'anything occurs satisfactory to them [...] as there appears to be a little uncertainty about the response'.[80] As members of the Advisory Committee on the Welfare of the Blind, both men were aware that the lowering of the qualifying age for blind pensions was already on the agenda. Clydesdale urged that the Minister should not announce his intention to improve the lot of blind people in any way before talking to the League's delegation and advised: 'Let this appear to be influenced by the deputation which might satisfy them.'[81]

The debate within the League also found its way onto the pages of the *Blind Advocate*. Under the heading 'The March must go on' Tom Parker defended the project in April 1936 as necessary because the Great Depression had left local authorities in the distressed areas unable to fulfil their responsibilities towards the blind community. Using his native Glamorganshire in Wales as an example, Parker stressed that only the national government was able to create equal conditions for all blind people in Britain, regardless of where they resided. Reminding his readers that the progress made since the 1920 march had been unsatisfactory, Parker tried to dispel fears of failure by pointing out that 'the entire Labour Movement, en route, would support the march'.[82] The project also represented value for money as it would cost only about £3,000, less than the amount 'which will be spent by our Organisation in the next year or two in endeavouring to induce Local Authorities, who either cannot or will not assume their responsibilities, to do so'.[83]

Clydesdale responded in the following issue of the *Blind Advocate* by stressing that the chances of pushing the government into fulfilling the League's demands were very slim. In addition, Clydesdale argued that there was 'a real danger in pressing for uniformity by Government action, even with further Government financial support'. As the Blind Persons Act was still a dead letter in many areas, these regions could easily bring the standard of blind welfare in other areas down, so that uniformity would be established at a low level. The League should therefore first concentrate on improving the lot of blind people locally before pressing for a uniform nationwide standard and an amendment of the Blind Persons Act. In addition, Clydesdale expressed doubts that the total cost of the march would be as low as Parker suggested.[84]

In arguing that the League should continue its strategy of pressuring local authorities to improve the situation of blind people on the ground, Clydesdale opted for a safe and uncontroversial strategy which had already yielded results in the past. Marching to London, in comparison, risked alienating the government as well as public opinion by using a tactic now closely associated with the NUWM and its Communist leadership. It was also expensive and the results of the first march in 1920, as well as of the five Hunger Marches to London to that date, had been far from impressive. As a veteran of the first march to London in 1920 Clydesdale was well aware of the risks this tactic involved. As a councillor and member of numerous committees whose service had been recognised by the Minister of Health through his appointment to the Advisory Committee on the Welfare of the Blind, Cyldesdale also had experience in working with, rather than against, the state. However, neither he nor Whittam were able to stop the march.

On 7 April 1936 Downing Street informed the Ministry of Health that the League had formally asked the Prime Minister to receive a deputation.[85] Only then was the PM's office informed about the League's plan but the Ministry of Health created the impression that it was very much in control of the situation.[86] Following Clydesdale's advice it expressed the conviction that the League would also be satisfied with seeing the Minister of Health, which turned out to be correct.[87] In preparation for this meeting the Ministry of Health also contacted Ian Fraser for information on the League and advice on how to deal with the deputation.[88] Kingsley Wood received the deputation which was led by the League's President Grierson and General Secretary Henderson on 19 May 1936. They were accompanied by MPs from the Conservative, Liberal and Communist parties. James Maxton, whose Independent Labour Party had disaffiliated from the Labour Party in 1932, had been planning to join the deputation but was prevented from doing so. No representative of the Parliamentary Labour Party was apparently available to support the League's demands, although the organisation had been affiliated with the Labour Party for over two decades.[89]

The deputation repeated the League's usual catalogue of complaints and demands. It was critical of local authorities that did not make full use of the permissive powers granted to them under the Blind Persons Act and pointed out that 53 out of 146 local authorities in England and Wales had even made little or no provisions for blind people in their area. The representatives of the League expressed disappointment over the fact that the Blind Persons Act fixed the minimum age for blind pensions at fifty years. The League wanted to lower the qualifying age to eighteen years and demanded that the pensions should be equal to those received by ex-servicemen.[90] As blind persons tended to move to areas where they received the best provisions the issue was national in scale. The government in London should therefore assume responsibility for 75 per cent of the welfare costs with local authorities covering the remaining 25 per cent. Once again the League advocated full public control of welfare services for blind people. Workshop employees should have at least the same standard of living as sighted workers and home workers should receive the same wages as workshop employees. Some local authorities still cared for blind people in their area under the Poor Law and some Public Assistance Committees included allowances to blind people in the Means Test, although the Unemployment Assistance Board had ruled that they should be disregarded in the determination of needs. Variations in the scales of assistance in different areas were too great and some areas still had not made proper provisions for blind people. This 'prevented blind persons from exercising the elementary right of moving from one area into another'.[91] The League also objected to the practice of piecework in blind workshops, as these institutions could not be commercial undertakings.[92]

Kingsley Wood promised to look carefully into the various points raised by the delegates, but emphasised that any legislation had to be coordinated with his colleagues and depended on the availability of Parliamentary time. He stressed the progress that had been made since the First World War, especially in the prevention of blindness and criticised the League's hostility to voluntary organisations. The Minister promised to support any agreement on the question of piecework, to look further into the striking differences in the scales of assistance and to urge local authorities to cease welfare provision for blind people under the Poor Law.[93]

The Minister's friendly but rather non-committal tone did not satisfy the League and the preparations for the march continued. A circular was published in which the March Committee asked Trades Councils, the Labour Party and trade union branches as well as Cooperative Societies

and Guilds for moral and financial support.[94] The League simultaneously also published an appeal to its 'Fellow Citizens' which explained
its reasons for marching and also asked for financial donations and
other forms of support.[95] While the appeal to the Labour Movement
stressed that working-class support had made success possible in 1920
and expressed the hope that the marchers would again be 'received
and treated most hospitably in each town', the appeal to the public
emphasised the hardships the marchers would endure on their way
to London.[96] They had 'decided to again face the possibilities of bad
weather, the inconvenience of being away from home for the necessary
period, and the increasing dangers and difficulties of the road' to secure
'a decent and secure future' for the blind community in Great Britain.[97]

With the appeals for support also came press coverage. Clydesdale was
named as one of the organisers and leaders of the march in the newspapers despite being one of its most outspoken opponents.[98] According
to Kerwood this was a form of disciplinary punishment administered
by the League. 'Mr. Clydesdale has publicly opposed the proposal to
organise a march and is suspected also of having taken clandestine steps
towards preventing it', he reported in August 1936. 'It is for this reason
that he has been given a prominent part, by way of punishment, in the
organisation of the march and the notices in the press emphasise the
part which he is taking.'[99] Kerwood also reported that he had received
'in confidence' further information about the march from Clydesdale
via Ben Purse who was now Head of Welfare Services at the National
Institute for the Blind.

Clydesdale had published a satirical poem about Purse's new trade
union in January 1922 in which he ridiculed 'The N.U.B. of great B.P./
And other folks of title'.[100] By 1936, however, the relationship between
the two men had apparently improved significantly. Purse explained to
Kerwood that the political aim of the march was to persuade the Labour
Party and the TUC to make further efforts to realise the programme
laid out in *The Blind Persons Charter*. An even more important objective was to raise funds and attract new members and Purse suggested
that this could be used to stop the march. 'In the opinion of Mr. Purse,
and presumably of Mr. Clydesdale, the main object of the march is the
financial one', Kerwood reported, 'and Mr. Purse told me that in his
opinion if the marchers could be prevented from marching through the
main streets of the towns en route and from making collections the
proposal would fall through.'[101] Kerwood subsequently inquired with
the Home Office about the possibility of implementing this suggestion.
After learning that local police enjoyed discretion in regulating the route

of a procession and issuing permits for the collection of money, he proposed that the Home Office should contact the police authorities along
the route of the march and 'suggest to them informally that it would be
inadvisable to allow collections to be made' and that the blind should be
kept from the towns' main streets for their own safety.[102] When Kingsley
Wood approached the Home Secretary John Simon shortly afterwards
for advice on what could be done to prevent 'this unnecessary march' he
also referred to the power of local police to regulate the route of marches
and refuse permits for street collections.[103] At the same time Kingsley
Wood also approached the Chancellor of the Exchequer regarding a
Bill to lower the qualifying age for blind pensions from fifty years to
forty years and conveyed his desire to announce the proposed legislation
publicly before the start of the march.[104]

The Home Secretary was 'most anxious to help' the Minister of Health,
'both because of the undesirability of putting blind people through such
an ordeal and because the general question of processions of demonstrators converging on London' was one which gave him 'concern'.[105]
By that time it was clear that the blind marchers would not be alone
on the road as the NUWM had begun preparations for another Hunger
March to London and the planning for the Jarrow Crusade had also
started.[106] However, Simon informed Kingsley Wood that he had no
authority to direct local police authorities as to how they should exercise their discretionary powers. He advised against Kerwood's suggestion
to issue a confidential circular to them as it would certainly leak out
and cause some criticism. When the same question had been discussed
with the Attorney General in connection with the NUWM's Hunger
March in 1934 it had been concluded 'that a circular would be unwise
on the above ground and because it could not give a sufficiently clear
lead to police authorities'.[107] Simon also listed other problems. The
blind marchers were not expected to create serious disorder or public
inconvenience and a deterrent effect could only be achieved if they
were informed ahead of the march that no street collections would be
allowed. However, neither the Home Secretary nor the local authorities
had the power to make such an announcement, nor was it possible to ban processions completely. The question of how to prevent
protest marches to London had already been discussed by the Cabinet
and an Interdepartmental Committee in 1932 but with little success.
Although Simon expressed his opinion that 'under modern conditions
such methods of making the views of people at a distance known are
quite unnecessary and out of date', there was nothing the government
could do to prevent these marches. Trying to enlist the help of the

Members of Parliament who had accompanied the League's deputation to the Minister of Health would probably only encourage the blind marchers.[108]

With the stick not available the carrot seemed the government's last chance to prevent the march. After the Chancellor had approved the lower age at which pensions could be drawn the measure was discussed by the Cabinet and announced by the Minister of Health in a speech in Worcester on 10 September 1936.[109] The Ministry of Health sent an outline of the speech to the League in the hope that this would cause it to cancel the march.[110] When that failed a letter was drafted on Kingsley Wood's order which pointed out that the government would introduce a Bill to amend the Blind Persons Act early in the next Parliamentary session. As it was to be expected that the Bill would be sympathetically received by all parties and as the Minister of Health would carefully consider any suggestions from the League regarding the Bill 'it would appear that a march of blind persons to London could serve no useful purpose, and moreover, it may well involve hardship and inconvenience to those who take part in it, and Sir Kingsley trusts that the National League will not proceed with it'.[111] The Minister's expectations were not fulfilled. While the League expressed its appreciation for the Minister's interest in its activities it pointed out that the proposals outlined by the government fell short of what was needed.[112] Preparations for the march were finalised in September 1936 and the three contingents of blind marchers left for London on 12 October 1936 – much later than the League had initially planned.

On the road to London: 1936

The 1936 march was essentially a repetition of the 1920 march to London. Manchester and Leeds were again two of the assembling and starting points.[113] The Leeds contingent marched via Sheffield, Nottingham and Derby to Leicester where it linked up with the Manchester contingent on 21 October 1936. The Manchester contingent, which included the marchers from Scotland and Ireland, arrived in Leicester via Macclesfield, Birmingham and Coventry. The South-Western contingent set out from Swansea. They had a longer route to travel alone, compared to 1920, and proceeded via Cardiff, Newport, Bristol, Chippenham, Swindon, Oxford and Reading to Watford near London, where they met the other marchers.[114]

Once again all marchers were male, although the proportion of female members of the League had increased markedly since 1920.[115] The

NUWM had first allowed women to participate in Hunger Marches to London in 1930, but only in a separate contingent. The Jarrow Marchers also excluded women from their ranks in 1936 with the exception of Ellen Wilkinson who, as Labour MP for Jarrow, headed the column ex officio for much of the Crusade. Logistical problems once again played a role in these decisions, for finding separate accommodation for female marchers often proved challenging on the road. Probably more important was the fact that only a revolutionary organisation like the NUWM could risk sending women on a punishing trip to London in often adverse weather conditions without worrying too much about alienating contemporary notions of femininity. Even Wilkinson had to stress her domestic credentials with a photo showing her 'busily assisting in the provision of food and refreshment for the men [from Jarrow] when they stopped at Springwell for their first meal'.[116] In contrast, men could confirm their masculinity by enduring the hardships of a march to London, especially if they were social outsiders by virtue of being unemployed or disabled.

Once again, most of the blind marchers were in paid employment and were 'leaving work to join the march' as Henderson explained.[117] In Nottingham, for example, the marchers were joined by ten men from the Midland Institution for the Blind, 'although they are provided with regular employment and good wages' as a local newspaper stressed. 'Apparently they desire to help their blind comrades who are not so fortunate as themselves.'[118] Three men from the Cardiff Institution even left their jobs without permission to participate in the march. They were dismissed as a result, but reinstated in January 1937 after pressure from the League.[119] In contrast to both the NUWM's Hunger Marches and the Jarrow Crusade, the working blind were marching for those who were either unemployed or unable to work. To make up for the loss of income, the marchers were paid by the League for the time they were away from work.[120]

While the routes of the march were similar to those taken sixteen years earlier, the political and economic context was very different in 1936. With large parts of the country dug in and waiting for better times, stressing voluntary hardships was not an appropriate tactic once the men were on the road. Contrary to 1920 the League emphasised that the marchers would 'not suffer any severe hardship' on their way to London.[121] As it was now common practice, local committees were formed to organise the reception of the contingents and letters were sent out to solicit support. While the marchers were again well received in many of the towns they passed through or stayed overnight in, they now frequently had to spend the nights in Labour Clubs, public baths, workhouses, chapels, army or public halls, police stations or other such places, with Public Assistance Officers providing blankets. The time of private accommodation in the homes of sympathisers was over.[122]

The economic depression was also felt in the disappointing income generated by the 1936 march, especially when compared to the substantial sums generated by its predecessor. The march fund was set up with a minimum levy of one shilling, which all members of the League had to pay.[123] The results of the collections were, however, lower than expected. In 1920, for example, the marchers had collected more than £65 in Stockport; sixteen years later it was less than £10.[124] At the final demonstration in London's Trafalgar Square less than £5 was collected.[125] The 1920 march had cost £7,000 and while Tom Parker had conservatively estimated in April 1936 that about £3,000 would be needed for the second march, the League was only able to spend roughly half of that amount.[126]

Despite the lack of financial success the marchers were once again described as a happy group. The men from Manchester 'came along the road to cheerful tunes played on mouth-organs and tin whistles, and headed by kindly police officers who protected them from the traffic'.[127] The Leeds contingent was led into Sheffield by the band of the city's Welfare of the Blind Department to the 'steady beat of a kettle drum' and 'cheery voices' singing songs.[128] 'It was not easy to realise that the men cheerfully tramping with knapsacks on their backs could not see the world around them,' one admiring journalist reported.[129] To alert the passing traffic to this fact the marchers carried yellow posters reading 'Caution. Blind marchers.'[130] As in 1920 they marched 'with linked arms and sticks tapping the roads' while others kept formation with the help of poles.[131] Police officers accompanied the contingents to the borough boundaries where they were met by officers from the neighbouring area. The blind gratefully acknowledged the help given by the police, which prevented the march from having the same revolutionary fervour as its predecessor.[132] In addition, the marchers had their own sighted guides who accompanied the columns.[133]

Once again the League protested that blind people did not want charity. Those who had 'lost their sight through disease and accident, or other cause' should receive a non-means-tested pension as a right, and potential supporters were once again reminded that a 'very large percentage of the blind population is recruited yearly from the ranks of the workers and our plight to-day may be yours tomorrow'.[134] Henderson assured the press that the blind did not like to draw attention to their situation in this way, but argued that it seemed 'to be the only effective way of bringing their position before the public'.[135] Again and again, the alleged success of the tactics used in 1920 was highlighted and the second march was presented as an effort to complete the achievements of the first through essentially the same means.[136] 'Justice, not charity' was again one of the marchers' slogans and it was only fitting that some of the veterans of 1920 turned out to march again.[137]

At every stop mass meetings were held at which the marchers explained their demands and resolutions were passed.[138] As the leader of the Leeds contingent, Clydesdale was one of the regular speakers and he used this position to convey an image of moderation. While he had to repeat the demand that Stanley Baldwin should see a deputation of marchers after their arrival in London, he also stated publicly that they would alternatively try to secure the support of MPs and that they were 'not going to burn down the Houses of Parliament or shoot the Prime Minister'. According to Clydesdale they only wanted 'an opportunity of converting the Prime Minister and the others to a realisation of the needs of the blind people of this country'.[139] Compared to 1920, this was moderate talk.

A novel feature of the 1936 march was that the League now had competition from three other groups, which lead an official in the Ministry of Health to exclaim that 'it seems now to be the open season for Marches!'[140] The NUWM's sixth National Hunger March started on 26 September and brought over 1,400 unemployed from all over the country to London, where they were welcomed by up to a quarter of a million people in Hyde Park on 8 November 1936.[141] The smallest march was organised by the British Campaigners Association, a group of ex-servicemen from Scotland. They started in Edinburgh but received little coverage in the newspapers and reached Hyde Park on the same day as the Hunger Marchers.[142] The Jarrow Crusaders started on 5 October and reached London on 1 November 1936. Their supposedly 'non-political' march presented itself as a civic protest of respectable unemployed petitioning the government for work and attracted the most publicity in 1936.[143] The Crusader's route overlapped with those of the blind marchers during the last stage and competition for attention came head-to-head when both the Jarrow marchers and the North-Western contingent of the League arrived at Northampton on 24 October.[144] In 1936 the blind were just one of the 'Armies marching on London from North, South, East and West', as the *Star* put it.[145]

The last contingents of the League united again at Watford near London on 29 October 1936. The following day they went on to

Figure 4.1 'Trafalgar Square, 1 November 1936'. Demonstration at Trafalgar Square, 1 November 1936 © National League of the Blind and Disabled

Willesden escorted by members of the Watford Labour Party and the National Unemployed Workers' Movement.[146] During the planning stage of the march the League had 'uncompromisingly rejected' a suggestion from the NUWM to join forces with the Hunger Marchers, or at least to cooperate with them on the road. The Metropolitan Police's Special Branch had nevertheless expressed concerns that 'this may not be sufficient to prevent the communists from forcing their cooperation upon the blind demonstrators' and a Communist speaker did in fact address the marchers during a meeting that evening.[147] On the last day before they reached their destination the NUWM had managed to break into the blind marchers' columns. Apart from that the League had been able to keep the radical left at arm's length.[148]

On 31 October 1936 the marchers arrived at Paddington Green where they were met by 130 London members of the League. From there they went to Battersea where they spent the next two nights at Gideon Road School.[149] On 1 November 1936, the same day the Jarrow Crusaders arrived at Hyde Park, the League's march reached its supposed climax with a mass meeting at Trafalgar Square. Contingents of the League's London branches and a few Labour movement organisations arrived at the Square before the marchers, headed by bands and banners.[150] Shortly afterwards the marchers arrived, bringing the number of people in the square up to a mere 500 according to the police. The speakers, who included a blind trade unionist from Melbourne, Australia, repeated the League's demands and a resolution was passed calling upon the government to amend the Blind Persons Act. It was emphasised that blind people wanted 'justice not charity' and that they could achieve this goal with the support of the masses. Given the rather disappointing turnout this seemed somewhat unlikely. The whole event lasted less than two hours.[151]

Most of the marchers returned home by rail on the next day, but an elected deputation of around fourteen people stayed behind with the purpose of meeting the Prime Minister.[152] After failing to achieve this aim they turned to the House of Commons as Clydesdale had announced in the press earlier. The deputation lobbied Members of Parliament on 4 November and the following day the men were received and entertained to tea at the House of Commons by a group of Conservative MPs brought together by Ian Fraser. The latter also promised to lay the League's demands before the government and the deputation returned home on 6 November 1936.[153] Ian Fraser kept his promise. Two representatives of the League were invited to discuss the government's upcoming amendment Bill with the Minister of Health on 11 November 1936, thereby allowing the League to have an input in the new legislation from the very start.[154] It was a pleasing conclusion to an otherwise disappointing affair.

Conclusion

The 1936 march was not a complete failure. As in 1920 'the general public was very sympathetically disposed' towards the marchers and their cause, as the police admitted in its summary and the momentum and publicity created by the event attracted new members to the League.[155] The government's desire to keep the League from marching to London helped to finally get a new Blind Persons Act through Parliament, although the legislation fell well short of what the League had wanted. The Act came into operation on 1 April 1938 and entitled blind individuals to start drawing non-contributory old age pensions from the age of forty. The League had demanded a lowering of the entry age to eighteen.[156] The new legislation also compelled local authorities to provide assistance exclusively under the Blind Persons Acts and not the Poor Law, unless this assistance was medical or given in an institution. This removed a major cause of complaint for which the League claimed credit. Furthermore, it allowed Councils in England or Wales to recover the costs for assisting blind people who had not resided for at least five years in their area from the local authority of their previous residency.[157] This fulfilled a demand made by the Joint Committee on Blind Welfare in July 1934, which represented the Association of Municipal Corporations and the County Councils Association. The League had vehemently opposed this demand, with the argument that the government should bear exclusive financial responsibility for the welfare of blind people and out of concern that the proposal would strengthen the existing system.[158] The new Act was therefore also at least in part a defeat for the League.

The interwar years showed the limits of what a small organisation such as the League was able to achieve. The League's failure to secure the desired amendment to the Blind Persons Act of 1920, even when Labour was in government, cannot simply be explained by the fact that neither of Ramsay MacDonald's two administrations had a majority in Parliament. After all, many of the League's demands had cross-party support. In an effort to demonstrate the Party's independence and capability to govern, however, the Labour administrations generally proved unresponsive to the trade unions' political agenda. When the League began to focus on County and County Borough Councils it discovered to its dismay that the same was true at the local level. Labour-dominated Councils often lacked the means or the will to make full use of the powers granted to them under the 1920 Blind Persons Act. 'I hardly know of one Labour Party or one Labour Council where there has been a serious effort to tackle this problem', Ben Tillett complained to the TUC in 1927 and stressed that he felt 'entitled rather to grumble against my own class in general and the Labour Movement in particular' as a result.[159]

The Labour Party's acceptance of *The Blind Persons Charter* was without doubt a success and a watershed event. However, it was only made possible by Labour's crushing defeat in 1931 when there was little prospect that the Party would return to government in the near future. Many Labour authorities also ignored *The Blind Persons Charter* and in June 1935 the League's Executive decided unanimously to send a deputation to the Labour Party's leadership 'to draw their attention to the reactionary labour groups in various parts of the country who refuse to accept and apply the policy of the party and also fail to take full advantage of their powers under the Blind Persons Act 1920'.[160] In the following year Tom Parker even claimed publicly

> that the best schemes for our people exist where Labour is still a minority [...] Despite our allegiance to the Labour movement we

must face the facts; we must realise that it is often much easier to persuade the 'Tory' local authority to give us a good scheme than it is to persuade a Labour authority. The overwhelming evidence is that the Tories respond more generously to our appeal.[161]

The 1936 march to London was, according to Purse, partly organised in order to put pressure on the Labour Party to implement *The Blind Persons Charter*, but the League decided to complain again to the National Labour Party at the end of 1937.[162] The League's Triennial Conference in 1940 once again criticised the failure of Labour politicians to adhere to their Party's official policies and the problem persisted.[163] 'The North East has been regarded as one of the strongholds of the Labour Party in the country', Clydesdale still fumed in 1950. 'Here if anywhere the Labour Party could carry anything they liked within the law and we are entitled to expect that the "Care of the Blind" would be as good here as any place else in England, but this is by no means the case.'[164]

Labour's reluctance to implement the League's demands caused the latter to reassess its commitment to the Party. By 1937 only 6 per cent of all League members paid the voluntary political levy in support of the Labour Party and the League's Executive decided not to send a delegate to the annual Labour Party Conference in that year.[165] The march of 1936 was therefore more of an attempt to get broader political support for the League's programme. No member of the Parliamentary Labour Party accompanied the deputation to the Minister of Health and Ian Fraser, who held the view that there 'ought to be no politics in the blind world', willingly provided access to Conservative MPs after the march.[166]

Although the 1936 march looked very much like its predecessor, the environment in which it took place was quite different. In 1920 a mood of optimism had prevailed and the League had attracted much support by stating that it wanted to remove blind people from welfare provision under the Poor Law. Sixteen years later many parts of Britain were still struggling to cope with the effects of the Great Depression and neither the situation at home nor events abroad offered much cause for optimism. The League's demand for more generous schemes in 1936 had therefore far less appeal than its earlier crusade against the Poor Law, especially since many British families in the distressed areas were also struggling to make ends meet. Their situation was highlighted by the Jarrow Crusade which captured the public imagination in 1936, although the lengths to which the Ministry of Health went to prevent the League's march shows that it still had the potential to embarrass the government.

However, some leading members of the League developed doubts as to whether confrontation was the right strategy in the first place. Following its policy decision in September 1933 the League began to shift from petitioning advisory, welfare or management committees to seeking representation on them. This process had already started earlier and was only officially ratified in 1933. It mirrored a similar trend of increasing cooperation between the voluntary sector and local authorities after the First World War, which Elizabeth Macadam famously labelled the 'New Philanthropy' in 1934.[167] Although the League did not explicitly refer to this development its leaders must have been aware of it. Achieving change through cooperation rather than confrontation was clearly in line with the spirit of the times in the 1930s and became increasingly attractive for the League as other tactics failed to bring the desired results. This approach acquired a new dimension and quality during the Second World War when working together for the common good became a question of national survival.

5
Success at Last? The League and the Consolidation of the Welfare State

As pointed out in the previous chapter, the League only gradually came to appreciate the influence which could be wielded through a cooperative rather than a confrontational approach. It had long felt ambivalent towards committee work as this usually involved cooperating with charitable organisations. The League had, for example, successfully petitioned the first Labour government in 1924 to restore its seat on the Ministry of Health's Advisory Committee on the Welfare of the Blind, but the value of such representation was already being discussed again just two years later.[1] Even its decision to sit on the Wireless for the Blind Committee triggered protests from branches in the early 1930s.[2]

However, the League's policy decision in September 1933 marked a turning point. The League subsequently managed to get seats on a growing number of local and regional committees, including three on London County Council's Advisory Council on the Welfare of the Blind.[3] In 1934 it even tried to gain a second seat on the Ministry of Health's Advisory Committee. Although it ultimately failed to achieve this aim, the League would retain its existing seat until the Committee ceased to exist in 1948.[4] In Scotland the League secured three seats on the newly formed Joint Advisory Committee in 1939 where it negotiated directly with representatives from all five Institutions in Scotland.[5] In December 1937 the League even accepted an invitation by the National Institute for the Blind to elect two representatives for the Institute's Executive Council.[6] Created in 1926, the National Institute's Council consisted of individuals interested in the welfare of blind people as well as representatives from the Associations of County Councils, the Associations of Municipal Corporations, the London County Council and organisations for and of blind people.[7] The League had already been invited to be represented on this body in 1931, although this invitation had been conditional on it publicly expressing support for 'a voluntary system in connection with work for the blind, strengthened and consolidated so as to be in a position to satisfy all future needs'. At that time the response of the League's Executive had been indignant. The General Secretary was instructed to inform the National Institute for the Blind 'that we regard the communication as an insult to our intelligence and a demonstration of their ignorance of the aims and objects of the National League of the Blind'.[8] Six years later, however, no conditions were attached although the League's aims and objectives had not changed. What had altered was the League's willingness to work for these objectives through committees and other bodies. This newly found spirit of cooperation would blossom even further during the Second World War and yield tangible results.

The Second World War

The Second World War's immediate impact on the League was, without doubt, profoundly negative. First and foremost, the conflict had a detrimental effect on the workshops which formed the League's strongholds. By 1939 there were over sixty workshops for blind people in Great Britain employing around 4,500 individuals.[9] These institutions found it difficult to attract orders or obtain raw materials once the conflict had started as their products were usually not classified as essential to the war effort. At the Birmingham Royal Institution for the Blind, for example, a number of workers became unemployed due to a shortage of imported materials for mat- and brush-making and by 1943 the League's Norwich branch complained that 'enormous amount of unemployment' existed in workshops and institutions all over the country.[10]

Other workers left sheltered employment as the war opened up new employment opportunities. The need to utilise all available manpower led to the creation of a wartime employment service for disabled people in 1941 and a growing number of workers migrated into open employment. Of the 240 people employed at the Birmingham Royal Institution, for example, 35 had gone into sighted industry by the spring of 1942. Twenty of them were directly engaged in the production of planes and tank parts.[11] According to the *Yorkshire Evening News*, a total of 700 blind workers found employment in war industries during 1943 and a number of other papers also ran stories about how the visually impaired contributed to the war effort.[12] In March 1944 the *Blind Advocate* reported that well over a thousand blind people had 'entered industries of National importance' and that the 'vast majority of these men and women have come from the class registered as Unemploy-able Blind Persons'.[13] By the end of that year the *Evening Standard* even claimed that a 'record total of two thousand sightless men and women' were 'fully employed on essential war work'.[14] 'The idea that blind people were restricted so far as useful employment was concerned to one or two ancient and almost forgotten industries has been exploded', Clydesdale noted with satisfaction in May 1945, but other members of the League expressed concern.[15] It was questioned whether blind war workers would be able to hold on to their jobs after the end of hostilities and industrial work in open employment was also portrayed as dangerous. Instead, members were urged to seek employment in welfare services for blind people where they could do their part by freeing non-disabled people for essential war work.[16]

The war also affected the League in other ways. Blind people in areas considered vulnerable to enemy air raids were offered evacuation at the start of hostilities. Participation was voluntary and the response differed from place to place. In Southampton, for example, the League's local branch collapsed in 1940 after most of its members had been evacuated.[17] In the North East, however, very few accepted the offer and most of the evacuees quickly returned due to the unpleasant living conditions they encountered in the receiving areas.[18] Regular German air raids on British cities began in September 1940 and affected many of the League's branches. The West Ham branch 'went out of existence during the continuous night raids on London', the Croydon branch likewise collapsed and even the London District Council ceased to function for a while as a result of the continuous raids.[19] The headquarters of the Manchester branch was hit in December 1940 and the Institutions at Cardiff, Sheffield and Swansea were damaged or destroyed in the following year.[20] In 1942 the Norwich Institution was damaged by bombs and the *Blind Advocate* found it necessary to publish advice on what to do 'If Your House in Bombed' in July 1942.[21]

With Britain fighting for survival the League's Executive decided to ban all revisions of the organisation's Rules for the duration of the conflict, despite the fact that a ballot on revisions had already taken place.[22] The 1929 Rules remained in force until 1946, which led to a resurgence of long-standing complaints about the Executive's supposedly undemocratic behaviour. In 1942 the League's Central Office at Gray's Inn Road in London was hit by a bomb which forced the General Secretary to run the organisation from a room in his own house in Sandridge, Hertfordshire.[23] It was only in 1948 and with great difficulties that new office rooms in Haringey, North London, were found.[24]

The General Secretary found it equally challenging to find accommodation for himself and his family in the capital after the war. In response the Executive decided in the same year to buy a house in London which would be let to each General Secretary during his respective term in office.[25] After years of exile from the capital, the League was determined to return for good.

The League spent the early years of the war arguing with local authorities for increases in wages and allowances to keep up with the rapidly rising cost of living.[26] It also continued its pre-war campaigns against the application of a family means test to domiciliary assistance schemes and for a 'minimum living wage' equivalent to the average wage municipal authorities paid their sighted workers.[27] The campaign was supported by circulars from the TUC's General Council and the Executive of the Labour Party. Issued shortly before the start of the conflict in 1939, the circulars urged local authorities, among other things, to pay the municipal minimum wage to all workshop employees and a minimum weekly allowance of twenty-seven shillings and sixpence for all unemployable blind people, without application of a family means test.[28]

Local authorities in Scotland proved to be the most responsive. Glasgow and Falkirk were the first to abolish the family means test in 1939 and by early 1941 most of the workshops in Scotland had adopted the municipal minimum wage, thereby bringing 'into being the realisation of what was for many years only a dream for the dim and distant future'.[29] By the end of 1942 the municipal minimum wage was paid in all workshops north of the border.[30] Outside of Scotland, however, the campaign found 'little support' as an official from the Ministry of Health put it in December 1944.[31] Nevertheless, a growing number of institutions at least accepted the principle of a minimum wage for their employees during the war, even though they did not grant the municipal minimum wage.[32] When the Second World War ended with the surrender of Japan in August 1945, fifty of the sixty-four workshops in England, Wales and Scotland were paying a minimum wage, including eighteen which paid the municipal minimum wage. The remaining fourteen paid piece rates plus an augmentation of a specific amount.[33] In addition a large number of local authorities raised wages and allowances under pressure from the League during the war and the *Blind Advocate* began to feature a steady stream of success reports as a result.[34]

Success led to a growth in membership and the founding of new branches during the Second World War. The Midland Organiser, for example, attributed the growth of the Stoke-on-Trent branch from 40 to 280 members to the improved conditions negotiated by the League in March 1942.[35] Total membership of the League rose from 5,769 at the end of 1942 to 6,847 in the following year and climaxed in December 1945 when the League reported 7,401 members.[36] This represented roughly 8.5 per cent of all registered blind individuals in Great Britain and was more than twice the number of all blind workshop employees in the country. For many of the League's leading members, the wartime experience confirmed their faith in the value of self-representation and activism. 'All the improvements in administration of blind welfare in England, Wales and Scotland are, in fact, due directly or indirectly to the work of the National League of the Blind,' Clydesdale argued in September 1940. 'Emancipation and improvement must be fought for [...] the only people who matter in the progress of blind welfare are the blind people themselves, organised so that they give atoms to the common ideals'.[37]

Despite such militant words the League's wartime campaign also held another lesson. The national emergency severely limited the opportunities for radical action. Wage disputes were settled by arbitration and the League organised very few public protests during the war.[38] A mass demonstration in Alloa, County Clackmannan, in August 1940 and a march of 139 blind people in Preston in March 1943 were the only events mentioned in the *Blind Advocate*.[39] Instead, the representatives of the League were forced to rely mainly on deputations and persuasion to achieve their aims. As a result, the organisation's local and regional officers further intensified their contacts with politicians during the war and the latter usually proved responsive to their demands.

The Scottish Organiser, for example, attributed significant improvements to the situation of blind people in Edinburgh to 'the untiring efforts of the officials of the local branch who have succeeded in establishing good relations between the corporation and the League'.[40] In the Midlands 'League history was made' in October 1943 when a Conference of Staffordshire local authorities received a deputation from the League. 'Speaking generally, the Conference must be regarded as a marked success', the regional organiser asserted and he expressed his hope that it had 'paved the way for a greater measure of League recognition in the future'.[41] From North East England, Clydesdale was able to report that representatives of four authorities had submitted a joint plan for the institutions at Middlesbrough and Sunderland to the League's Executive 'for their approval and comment before submitting the scheme to their councils for approval'.[42]

The drive towards direct representation on workshop or local authority committees also carried on during the war. Although some official bodies continued to 'regard the League as a cross between Bolshevik poison and a contageous [*sic*] disease', many others began to accept it as a partner during the Second World War.[43] A few councils and committees which had previously refused to recognise the League now agreed to receive deputations, although usually only after pressure from the local Trades Council. The hitherto 'impenetrable barrier' between the League and Warwickshire County Council, for example, was broken down in Summer 1942 'thanks to the kindly assistance of the Rugby and Nuneaton Trades Council'.[44] In the following year the County Council even initiated negotiations between the Voluntary Association in Warwickshire and the League, which led to increased payments to blind people in the county. A clearly puzzled George Custance, the League's Midland Organiser, expressed in the *Blind Advocate* his appreciation to the Association's Secretary for 'the spirit of co-operation which she has shown towards our organization'.[45] However, he also added that it was 'very seldom (all too seldom, in fact)' that the League could 'compliment, congratulate or thank any official of a voluntary society on some definite piece of good work, or for some really tangible assistance to the blind'.[46] The wartime spirit had encouraged an atmosphere of negotiation, but not changed the League's hostility towards charity officials who were still described as 'carping, parasitical, voluntary humbugs'.[47]

In 1945 the League's two representatives resigned from the Executive Council of the National Institute for the Blind, a step Ben Purse attributed to 'a sudden return to doctrinaire policy on the part of the League's executive [*sic*]'.[48] However, the reasons must have been more complicated as the League's Executive agreed in December 1945 that a future invitation from the Institute to refill these seats would be given 'favourable consideration'.[49] This invitation arrived in November 1949 after the Institute had received a Royal Charter and was re-incorporated. Its Secretary-General stressed especially 'the genuinely democratic character of the Institute's constitution', which suggests that this was the issue which had caused the League to withdraw from it four years earlier and the invitation was accepted unanimously by the League's Executive.[50]

The Beveridge Report and the arrival of the welfare state

Although the war had not changed the League's hostility towards charity, it had changed people's expectations of what the state could and should do to protect its citizens against poverty, ill-health and unem-ployment. The collective hardships endured demanded a vision of a better post-war world and politicians responded to this demand.[51] In August 1941 the Atlantic Charter proclaimed that Great Britain and the United States were also fighting for 'improved labor standards, eco-nomic advancement and social security'.[52] Two months later the British government announced the creation of 'a comprehensive hospital ser-vice' for all who needed it after the war, while Parliament expressed its support for family allowances. In response to trade union pressure for a more streamlined and efficient system of insurances and benefits the Inter-Departmental Committee on Social Insurances and Allied Services was set up under the chairmanship of William Beveridge in June 1941. Beveridge went considerably beyond his rather narrow brief to study the 'existing national scheme of social insurances and allied services' in Britain and make recommendations regarding their reform. His Report provided a blueprint for a comprehensive welfare state after the war and received an 'ecstatic' reaction from the public when it was published on 2 December 1942.[53] Although the Conservatives, Labour and the Liberal Party all had different opinions on how Beveridge's recommendations should be implemented, they did agree with the broader principles outlined in the Report. A consensus emerged that the state should pro-vide full employment as well as 'national compulsory insurance for all classes for all purposes from the cradle to the grave', as Prime Minis-ter Winston Churchill put it in a radio broadcast on 21 March 1943.[54] Only a few years after the disappointing second march to London, the League's vision of a state which provided training, employment or a minimum income for those unable to work had become the mainstream consensus.

However, the League was not directly involved in the creation of the Beveridge Report. Encouraged by the momentum generated by the war the League's Executive decided in the summer of 1941 to start a new campaign to amend the Blind Persons Acts. The General Coun-cil of the Scottish TUC signalled its backing in August 1941, but the British TUC requested that the League stopped its campaign when it was approached by the Executive.[55] The General Council pointed out that the matter was due to be dealt with by Beveridge and that the TUC was scheduled to submit evidence to the Inter-Departmental Commit-tee. In light of this, the General Council apparently felt that the League's campaign was badly timed. Trades union support had been crucial in the League's wartime campaign for higher wages and allowances and it therefore had little choice but to agree to the General Council's request.

The Executive reluctantly consented in January 1942 to leave the matter in the hands of the TUC, although the decision triggered criticism from within the League.[56] Members of the League realised very well that the Beveridge Report could become ' "the new charter for the blind" in the post-war world', as the President of the Merthyr and Mid-Wales Institution for the Blind put it, who also submitted a memorandum to the Inter-Departmental Committee.[57] The National Institute for the Blind also provided a memorandum praising the partnership the Blind Persons Act of 1920 had created between local authorities and voluntary organisations.[58] The League, however, had to work through the TUC to present its position to the Beveridge Committee and felt marginalised as a result. 'We are all awaiting, some with confident anticipation, some with gloomy forebodings, the presentation of the Beveridge Report on Social Insurance and Social Security,' the League's Midland Organiser summarised the mood in the organisation in October 1942.[59]

The published Report was greeted with equally mixed feelings. Much of Beveridge's vision overlapped with the League's own programme: Work for those who were capable, education or training for those preparing for the labour market and state-financed support as a right for those incapable of maintaining themselves were all long-standing demands of the League. Beveridge's assertion that blindness was 'a special problem, to be dealt with within the general framework by methods appropriate to the special conditions of the blind' was likewise noted with approval and later quoted in position papers prepared by the League.[60] The recommendation that 'the Ministry of Social Security should assume general responsibility for the blind' also promised to finally fulfil a central part of the League's agenda.[61] However, Beveridge proposed that the Ministry should exercise its responsibility in cooperation with local authorities and voluntary agencies. In its reaction to the Report the League's Bolton branch blamed this recommendation on 'the ulterior influence of charity organisations in its preparation, and the absence of effective representation from the blind through this League'.[62] Belfast likewise warned 'that the emancipation of the blind is not to be achieved by the continued cooperation of the State with the charity organisations' and urged the Executive 'to fight for full State control in carrying out the Beveridge Plan'.[63] The Glasgow branch expressed hostility to any plan involving charitable organisations and urged the Executive to 'press for the participation of the League' in any discussion of a 'national policy on Blind Welfare'.[64]

The League's Executive did certainly try. The publication of the government's White Paper on Social Insurance and Social Security and the passing of the Disabled Persons (Employment) Act in 1944 both had a profound impact on blind people in England, Wales and Scotland. The League responded by calling a Special Conference which was held in Blackpool on 30 September and 1 October 1944. The delegates from 63 branches welcomed the Disabled Persons (Employment) Act, but instructed the Executive to press for the retention of special workshops for blind people, the transfer of all workshops to direct public control and the creation of rehabilitation and vocational centres by the Ministry of Labour and National Insurance.[65] The White Paper had only been published a few days before the conference and was apparently not debated as a result.[66] However, the Executive considered it together with the conference resolution in November 1944 and decided to create a Special Committee, which included members of the Executive as well as the League representatives on the Advisory Committees. This Special Committee drafted memoranda outlining the League's views on the government's social and employment policies. In addition, a delegation of six was appointed to meet, if possible, with the Minister of National Insurance, the Minister of Labour and National Service, the TUC, the Labour Party and Members of the House of Commons.[67] The aim was not just to secure the position of blind workers, but also of those who were unable to perform paid employment.

Welfare and wages

While the League welcomed the principles expressed in the government's White Paper on Social Insurance and Social Security, it immediately became concerned with preserving the established standards of living of blind people in receipt of domiciliary assistance. The League's Special Committee cheered 'the Government's decision to give direct State Aid to all blind persons', as this was 'in conformity with the policy of the League since its inception'. However, it also expressed regret that the White Paper did not indicate 'to what extent a blind person may be assisted'.[68] George Custance also acknowledged in the *Blind Advocate* that the document 'laid down a definite principle for which we have always clamoured', but expressed concern that many members would be financially less well off under the new system.[69] Clydesdale had warned before the 1936 March to London that, if the national government could indeed be brought to assume full financial responsibility for all blind welfare services and introduce a uniform national scale of assistance, the latter would be lower than the allowances paid by the most progressive local authorities.[70] This threat was now becoming real and the League was determined to ensure that none of its members would be worse off because of the new legislation.

The League's campaign to prevent this reflects the somewhat chaotic state in which the organisation found itself during the war. On 27 November 1944, the League's General Secretary Henderson wrote to William Jowitt, Minister of National Insurance and member of the Labour Party, asking him to receive a deputation to discuss the government's White Paper.[71] A few days later J. Whittam approached the Minister after a public meeting at Manchester's Albert Hall. He handed him a letter with four questions on how the scheme would affect blind people to which Jowitt promised to reply. Whittam was the League's President as well as the Secretary of the Bolton branch. As the letter was written on paper from the Bolton branch the Ministry was apparently unaware that Whittam was also the leader of the National League of the Blind.[72] In fact, the staff at the Ministry of National Insurance had very little information on the League and asked the Ministry of Health to clarify 'the size and standing of this particular organisation'.[73] The reply suggested that the League should be asked to first submit its views in writing after which 'the Minister, or somebody on his behalf, should receive a deputation, hear what they have to say, and give a non[-]committal reply'.[74] The Ministry of National Insurance accepted this advice and also began to work on a reply to Whittam's letter. A few days later a letter from the Secretary of the League's Stockport branch arrived at the Ministry with further questions. He, too, had been at the Albert Hall meeting in Manchester, but Jowitt decided not to reply to his questions.[75]

Following the advice of the Ministry of Health, the League's Executive was invited on 13 December to submit a position paper on the so-called unemployable blind.[76] Not all details of the new insurance scheme had yet been worked out and the request for a written statement therefore bought valuable time for the government.[77] The League's reply arrived in late February 1944 and expressed concern that many blind people would actually be worse off under the new nationwide scheme of assistance than they were under the old system.[78] It pointed out that many local authorities had operated the Blind Persons Acts generously in the past, although it failed to mention that substantial pressure from the League and local Trades Councils had often been necessary to achieve this. Around 75 per cent of the unemployed blind population received a weekly income of at least thirty shillings, supplemented by allowances for their dependants. No less than 54 out of 200 local authorities even paid thirty-five shillings or more. The government's White Paper had suggested an invalidity benefit rate of only twenty shillings.[79]

The League wanted 'an immediate guarantee that the best conditions obtained under existing legislation shall not merely be maintained but augmented', preferably through a 'handicap allowance of not less than £2.0.0 [*sic*] per week plus payments for a wife and the first child'.[80]

The Ministry saw its own position confirmed by the League's statement as it outlined 'the chaotic position which at present obtains regarding the blind'.[81] The need for a national scheme clearly existed and even the demand for a special allowance was seriously considered. The level of assistance was identified as the most contentious issue, since the League's demand was quickly rejected as unrealistic. However, the Ministry did not have information on how much local authorities did indeed pay in their respective areas and acknowledged that it needed the League to provide this data.[82]

Jowitt, supported by members of the Ministry of Health and the Assistance Board, received the representatives of the League on 5 April 1945. The deputation was led by Whittam who had already received a written reply to his questions in December.[83] Once again, the League's focus was on those incapable of work, despite its formal status as a trade union. According to Whittam, 73,000 of the 85,000 blind people in Britain 'were unable to do work of any kind'.[84] These people, Whittam argued, deserved financial support 'not on the basis of relief, but as a compensation for their handicap'. Sight loss was 'no ordinary handicap' and in economic terms 'perhaps the most severe of all physical handicaps'. Many of those who were afflicted by it were over fifty years of age and had helped to build the wealth and prestige of Britain through their work before losing their eyesight. They therefore 'had a strong claim to the special treatment they had received in the past from successive governments'.[85] Whittam repeated the demand for a handicap allowance which should not be means-tested and of the same scale as the planned allowances for those disabled in war or industrial accidents.

Beveridge had suggested such a 'partial incapacity allowance additional to disability benefit for special expenses' in his Report, to cover the 'special needs of blind persons'.[86] The National Institute for the Blind had also adopted the idea and demanded a non-means-tested allowance 'in addition to any benefit, pension, or assistance that the blind may receive under the National Insurance scheme'.[87] As a spokesperson for the Institute later put it, the purpose of the allowance was not 'to pension off blind people but to put them, whether working or not, in as good a position as sighted persons'.[88] With both the League and the National Institute lobbying for an allowance the government was willing to give it serious consideration.[89] In his reply to Whittam's presentation, Stuart King from the Assistance Board expressed his expectation that the level of assistance paid under the new scheme would be 'somewhere about the level of the good authorities'. The League was asked to provide an estimate of the additional expenses blind people incurred on account of their disability, which the deputation promised to do. The National Institute for the Blind, whose deputation was received by Jowitt on 17 May 1945, likewise agreed to produce such a statement. However, it did not deliver on this promise.[90]

The League provided its statement in July 1945, but the document failed to impress. Written in the form of a letter and signed by Henderson, it argued that especially individuals who had lost their sight late in life found it difficult to adapt to their new situation and had to rely on paid sighted helpers for many tasks. Special equipment for blind people was expensive and blind people were also bound to be less efficient in managing their resources. No figures were put on the extra costs incurred by them which caused an official from the Assistance Board to complain that the document lacked 'meat'.[91] Henderson concluded his letter by stressing the long history of, and continuing need for, special legislation for blind people in Britain and the 'measure of comfort and contentment' they had achieved as a result of such special treatment.[92] At the dawn of the welfare state in Britain, the League was most worried about defending existing privileges and living standards. While this was a testimony to what had been achieved in the field of blind welfare, especially since the beginning of the Second World War, it also put the League in a difficult position rhetorically. The demand for special treatment was hard to justify in the light of Labour's plans for a universal insurance scheme. Jowitt himself publicly pointed out that he 'had to reject appeals by spinsters, the blind, and many other people with excellent cases for preferential treatment' because of the negative effect this would have had on the larger economy. Giving in to these demands would have inevitably led to a sharp rise in prices, Jowitt argued, which would have offset the increase in benefits and endangered 'the savings of thousands of people'.[93] When the government made it clear in the House of Commons that blind people would be treated 'as a normally handicapped person, thus doing away with special claims that have been recognised for so long by succeeding Governments and also by Sir William Beveridge in his report', the League's response was gloomy. Clydesdale predicted that this would force blind people to return to begging in the street or 'allow the organised professional beggars [i.e. charitable organisations] to continue their work on their behalf'.[94] According to the League's Midland Organiser, the White

Paper envisioned 'the return to poor law conditions, and all that that conveys'.[95]

The League therefore started a lobbying campaign and once again enlisted the help of Ian Fraser for support. Its long-standing hostility towards voluntary organisations did not extend to Fraser's organisation St Dunstan's, whose work for blind veterans had often been covered in the *Blind Advocate*. Fraser presented the League's position to James Griffiths, Jowitt's successor as Minister of National Insurance and was given assurances that no blind person would be less well off financially after the new national scale went into effect in July 1948.[96]

The League also became concerned that a number of local authorities refused its demands for higher allowances by pointing out that the National Insurance Bill was pending in Parliament. It therefore sought and received confirmation from the Ministry of National Insurance that the Bill was not intended to supersede the Blind Persons Acts. The Ministry also expressed the hope that local authorities would administer the latter 'in the most humane and progressive manner' until the introduction of the National Assistance Bill in the next session of Parliament, which would abolish the Poor Law as well as the Blind Persons Acts.[97] Backed up by this statement the League continued to press local authorities for higher allowances and wages. These appeals were often successful and a growing number of local authorities in England and Wales also began to introduce the municipal minimum wage in their workshops.[98] After a long struggle even the London County Council granted workshop employees the municipal minimum wage in July 1947, although it was conditional on workers' age and duration of service.[99] The League heralded this as a step of national significance, since the Minister of Labour had already proposed setting up a national negotiating body to determine wages and conditions in blind workshops.[100] 'The whole of the Workshop position is in the melting pot, and there is no doubt that London formerly provided a menace to the conditions already established elsewhere,' Tom Parker wrote in August and argued that the League was now 'in a much stronger position when it comes to the question of the National development'.[101]

Many local authorities also increased their allowances to individuals incapable of work in the knowledge that the national government would assume responsibility for these payments after the passing of the National Assistance Bill.[102] A number of them even began to coordinate their scales of assistance across county and borough lines and the Association of the Workshops for the Blind tried to get local authorities to accept its own employment and wages scheme in 1948. The League opposed this attempt and supported the Minister of Labour's proposal for a national negotiating body.[103] Employers rejected this initiative and various other models were tried until a National Joint Council for Workshops for the Blind was created in July 1964, on which the League acted as sole representative of workshop employees.[104]

The National Assistance Act finally came into effect on 5 July 1948. The efforts of the League and the National Institute to secure existing standards had been successful as the government had agreed to a non-detriment provision. About one quarter of the 40,000 blind people who were taken over from local authorities would have been worse off under the new scheme but for this provision.[105] Due to the efforts of the League and the National Institute they now continued to receive their higher payments until the national scale caught up with them, which in some instances took up to four years. In rural areas, however, the National Assistance Act brought an immediate and marked improvement for many sightless individuals. The League did have its strongholds in urban areas where the workshops were located. Local authorities in rural areas had therefore often found it possible to make little or no use of their powers under the Blind Persons Acts of 1920 and 1938.[106] The new national scale ended this problem.

However, the League had not achieved all it had hoped for. The National Assistance Act did not only abolish the Poor Law, but also the Blind Persons Acts of 1920 and 1938.[107] The League had argued in vain that the special problems blind people faced merited special legislation for this group. While blind people retained some privileges compared to other groups, they were now, in principle, treated as part of the larger group of disabled people.[108] Another cause for complaint was that the National Assistance Act left those blinded by illness less well off than those who had lost their sight as a result of industrial accidents or war-time military service.[109] The League strongly criticised this fact and would continue to argue that all blind people should be treated equally as they all had the same needs.[110]

Finally, the National Assistance Act did not introduce the special allowance both the League and the National Institute for the Blind had demanded. The importance both organisations attached to this demand was demonstrated by the fact that Griffiths invited them back to the Ministry to explain this decision personally. The deputations of the League and the Institute met with the Minister at Carlton House Terrace on 6 November 1947. Griffiths told the delegates that a special allowance for blind people would create similar demands from other disabled groups. Even if an allowance was introduced many blind people would still have to apply for additional assistance to have their needs met. This, Griffiths argued, would cause administrative difficulties and was not the best way of helping them. The Minister pointed out that the government nevertheless recognised the special position of those with visual impairments. They would still be entitled to apply for a non-contributory pension from the age of forty and the National Assistance Bill made it mandatory for the National Assistance Board to provide special assistance for blind people.[111]

The delegates from the Institute and the League, as well as the Members of Parliament who accompanied them, all expressed their disappointment about the decision.[112] However, Griffiths kept his word and the Regulations adopted after the passing of the National Assistance Bill introduced an additional weekly allowance of fifteen shillings 'to meet special needs arising from blindness'.[113] The sum fell well short of what the League had demanded, but the allowance brought blind people an increase of 62 per cent over the standard scale rate of twenty-four shillings for a single householder.[114] No other group, except those receiving treatment for pulmonary tuberculosis, received such special treatment and the League welcomed it as 'evidence of a generous and humane approach to the question'.[115]

Overall, the League was well satisfied with the new legislation and claimed a share of the credit for it. 'We regard the National Assistance Act as a partial response to our prolonged agitation', the League's General Secretary T. H. Smith confidently proclaimed in July 1948. While he acknowledged that the Blind Persons Acts of 1920 and 1938 had improved the lives of many individuals, he also stressed that the two pieces of legislation 'would have remained a dead letter in many respects if it had not been for the work of this Society. [...] The National League of the Blind was the only Organisation to initiate approaches to local authorities to secure the appointment of [a] Blind Persons Act Committee, and a substantial increase in domiciliary assistance'.[116] Smith made it clear that the National Assistance Act did not end the need for further lobbying and campaigning. The officers of the National Assistance Board had great discretion for making additional payments to individuals with special needs and the League's General Secretary urged all branches and District Councils to ensure 'that these discretionary powers are used to the full on behalf of the blind'.[117]

And there was more work to do. Under the National Assistance Act, local authorities retained the responsibility for organising welfare services for disabled people. The legislation allowed them to either assume direct control of this task or to delegate it to a voluntary organisation and the League urged its branches to prevent the latter. 'It would be disappointing if the larger measure of direct interest assumed by the State in the employable and unemployable blind person should coincide with a development of blind welfare services under voluntary direction financed to a major extend by public funds,' the *Blind Advocate* argued in January 1949.[118] Finally, the Act conferred upon local authorities a duty to promote the social rehabilitation of disabled people, which the League interpreted as helping them 'to get back into the ordinary social life of the community'. It suggested that this could be best achieved through collective instructions in educational centres outside of the home and the lobbying of local authorities for the creation of such centres was identified as 'a real humanitarian work for the Branches and District Councils'.[119]

Nevertheless, 'the nationalisation of domiciliary assistance' in 1948 was recognised by the League as a watershed moment. After decades of agitation and lobbying it had achieved its aim of direct state aid.[120] From then on the League would focus on improving the system rather than changing it. The agitation for direct state aid had been largely led by those employed in the workshops for blind people. The League had been formed around these institutions which provided crucial resources as well as a pool of recruits for local branches. However, the workshops and their employees were also significantly affected by the Second World War and the welfare state legislation it triggered.

Work and training

As already discussed, the Second World War dramatically shifted perceptions of what disabled people were capable of in the workplace. The manpower needs of the Second World War had also allowed many partially sighted and blind individuals to enter open employment and take up industrial jobs for which they had hitherto been deemed unsuited. Once again, pioneering work was done by St Dunstan's which set up an Industrial Department for sightless veterans after a conference with employers in 1940.[121] Bowing to pressure from the TUC as well as the voluntary sector, the Ministry of Labour and National Service assumed responsibility for the vocational training of disabled people in the following year. An 'interim scheme' was started under which Disablement Resettlement Officers interviewed people with disabilities and offered advice on training and employment.[122] In addition an Inter-Departmental Committee was appointed under George Tomlinson, Joint Parliamentary Secretary at the Ministry of Labour and National Service, to develop plans for a comprehensive post-war rehabilitation, training and employment programme. The Tomlinson Committee published its report in January 1943 and it subsequently became the blueprint for the Disabled Persons (Employment) Act of 1944.[123]

The Act defined disability in relation to one's capability to perform work, very much like the Blind Persons Act of 1920 had defined blindness as the inability 'to perform any work for which eyesight is essential'.[124] A disabled person was someone 'who, on account of injury, disease, or congenital deformity', was 'substantially handicapped in obtaining or keeping employment, or in undertaking work on his own account'.[125] The first sections of the Act to be enacted by Order in Council in August 1944 were those providing training and industrial rehabilitation courses.[126] The Ministry of Labour and National Service was authorised to set up such courses with the approval of the Treasury in order to facilitate the integration of disabled individuals into the open labour market. Disabled people could sign up on a special register maintained by the Ministry of Labour and employers of a certain number of people were required to hire a percentage of their workforce from the pool of registered disabled persons. The quota was negotiable, depending on the specific circumstances of an employer, but it was compulsory. Unlike the voluntary quota under the King's National Roll Scheme introduced in 1919, employers who did not fulfil their obligation faced a penalty of up to £100 or three months in prison. The Minister of Labour could even reserve specific occupations for registered disabled people, although this power was rarely used out of concern that it might limit disabled workers to these types of jobs.[127]

Furthermore, the Ministry of Labour and National Insurance was empowered to create sheltered employment or training opportunities for severely disabled individuals by setting up a non-profit-making corporation. The 'Disabled Persons Employment Corporation', which was later rebranded 'Remploy', came into existence in March 1945 and opened its first factory in April the following year. Seventy more would follow before the end of 1949.[128] Local authorities or voluntary organisations were allowed to provide their own sheltered employment for disabled people, but these facilities would also be financed by the Ministry of Labour and National Service.[129] For the next thirty years, this would be the framework in which employment for disabled people would be provided.[130]

The League's reaction to the Disabled Persons (Employment) Act was mixed. On the one hand it was perceived as a triumph. 'State responsibility for the care and well-being of blind persons has been the primary object of the National League of the Blind for more than forty-five years, and we welcome with profound satisfaction the acceptance of this principle by the Government in passing into Law the Disabled Persons (Employment) Act,' Henderson told the Minister of Labour and National Service in August 1945.[131] The League had long demanded industrial training schemes organised, financed and run by a department of the national government. The creation of national and municipal work-shops which paid 'a real living wage' had been another core goal and the League expressed the hope that the Act would bring all existing workshops under the control of the Ministry of Labour and National Insurance.[132] The Act also fulfilled another long-standing demand of the League by applying to both civilians and former service personnel. While the latter were still given preference over civilians in the adminis-tration of the Act, the legislation nevertheless provided equal provisions for both groups.[133] Finally, the aid given by the State was not framed in the language of charity. Training and support were provided so that dis-abled people could realise their potential, succeed on the labour market and contribute to society. These services were a form of compensation to level the playing field with non-disabled workers, not an attempt to keep disabled people occupied.

As a general rule, Remploy tried 'to run its factories, so far as possi-ble, on commercial lines and to reproduce closely the atmosphere of ordinary industry'.[134] Sheltered workshops had traditionally focused on handicrafts like basket-, brush- or mat-making, partly because they were credited with a therapeutic value. In contrast, Remploy offered jobs in the industrial manufacturing of furniture, clothing, electrical appliances or other such items.[135] Those working in open industry were likewise employed in a wide variety of occupations. This was a deliberate pol-icy and a direct result of the experiences undergone during the Second World War. 'We developed what I call a brush-and-basket complex', Tomlinson summarised the previous approach in a speech organised by Henshaw's Institution in November 1944. 'If they could not make brushes and baskets we said they were unemployable. We did not give them the opportunity of being trained for jobs they could do.'[136]

The League's reaction to the Disabled Persons (Employment) Act once again showed a concern for its immediate economic consequences. On the initiative of the Executive, another special conference was called for 17 March 1945 to discuss the League's position on remuneration for workshop employees.[137] With regard to the future of the workshops, however, the League was caught in a dilemma. On the one hand it supported the aim of broadening employment opportunities for blind people by placing them in open industry or professional positions. The special conference at Blackpool in 1944 had openly criticised workshop managers for allegedly blocking the transfer of their employees into such jobs.[138] A deputation to the Ministry of Labour and National Insurance in August 1945 emphasised the League's view that as 'many blind persons as possible should be employed in normal industry' and that training should be developed 'so as to provide a wider range of occupations'.[139] In particular the League stressed the desirability of employing more blind people in the administration of welfare services for blind people, as well as the need to place more of them in professional jobs. However, the special workshops for blind people were also the centres around which the League had grown and from which it derived much of its strength. The Blackpool conference therefore instructed the Executive to work for the preservation of the special workshops as well as 'the elimination of voluntaryism [*sic*] in the direction of such institutions'.[140] The government's plan for inclusive factories open to all disabled people was perceived as a threat to the League's institutional strongholds.

Somewhat surprisingly, the League justified its demand for special workshops for blind people with the claim that the latter were significantly less efficient than sighted disabled workers.[141] The League's deputation to the Ministry of Labour in August 1945 expressed the view that 'the capacity of the majority of the blind averaged not more than 50% and it was thought that it would be prejudicial to blind workers for them to train or work alongside sighted persons'. Speaking for the deputation, the League's President also argued that blind people working in open industry 'had experienced certain difficulties' working alongside sighted employees.[142] The representatives of the Ministry of Labour were unsympathetic. They emphasised that the government was generally opposed to the segregation of blind workers and stressed that the latter should be treated 'as far as possible as normal persons'.[143] Nevertheless, the Ministry of Labour and National Insurance financed the specialised blind workshops, despite the rapid creation of new Remploy factories between 1946 and 1952. By 1958 there were around seventy such workshops providing training or employment for over 4,000 visually impaired individuals.[144] Two-thirds of them were run by charitable organisations, despite the League's long-standing campaign for the municipalisation of all workshops and the League continued to denounce this system as 'cumbersome, inefficient and uneconomic'.[145]

The network of Remploy factories, in contrast, represented the model the League had demanded since the late nineteenth century. Nevertheless, blind people were effectively barred from employment in Remploy factories as demand for these jobs was high among other disabled groups and the special blind workshops continued to exist.[146] The League's General Secretary pointed out that it was

> somewhat ironical that while the policy of the League has been followed in relation to the workshops employing other severely disabled people, it has still to be given effect to in workshops for the blind [...] If the provision of work in special factories for seeing handicapped persons is a matter for national action, there is no reason why the employment problem of the blind should not be dealt with on similar lines.[147]

The government, however, had different ideas. Encouraged by the Ministry of Labour, local authorities began to place sighted disabled workers in workshops formerly reserved for blind people.[148] The process was a slow one: By March 1962 thirty workshops had admitted a total of 158 sighted disabled people, but the trend was clear and the numbers were growing.[149] A Working Party on Workshops for the Blind set up by the Ministry of Labour in 1960 approved this development and recommended that local authorities should combine sheltered employment for sighted disabled people with those provided for blind people. The League's General Secretary had been a member of the Working Party and the League officially supported this policy. However, it became concerned that the sighted disabled workers were not organised and sometimes less well-paid than its own members. The Working Party's Report, which was published in 1962, in fact recommended separate representation for sighted disabled workshop employees on a yet to be created Joint Industrial Council, while the League was earmarked to only represent visually impaired workers.[150] Rather than watching the creation of a separate trade union in the workshops the League tried to change its Rules in 1962 in order to allow sighted disabled people to become members. However, this move failed due to the fact that the proposed amendment did not provide for a change of the League's name.[151] The problem was discussed again at the League's Triennial Conference in 1964 and four years later the League officially opened its ranks to disabled sighted workers and changed its name to the National League of the Blind and Disabled of Great Britain and Ireland.[152]

The changing status of sheltered employment in British society also began to worry the League from the 1940s onwards. In the past, skilled workshop employees had formed a distinct group of relatively well-paid, confident and class-conscious activists able to provide leadership for those who were less well off. Since the Second World War, however, individuals who successfully competed with sighted workers in modern industries became the heralded role models.[153] 'Segregation with all its attendant evils has obviously been left behind, and a complete understanding between sightless and sighted is at last in prospect,' J. E. Rose wrote in *Industrial Welfare* in 1947 and proclaimed the beginning of a new era 'in which both will work side by side to enjoy companionship and the amenities of industrial life'.[154] A Working Party created by Minister of Labour George Isaacs in the following year dealt with the question of how to develop the employment of blind people in industry and services and likewise promoted employment in either sector as preferable over sheltered employment. In its report, which was published in 1951, the Working Party recommended measures to allow young people, as well as those who had lost their sight in adult life, greater chances to find jobs in open employment.[155] Sheltered employment increasingly became seen as a refuge for those who were perceived as too old and not productive enough for other occupations. 'In general, the new recruits who have come into the workshops in recent years have been older, less capable, and less adaptable than the pre-war entrants,' the Working Party of Workshops for the Blind summarised in 1962.[156] Eight years later Rose was still able to write with confidence that the 'blind in the workshops today are nearly all older men, over forty. The younger blind would prefer to work in a sighted world.' For Rose, the workshop had become the domain of 'the less able blind, who find difficulty in competing and living in a sighted world'.[157] Regardless of whether this assessment was fair or not, it signalled a loss of status for the workshops which reduced their usefulness as recruitment grounds for a new generation of militant leaders.

Conclusion

When the League prepared for its Golden Jubilee in 1949 it had cause to look back with pride over the fifty years of its existence as a trade union. Yet Midland Organiser J. Perry sounded defiant when he told his fellow trade unionists in April 1948 that they had a 'right to celebrate' the anniversary. Membership figures had grown beyond all expectations and the organisation had 'recorded success after success for the Blind' despite the persistent efforts of charity officials to 'destroy, frustrate and hinder the work' of the League.[158] However, Perry reminded the members of the League that there was still work to be done. The League had been founded to win 'State Aid for the Blind, and the abolition of the Charity System' and while the former had been largely achieved, the latter had not.[159]

Voluntarism had flourished during the Second World War, but charitable organisations found themselves in crisis as a result of the conflict. The war had caused substantial damage to buildings, depleted funds, reduced the number of volunteers and forced many organisations into closer cooperation with the state, with the latter providing essential services and charitable organisations supplying only amenities. In an increasingly egalitarian, secular and mobile society, charity came to be regarded as demeaning and the introduction of a comprehensive welfare state posed the question as to whether it was still necessary at all. By 1948, over 90 per cent of the British population thought that charity no longer had a role to play in society.[160]

However, charitable organisations for blind people or other disabled groups were somewhat sheltered from this trend. The granting of a Royal Charter to the National Institute for the Blind in 1948 was a warning sign for the League that some organisations still enjoyed widespread respect.[161] Private charities provided highly specialised services for a relatively small group of people and the Minister of Health himself stressed in a speech in December 1948 that they still had a role to play. Aneurin Bevan declared that the success of welfare schemes for disabled people depended on the crucial support voluntary associations provided for local authorities and argued that they offered a personal level of care which civil servants were unable to give: 'You can't possibly get officials to provide that sympathy, personal contact, and unremitting attendance, which is provided by voluntary means.'[162] The League's General Secretary was quick to point out that Bevan's statement was at odds with official Labour Party policy and that the very same argument had been used to oppose Bevan's National Health Service which had started in July 1948. 'The fact that the National Assistance Act has superseded the Blind Persons Acts in no way makes our criticisms of the voluntary system less valid, or the needs for a public welfare service for the blind any less,' Thomas H. Smith stressed and the League's President also emphasised this point at the Golden Jubilee celebration the following May.[163] In a direct reference to Bevan's remark, the League's President declared that 'in the view of its members, a view founded on personal experience, the Government was preferable to the charity official at any time'. While

civil servants might have a tendency to interpret regulations rigidly, regulations 'could be amended by agitation and persuasion'. The prejudices
of most charity officials, however, were often impossible to change, especially as they had a vested interest in preserving the existing voluntary
system.[164] Democratic accountability, in other words, was more important than personal relationships which were reminiscent of old patterns
of paternalism and deference. It was a position many supporters of the
Labour Party subscribed to at the time.[165]

The League therefore celebrated its Golden Jubilee in 1949 with a mixture of pride and determination. Many of its aims had been realised and
its standing with local authorities and central government had reached
new heights. The Golden Jubilee Celebration of the League's London
District Council on 15 October 1949, for example, was attended by the
Minister of Labour and National Service. George Isaacs, MP, assured the
League that it still had an important role to play and urged its members
to continue working for better conditions for the visually impaired in
Britain.[166] Based on the experience of the past two decades, the League
concluded that this could be best achieved from an insider position. For
the first time in its history, the 1952 Code of Rules contained a commitment to securing 'direct League representation on all bodies charged
with the administration of the various services concerned with the education, employment and welfare of the blind'.[167] The League had started
this policy in 1933 and it yielded results once public opinion came in
line with the League's vision of state-funded and centrally administered
welfare during the Second World War. By that time the League had managed to build an organisation which covered the whole of the United
Kingdom and was ready to exploit the shift in public attitude to the
fullest.

To what degree the League had contributed to this shift is ultimately
impossible to answer. Even within the trade union movement, many
people had never heard of the organisation. Nevertheless, the League
constantly pushed the boundaries of the discourse on how visually
impaired people should be treated. It also publicised – and sometimes
exaggerated – the shortcomings of the existing system and provided suggestions for how to remedy them. Rather than being a radical voice in
the wilderness the League gained increasing access to policy formulating
bodies and decision-makers over the first half of the twentieth century. It
also had the active backing of the TUC from 1902 onwards and by 1947
the Assistance Board described the League as one of the 'two principal
associations representing the interests of the blind' in the country. Government Ministers were willing to listen to it and came to appreciate its

experience and expertise.[168] The fact that blind people enjoyed considerable privileges compared to other disabled groups in British society even
after 1948 was also partly, although not exclusively, due to the League's
constant activism. The 'state aid' the League had demanded and helped
to win for blind people provided a blueprint for the government when
it finally turned its attention to other disabled groups in the 1940s. By
helping to shape the pioneering services provided for blind people in
the first half of the twentieth century the League also helped to shape
the British Welfare State after the Second World War.

Case Study C: Tom Parker

Like Ben Purse, Thomas ('Tom') J. Parker also grew up in one of the traditional strongholds of British trade unionism. Born in the Rhondda Valley on 18 June 1909 as the son of a miner and committed trade unionist, Parker also lost his sight during childhood. At the age of eleven he accidently pushed a meat skewer into his right eye while trying to mend a football.[169] His mother immediately took him to an eye specialist who demanded the prohibitively high sum of £20 to perform the necessary operation. This caused a crucial delay of twelve hours before Parker finally received treatment at Cardiff Infirmary.[170] He later told a reporter that 'there wasn't £20 in the whole village let alone in our household' and the incident clearly had an impact on Parker's attitude towards sighted professionals and his perception of class.[171] Although the operation at Cardiff Infirmary was thought to be successful, Parker lost the sight in his right eye and half the sight in his left. When another operation to restore his sight went wrong in 1925 he became completely blind and remained so for the rest of his life.[172]

Parker resumed his education at a residential school in Bradford until he returned to South Wales at the age of sixteen. He found employment as a basket maker in the Rhondda Workshop for the Blind, which was run by the local Institute for the Blind and financed entirely by contributions from the local mining community. This experience of working-class solidarity with blind people was the other formative experience of his life and over six decades later he still spoke 'with great pride of how it all came about'.[173] Workshop employees were required to join the Rhondda branch of the National League of the Blind which had been formed in 1919. Parker became Chairman of the branch in 1927, later advanced to the position of area Secretary and finally joined the League's Executive Council in 1933. Three years later he was elected to the post of Organiser for London and the Home Counties.[174] He was so successful in his new position that the Executive officially commended him for his work after only one year in office.[175]

After the Second World War, Parker ventured into electoral politics and in 1946 became the first Labour candidate to win a County Council election in Uxbridge. He lost his seat on Middlesex County Council in 1949 but was elected to Uxbridge Urban District Council (later Uxbridge Borough Council) in the following month. Parker led the Labour Group on the Council between 1949 and 1964 and also sat on its successor, Hillingdon London Borough Council, until 1968.[176] He was chairman of the local National Insurance Advisory Committee and elected Mayor of Uxbridge for 1960-1. Parker was one of three blind men to hold such a post in that particular year: Alderman Shakeshaft, who was also a member of the League, was elected Mayor of Birkenhead for the same term and Councillor Norman Preedy became Mayor of Dudley. Parker and Shakeshaft were neither the first nor the last members of the League to achieve such a high profile office. James A. Clydesdale had already served as Lord Mayor of Newcastle upon Tyne in 1945-6, while A. Chrisp was elected Mayor of Greenwich and E. A. Dickinson Mayor of Middlesbrough in 1958-9. Dan West, the League's President, would later serve twice as Mayor of the London Borough of Hackney.[177] As Parker himself pointed out, this was 'an impressive record of public service from the members of a small organisation'.[178] It was also an impressive record for an organisation which had for a long time depended on allies within the political establishment.

Parker's quest for a seat in Parliament was, however, less successful. In 1951 he contested the Ruislip-Northwood Division of Middlesex but was defeated despite achieving the highest vote for Labour ever recorded in this constituency.[179] In 1964 he tried to unseat the Tory MP for Uxbridge, TV personality and regular *Evening Standard* columnist, Charles Curran and came within 653 votes of achieving this goal.[180] After the sudden death of Thomas H. Smith in 1969 Parker decided to run for General Secretary of the League. He comfortably won the election and remained in office for the next ten years. In contrast to previous officers of the League, with the exception of Purse, he started to take an active role in the affairs of the Royal National Institute for the Blind.

Parker successfully encouraged the League to resume its cooperation with the Institute and became a member of its Executive Council in 1970.[181] He would continue to serve on this body until 1995. Parker helped to create, as well as chaired, the Institute's Consumer Sub-Committee in 1975, which tested new goods designed for blind people and also became Vice-Chairman of the Rehabilitation, Training and Employment Sub-Committee in the following year.[182] Radio was one of Parker's passions and he was one of the first blind people in the country to acquire a Radio Amateur's Licence in 1938. As a result the Institute appointed him as one of its representatives on the Committee of the British Wireless for the Blind Fund of which he was Vice-Chairman until 1995. He also served as Chairman of the Institute's Technical Committee.[183]

International affairs were his other passion and Parker eventually became the League's representative for this field. His first official trip abroad led him to the Netherlands in 1949 where he helped blind organisations rebuild their facilities after the destruction caused by World War Two. Many more journeys abroad would follow. His first visit to the United States took place in 1965 at the invitation of the National Federation of the Blind to speak at its 25th jubilee in Washington DC. Two years later Parker became a member of the Executive of the International Federation of the Blind (IFB) after the League had joined the organisation and he served as the IFB's Honorary Vice-President until it dissolved in 1984 to make way for the World Blind Union (WBU). Parker was made an Honorary Life Member of the WBU on its foundation and was also appointed to its Rehabilitation, Training and Employment Committee. He also received an Honorary Life Membership of the European Blind Union.[184]

Despite officially retiring in 1979, Parker continued as Vice-Chairman of the Royal National Institute's Rehabilitation, Training and Employment Sub-Committee. Three years later he also became chairman of the Institute's Vocational and Social Services Committee, thereby following in Purse's footsteps. He held both positions until 1992 when he also left the Consumer Sub-Committee. From 1980 to 1988 Parker was also Vice-Chairman of the Institute's International Committee.[185] In addition to his manifold activities in the League and the Royal National Institute, Parker also became the first chairman of the European Economic Community's Liaison Committee for Visual Handicaps and played an active role in the European Blind Union and other organisations.[186] He received many honours, including an OBE, the Louis Braille Medal and the Ordre du Mérite from the French Organisations of the Blind.[187] In 1989 Princess Diana also presented him with the Help the Aged Golden Award for being an 'Intrepid Traveller'.[188] He died peacefully at his home in Pontypridd, South Wales, on 11 August 1995. His wife had died before him.[189] The memorial meeting for him on 31 January 1996 was attended by about one hundred people. Among those paying tribute to Parker were 'Jack' [James] Jones, the former General Secretary of the Transport and General Workers' Union and Parker's son, Brian.[190]

Parker's impact on the League and the blind community at large easily rivals that of Ben Purse. However, Parker did not write books, nor did he show great interest in broader philosophical questions and he is therefore far less well known than Purse.[191] 'He was essentially a practical man who was much more at home looking at new equipment for blind people than in tackling abstract ideas,' the chairman of the Royal National Institute put it in his obituary.[192] Parker did, of course, also participate in demonstrations. He was one of the leading advocates of a second march to London and in charge of the marchers during their stay in the capital in 1936. He also led a contingent of marchers from Uxbridge on a CND march to Aldermaston after the war.[193] But Parker's real impact was in the committee rooms, which illustrates the changing nature of blind activism after the Second World War. Rather than fighting the system the League was now part of it and Parker, unlike Purse, received recognition and praise for his cooperation with voluntary organisations.

6
A Changing Relationship: The League and Charity in the Post-War Era

Despite the self-congratulatory tone of the Golden Jubilee celebrations in 1949, the League already had reasons to worry by that time. Membership figures had peaked in 1945 when a record of 7,401 men and women were paying fees. The number of branches had reached its highest figure ever in the following year when 109 local committees were recognised by the League's Central Office.[1] From then on, however, the League began to shrink. In the year of the Golden Jubilee, membership had already declined to 6,665 individuals and the League had lost nine branches. On its 75th Anniversary in 1974, the League had only 4,250 members. By February 2000, when the League ceased to file independent returns, this had fallen to 1,755 people.[2]

The welfare state legislation of the 1940s was one of the reasons for the League's seemingly unstoppable contraction after the Second World War. Despite the League's best efforts the visually impaired largely lost their distinct position in the landscape of welfare after 1948, when they were merged into the larger group of disabled people.[3] This did not only lead to a reduction of the specialised welfare services local authorities provided for the blind community.[4] Existing committees dedicated to the welfare of blind people were replaced by those concerned with disabled people in general and the League struggled at times to gain representation on these new bodies. For example, the League had long held a seat on the Ministry of Health's Advisory Committee on the Welfare of the Blind, as well as on its Scottish equivalent. When both were abolished the League was invited to nominate candidates for the new Advisory Council on the Welfare of Handicapped Persons which replaced them, but none of its nominees were appointed.[5] The Minister of Labour and National Insurance likewise appointed a National Advisory Council, but again the League was not directly represented on it.[6]

On the local level the problem was of a slightly different nature. Here the League was usually able to secure seats on the bodies which replaced the old Blind Persons Act Committees, but some of them granted their co-opted disabled members fewer rights than they had before 1948.[7]

In other words, the welfare state legislation of the 1940s diluted the voice of the League in the decision-making process as visual impairment became just one of the many disabilities the welfare state was concerned with. The League's previous successes had resulted from its ability to take on local authorities individually and play them off against each other. Individuals had an incentive to join their local branch and were entitled to feel that their individual activism made a difference. 'In the years up to 1948 we had almost one hundred branches scattered around the country', Tom Parker ruefully recalled 25 years later: 'Many thousands of non-employed blind people were in the ranks of the League. They had been able to apply pressure on County and County Borough Councils [...] Those days saw the League at its best'.[8] After 1948, however, the League had to negotiate with the central government, and civil servants and government ministers ultimately proved less responsive to deputations and demonstrations than local politicians. Many members of the League who were unable to work saw little point in continuing to pay membership fees. They 'thought that now the League had achieved a long cherished dream of state aid for the blind, their struggle was over and they could relax', Parker stated as he summarised their attitude and he called this the 'great tragedy'.[9]

The workshops in the post-war era

People in open employment also began to avoid the League and if they joined a trade union they usually preferred one associated with their respective profession. The League did consider ways of addressing this issue, for example by lowering membership fees for those in open employment and by setting up dual membership schemes with other trade unions. However, the long-term trend was one of declining numbers and failure to recruit enough new young people also led to a rise in the average age of the League's membership.[10]

The opening of the specialised workshops for blind people to sighted disabled workers created further problems. It generated divisions within the League because the interests of the new members were not always represented adequately within the organisation. More importantly, however, it destroyed the League's hitherto sharp profile as a self-representation group of people who shared a specific disability.[11]

Employment in a sheltered workshop now became the common denominator of the League's members and this bound the fortunes of the League to an institution whose prestige was clearly in decline since the Second World War, when placement in open employment became the preferred option. Local authorities increasingly 'considered sheltered employment as a means of providing employment for those who are most severely disabled and regard them more as simply occupation centres, and not as a viable means of efficient employment'.[12] Even within some parts of the Labour Party and the Trade Union Movement, sheltered workshops were perceived as segregating or 'ghettoising' disabled people and the League's General Secretary still had to defend their existence vis-à-vis other trade unionists and government ministers in the 1990s.[13]

The League's increasing focus on workshop issues was a major reason why it eventually lost its place at the forefront of the struggle for disability rights after the Second World War. Martin Milligan, the President of the National Federation of the Blind, made this clear when he addressed the League's Triennial Conference in 1988. Milligan had joined the League in Edinburgh in 1941 and retained his membership after joining the National Federation of the Blind. Now a professor of philosophy at the University of Leeds, he argued that the League had become too much of a specialised trade union since the Second World War:

> The almost total absorption with workshop affairs of all but one League Branch of which he has been a member and the fact that he did not work in a workshop, and was therefore unable to participate, made him conclude that help with the things with which he was concerned could come from the Federation.[14]

When Joe Mann was elected General Secretary in 1995 he still found the League to be 'very insular' and restricted to 'what was going on in the trade union movement'. The desire to make the League more outward looking and proactive was hampered by the organisation's lack of resources and eventually caused it to join forces with the ISTC in 2000.[15]

The League had always assumed that the introduction of direct state aid would bring with it the end of 'voluntaryism' as statutory services would simply replace voluntary services. Many people outside of the League had shared this assumption when the Labour government consolidated and completed the welfare state between 1945 and 1948, although by far not everyone rejoiced at the idea.[16] William Beveridge, for example, was very much concerned about the future of the voluntary sector and mounted a sustained argument for its continuing useful-ness in his third report *Voluntary Action*. Published in 1948, the report correctly identified blindness as one of the problems which had 'not been removed from the scope of Voluntary Action'.[17] Government offi-cials made it clear repeatedly that they had no intention of curtailing 'the activities of the various voluntary associations interested in blind welfare'.[18] On the contrary, specialised services for the visually impaired remained one of the areas in which private charities continued to ful-fil a crucial role without much competition from overstretched local authorities.[19] The League was not alone in complaining about 'a seri-ous deterioration in the specialised services provided for blind people' since the Second World War, and the decline of the Home Teacher Service especially was frequently mourned.[20] The League criticised this development but was largely powerless to stop it.

Its hostility towards the voluntary sector remained unchanged in the first decades after the Second World War. Fundraising campaigns by charitable organisations were criticised as unnecessary and disingenu-ous after 1948 due to the fact that the state had now assumed financial responsibility for blind and partially sighted people.[21] In particular, 'beg-ging appeals from voluntary societies for the blind by the use of child statuettes and street collections' were considered to be 'humiliating' and 'disgraceful' as they created the impression that the education of visually impaired children depended on charitable donations.[22] The continu-ous role of charitable organisations in the provision of welfare services was criticised as 'both inefficient and wasteful' and the League already stressed in 1949 that it remained determined 'to convince public opin-ion of this fact'.[23] This was partly done by continuing its attacks on workshops, most of which were still run by voluntary organisations, although the government and local authorities now provided much of the funding.

Many workshops struggled economically in the post-war era and the League blamed their problems on a 'lack of proper commercial organisa-tion, lack of enterprise and lack of cooperation'.[24] Efforts to modernise the workshops were welcomed, but 'inefficient management' was identi-fied as a major reason for lack of commercial success in the early 1950s.[25] This assessment was not unfounded as workshop managers very rarely had previous business experience. The political preference for placing as many blind people as possible in open employment led to a declin-ing demand for workshop places and to the admission of individuals whose productivity was not high enough to make the workshops eco-nomically viable. This development was already severely criticised by a Joint Committee set up by the Minister of Labour, the Minister of

Health and the Secretary of State for Scotland. Chaired by Lord Piercy, the Committee's Report in 1956 expressed the view that 'all sheltered workshops, whether for the blind or the sighted, should be regarded as places of employment with as high as possible a rate of individual productivity'.[26] Following the Report's recommendations, the Disabled Persons (Employment) Act of 1958 therefore implemented a number of measures to highlight the character of the workshops as productive economic units rather than facilities providing divisionary occupation. Nevertheless, the workshops remained the responsibility of local authority Welfare Committees and Officers. Workshop managers were often picked based on their previous experiences of working with blind people rather than their business expertise and many of them were expected to cover welfare issues as part of their duties.[27]

Another consequence of local control was a failure to market workshop products on a national scale, or to combine with other such institutions to procure the necessary raw materials more cheaply.[28] Outdated trades were another problem, as traditional crafts like basket-, brush- or mat-making were in quick decline and often unsuitable for those who were unable to find employment in open industry.[29] Finally, workshop employees were remunerated in a way which gave them little incentive to increase their output, despite the widespread introduction of an 'incentive bonus' in the 1950s.[30] The combined results of these factors were rising costs and declining revenues. By the early 1960s the annual cost of providing sheltered employment for less than 4,000 blind individuals had reached around two million pounds. The Ministry of Labour's Working Party on the Workshops for the Blind wryly observed in its 1962 Report that it would have been actually cheaper to 'close down all the workshops while continuing to pay the blind the same wages and augmentation as before'.[31] By that time only a very small proportion of the income of workshop employees came from 'earnings', while the rest were 'augmentation' payments from local authorities. The authorities had agreed to the introduction of a minimum wage for workshop employees throughout the nation in 1951 and the augmentation payments were made to bring the workers' income up to the agreed level. These payments were income tax-free welfare payments paid on the basis of need and the Working Party therefore called it 'fiction rather than fact to say that the worker is contributing substantially to his own maintenance'.[32] The workshop which the League had once regarded as essential for lifting its members out of charity had failed to deliver on the promise of independence and respectability.

The Working Party's Report affirmed that workshops still had a useful role to play, but also expressed the view that employment in open industry was generally preferable. It also supported the position of the Piercy Committee that all workshop employees should be able to make 'a significant contribution to production' but identified 'tradition and the system of local control' as the main obstacles to modernising the workshops.[33] Following its recommendation a non-profit organisation called the Industrial Advisors to the Blind Ltd. was set up in 1964 to help workshops become more competitive and successful in marketing their products, but these institutions nevertheless continued to struggle.[34] 'Traditional markets are shrinking', Tom Parker admitted in 1970: 'New materials and new articles are being used by the former customers who provided work for the Workshops.'[35] In an effort to adapt to changing market conditions workshops slowly began to replace traditional handicrafts with mechanical jobs. The League did not oppose the introduction of new trades in the workshops in order to make them more competitive, although it also claimed that many employees found 'working at a skilled craft more interesting and congenial than doing a repetitive job'.[36] The organisation also became increasingly concerned about the impact the switch from skilled handicrafts to industrial work had on the wages of its members.[37]

This concern was only matched by the fear that the workshops would disappear altogether. The institutions were so expensive to maintain that their future came under threat once the country's economic situation became more difficult in the 1970s. The 'Sheltered Placement Scheme', which provided subsidies for disabled people in open employment, was regarded as more cost-effective and grew at a relatively high pace from 1985 onwards. This led to the closure of workshops as scarce resources were allocated to the new scheme rather than the established workshops.[38] By 1991 the League's General Secretary admitted that defending workshop wages and ensuring ongoing state funding for these facilities constituted the League's 'two main struggles'.[39] After Joe Mann took office in 1995, the focus shifted on helping to make workshops commercially viable and the League even looked into the possibility of setting up cooperatives.[40] Mann also tried to change the image of the workshops by promoting the terms 'supported factories' or 'supported businesses'. Nevertheless, the number of factories outside of Remploy dropped from 129 in 1995 to fewer than 60 in 2014.[41]

Adapting to a changing world

Contrary to what the League had hoped for in the 1940s, voluntary organisations did not disappear as they promised to deliver better value for money for specialised services than government agencies. Given the often precarious position of Britain's public finances after the Second World War, the League was simply unable to win the fight against charity and its attitude towards working with them began to change. This is probably best demonstrated by the very active role Tom Parker played in the Royal National Institute between 1970 and 1995.[42]

The relationship between the League and the Institute had come under severe pressure when the League tried to organise the Institute's kiosk managers in London in June 1959. The Institute refused to recognise the League as the appropriate bargaining partner, to which the League reacted by withdrawing its two representatives from the Institute's governing body in 1962.[43] It was only in 1970 that the League decided to return its delegates to the Institute's General Council. A delegate at the League's Triennial Conference in that year stressed 'that isolation and cutting oneself off from other organisations served no useful purpose' and other delegates also expressed support for working together with 'all possible bodies dealing with blind welfare'.[44] Most of these bodies were registered charities, but the pattern for cooperation was now set. Shortly after the 1970 Triennial Conference the League began to work with the National Federation of the Blind in campaigning for a 'Blindness Allowance' for all registered visually impaired people in Britain. The Royal National Institute would later also join the campaign and a committee was set up in 1980 to coordinate the work of the three organisations.[45] By the middle of the 1980s the League was affiliated with voluntary organisations such as Disability Alliance, the British Council of Organisations of Disabled People, Maternity Alliance and others and the list would grow even longer in the 1990s.[46] The leadership of the League and the Royal National Institute even discussed the possibility of a joint membership base in the mid-1990s, but this plan did not find enough support.[47]

Making its peace with charitable organisations stripped the League of its special character. For half a century the fight against charity and for direct state aid had been an effective mobilisation tool which gave the League an appeal beyond the narrow confines of the blind workshops. Once the welfare state had arrived and charitable organisations had adjusted to the new landscape of welfare in Britain, the League became in the public eye increasingly reduced to its trade union functions. Being seen as an organisation just for workshop employees bound the League to a shrinking and ageing membership reservoir, while new organisations such as the Disablement Income Group appealed to a broader constituency and effectively took over the League's 'justice' frame in the 1960s and 1970s.[48]

The League continued to campaign on broader economic issues which affected all or most visually impaired people, such as income tax concessions, higher Social Security Supplementary Benefits, or the already mentioned struggle for a universal 'Blindness Allowance'.[49] However, it increasingly did so in cooperation with charitable organisations because the latter had greater financial resources. 'We have to cooperate with these people because they have the money', Gareth Davies put it in July 2014 and explained that 'the relationship with them is now much better than it was because the game plan has changed over the years. It can accordingly be said that the relationship is often mutually advantageous as they cannot be too overtly political.'[50] The law prevents charitable organisations from overt political work, but the League ceased to be a registered charity after the passing of the Charities Act of 1960. When the Act came fully into operation in 1962 the General Secretary contacted the Charity Commission and was advised that the League was not regarded as a charitable organisation under the new Act.[51] The League subsequently tried to register anyway in order to become exempt from paying Selective Employment Tax, but these attempts were denied by the Charity Commission and the Chancellor of the Exchequer, as its 'objects were not confined to charitable purposes'.[52] The decision at least allowed the League to remain politically active and gave it greater freedom of action and expression than its new partners in the voluntary sector. The fact that it celebrated its centennial in Downing Street in December 1999 shows that it also remained well connected with the leaders of the Labour Party.[53]

Faced with a declining membership base the League tried to find a new sense of purpose by intensifying its contacts with organisations outside of the United Kingdom. The *Blind Advocate* had always reported on the situation of blind people in other countries, partly in order to highlight the shortcomings or achievements of the welfare system in the United Kingdom.[54] Representatives of the League began to attend international conferences well before the First World War and in 1920 the League's Executive made preparations to directly contact, and if possible visit, organisations in other countries to gain first-hand information on the situation of blind people there.[55] Arguing that 'no organisation that has for its object the raising of the social and economic position of the blind can fail to be interested in the struggles and triumphs of similar organisations in other lands', the 1934 Triennial Conference unanimously welcomed the founding of the Universal Association of Organisations for the Blind.[56]

After the Second World War the League took its international engagement to a new level and even established contacts with organisations in Africa in the 1960s. The Kenya Union of the Blind received financial support from the League, while the General Secretary advised the President of the National League of the Blind of Zambia on organisational and policy matters.[57] After a visit from two representatives of the Tanzanian League of the Blind in 1983, a delegate of the League visited the African country in late 1984 'to see what the situation was, and how the National League and the International Department of the Trades Union Congress and other organisations could assist'.[58] Such activities inevitably triggered criticism from the grassroots given the League's increasingly precarious financial situation in the 1980s, but the Executive defended its international agenda.[59] The international stage still offered the prospect of prestige and recognition even though the League's size and influence was declining at home. The General Secretary admitted in 1982 that

> Of course international activities are expensive, but as the League is the largest organisation of the blind in the United Kingdom and the oldest with a very proud record to proclaim to Europe and the World, it is inevitable that we will be the major organisation of Blind people promoting international co-operation and good will amongst blind organisations throughout the world.[60]

The crisis of trade unionism and its effect

While the number of registered charities in Britain began to grow dramatically in the 1970s, trade unionism went into decline by the end of the decade.[61] The League's financial fortunes had been tied to the trade union movement since 1916 and it quickly felt the impact when the latter began to struggle in Thatcher's Britain. By the early 1980s income from membership fees covered only around one-third of the League's expenditure. Much of the rest was provided by donations from other trade unions, but getting these donations became more difficult as well as less dependable.[62] In the years 1982, 1984 and 1985, the League's overall expenditure exceeded its income and in August 1985 the six Area Council Secretaries came together to create the 'Friends of the National League of the Blind and Disabled' as a fund-raising support group with charitable status. The initiative had the active support of the League's General Secretary Michael A. Barrett, who also was the League's Treasurer. Barrett stressed that action was needed 'to offset the shortfall that we are now experiencing in the receipt of donations from other Trade Unions' and warned: 'If we are unable to do something collectively, then we would be forced to start running down our activities and information service so that we do not run into debt.'[63] However, the organising of 'a Lottery based upon football fixtures carried out over a period of 30 weeks' by the Friends of the National League of the Blind and Disabled in 1985 was never likely to solve the League's financial problems.[64] The early 1990s again saw 'a drastic drop in revenue [. . .] in donations from other trade unions', with the League receiving £15,000 less in 1993 than it did the year before.[65]

The trade union movement in Great Britain was experiencing a difficult period and reacted by pooling its resources. The 1980s and early 1990s saw 'trade union merger mania' in response to falling membership numbers and declining resources.[66] Smaller specialised trade unions which amalgamated or merged with other trade unions often insisted on maintaining their structure and identity within the new organisations, or they affiliated with the General Federation of Trade Unions (GFTU) which provided education, legal advice and research for them.[67] The League did both. According to Joe Mann, who also served as President of the GFTU from 2011 to 2013, the League flooded the GFTU's courses with its members from the 1990s onwards.[68] In addition, it also merged with the ISTC on 8 February 2000. The move received the support of nearly the entire membership of the League as the organisation was allowed to continue as a distinct entity within the ISTC.[69] It still continued to do so after becoming part of the new trade union Community in 2004 and had a membership of around 800 people in late 2014.[70]

Conclusion

When the House of Commons debated the Royal Patriotic Fund Corporation Bill in April 1950, Commander Harry Pursey, Labour Member for Hull East, vividly expressed his opposition to charity for ex-service personnel and their families. Pursey announced his intention to campaign 'wherever possible, to have the Royal Patriotic Fund Corporation closed down lock, stock and barrel, and its funds amalgamated and transferred elsewhere, because only in this way can the fullest value be obtained from the money which is available'.[71] Secretary of State for War John Strachey replied that he had 'a certain sympathy' with Pursey's view 'that charitable bodies of the type of which the Royal Patriotic Fund Corporation is an example have become anachronistic'. He argued that

> These very numerable charitable bodies, many of which have served excellent purposes, and many of which [...] still do so, require looking at in the considerably changed social conditions of today to see whether, quite properly, within the powers of this House, their functions and administration should be reviewed.[72]

The League was delighted with these statements. 'Commander Pursey admirably summarises the policy of the League but transfers it to another field', the *Blind Advocate* proclaimed and argued that Strachey 'would find equal, if not more, reason to pass such observations if his attention had been directed to the field of blind welfare'.[73] At that time it still felt possible to win the fight against charity.

Over six decades later, however, charitable organisations are thriving while the League is no longer the force it still was in 1950. Far from having become 'anachronistic', charities for ex-service personnel and their families, such as Help for Heroes, are currently among the best known and most popular in the voluntary sector in Britain.[74] Charitable organisations such as the Royal National Institute have successfully adapted to the changing times. While the League had always been proud to be an organisation 'of' rather than 'for' blind people, the Royal National Institute can now make the same claim. The Institute, which had always been more widely known than the League, renamed itself the Royal National Institute of the Blind in 2002 and started to admit individual members for the first time. Only five years later it changed its title again to the Royal National Institute of Blind People. More than half of the Institute's Board Members have to be completely or partly sightless. In other words, the Institute is now entitled to speak with some legitimacy for all sightless and partially sighted people in Britain.[75]

The League, however, does now mainly represent those in sheltered employment. From the very beginning its fate was closely tied to the workshops for blind people and when these institutions changed their character during and after the Second World War the League's appeal also narrowed. By the 1970s it had to make its peace with the charitable organisations and its ability to campaign on issues beyond sheltered employment came to depend on its former enemies providing crucial resources. The League's fight against charity had been lost.

Evaluating the League's Legacy

The 1960s are often treated as a watershed decade in the history of voluntarism. Established charitable organisations began to modernise, while new pressure groups appeared and tried to instigate legislative change from inside the political framework by lobbying decision makers and providing evidence and expertise. The 1960s also saw the rise of the so-called New Social Movements which strove to achieve change from outside the political system by organising demonstrations, rallies or other such public protest events. While the pressure groups wanted to get recognised and be accepted as partners by those in power, New Social Movements were involved in a public struggle with the latter. In contrast to trade unions, the main representatives of the 'old' social movements, New Social Movements did not focus predominantly on the economic interests of their supporters, but were also concerned with issues of identity, participation in society, rights and ways of life.[76]

As Virginia Berridge and Alex Mold have recently pointed out, however, such a dichotomist view of 'old' versus 'new', or 'insider' versus 'outsider' is too simplistic. A number of features which supposedly distinguished the New Social Movements of the 1960s can also be found in social movements of the nineteenth century, while during the interwar period many non-governmental organisations already bridged the outsider/insider divide by pursuing 'a strategy of cultivating relations with ministers and officials inside the state [...] whilst at the same time practising the long-established politics of moral pressure outside' by organising marches, rallies and petitions.[77]

The history of the League supports this criticism. From its inception in the late nineteenth century the League displayed key features of New Social Movements by talking the language of rights and trying to re-shape the image of blind people in society. The perception of blind people as deserving recipients of charity had been firmly established since Tudor times and was identified by the League as a major obstacle to their integration into society. It therefore argued ceaselessly that many visually impaired individuals were capable of playing a useful role in society by participating in the market economy through working in special workshops. The failure to do this in adequate numbers or with enough efficiency was blamed on the charitable organisations and their representatives who were portrayed as either incapable or unwilling to integrate them into the production process. Hence, the League argued, it was necessary for the state to take over from the voluntary sector. Politicians and civil servants were supposedly more professional, efficient, not hampered by self-interest, impartial and, above all, willing to respond to outside pressure. State financed and administered services were also desired for their symbolic significance. The call for direct state aid was not just based on socialist ideals or the expectation of better wages and working conditions, but in the belief that only by escaping charity could blind people acquire full citizenship. State funded welfare services and payments signalled inclusion as well as recognition, while private charity signalled the opposite. Charity was provided voluntarily on the basis of individual need, not as an entitlement based on citizenship.

The outcry which followed Lord Freud's comments at the Conservative Party's conference in September 2014 demonstrates that the link between equal pay and equal rights still exists. The Minister for Welfare Reform had stated at a fringe meeting that some people with mental disabilities were 'not worth' the minimum wage. The comment was made in the context of a question regarding how more disabled people could be brought into 'the workplace' so that they were able to feel that 'they were adding something and gaining worth'. Lord Freud quickly had to issue a 'full and unreserved apology', since his statement implied an inferior status for some disabled people.[78] The League, which had successfully won the first national minimum wage for workshop employees in 1951, had always understood that equality of wages was not just an economic question.

Reading the fight against charity as a struggle for equality, inclusion and citizenship avoids interpreting the history of the League as a conventional narrative of rise and decline. True, the League came into existence at a time of social reform and expanding state services in the late nineteenth century. Although its membership figures fluctuated during the first half of the twentieth century the overall long-term trend was upwards until the post-World War Two period when the League saw many of its demands implemented. From the 1950s onwards the

League's membership and resources steadily began to shrink and finally went into sharp decline in the late 1970s. Interpreted in this way, the story of the League mirrors the development of British trade unionism, the British welfare state and, to a certain degree, the history of Britain itself which supposedly experienced its 'finest hour' during the 1940s only to go into a period of steady and seemingly inevitable decline and recurring crisis afterwards.

However, such narratives of rise and decline are rarely convincing and the League's importance was not directly tied to its size. Membership numbers clearly mattered as they brought income, power and legitimacy, but the League was also important for other reasons. By enduring when other groups had collapsed, the League established that disabled people could indeed represent themselves in the public sphere on a permanent basis. Previous organisations founded by blind individuals for their community had often provided services within the paternalistic framework of charity. Organisations which did not operate within this framework, such as the British Blind Association, had found it difficult to survive or have an impact beyond the local level. The League, however, managed both which helped to establish the notion that the continuous self-representation of disabled groups in the political arena was possible or even desirable. The League also became a training ground and the institutional base for leaders such as Purse, Clydesdale and Parker, who eventually had an impact well beyond the organisation's narrow confines. Other individuals, such as Martin Milligan, were mobilised through the League before joining organisations such as the National Federation of the Blind. As this study has demonstrated when discussing the numerous internal conflicts which rocked the League throughout its history, its members often took an active interest in the affairs of the organisation. According to Joe Mann this is still the case today, as for example demonstrated by the persistently high level of participation in League elections.[79] Out of this active membership emerged a range of politicians and trade unionists throughout the years who had received a thorough schooling in organisational politics. This book has only been able to focus on two of them in greater detail, but a collective biography of the League's leadership would be a worthwhile project for future research.

When the League appeared on the scene in the 1890s, no template existed for how to organise a radical and politically active self-representation group of disabled people on a national basis. The only comparable organisation which existed was the British Deaf and Dumb Association, but its goals were much more limited than those of the

League. As this study has shown, the League experimented with different organisational templates and also changed its character from time to time. It started out as a loose federation of corresponding committees, then became de facto a friendly society before highlighting its trade union identity from 1916 onwards in response to a growing financial dependency on trade union donations. It was forced to register as a charity in 1934, only to be increasingly reduced to its trade union functions after the Second World War. Faced with the prospect of total collapse in the 1990s the League again reacted and amalgamated with other organisations, while at the same time retaining a distinct identity as a 'section' within Community.

This remarkable ability to adapt to change was one of the reasons why the League managed to survive against the odds. Another reason was that it was the first self-representation group of disabled people in Britain with a truly national membership base, a clear message and programme and a well-defined opponent. The League's 'Justice not Charity' slogan had a huge mobilising potential throughout the nation and linked well with similar frames employed by the TUC and the Labour Party. The League managed to commit both organisations to supporting its demand for direct state aid and, while the Labour Party often proved reluctant to act when in power, support from the TUC was reliable and often decisive. Trade union support brought success and recognition not only at the national but also the local level. From the annual Congress to the General Council to local Trades Councils, trade unionists were ready to actively support the League when needed and thereby amplified its influence significantly.

Affiliation with the labour movement brought a number of crucial successes over the years and these are another reason for the League's longevity. Its contribution to improving working conditions and wages for workshop employees is beyond doubt and was also acknowledged by the Working Party on Workshops for the Blind in 1962.[80] The League showed pragmatism when it cooperated with the voluntary sector before the First World War in order to get Parliament to support special legislation for blind people. It kept the issue on the agenda after the First World War and thereby contributed to the passing of the Blind Persons Act of 1920, even though the latter fell well short of what the League had demanded. Its second march to London triggered the second Blind Persons Act in 1938 and the League helped, together with the National Institute, to preserve, at least in part, the privileged position of visually impaired people in the post-war welfare state. While the League complained about the permissive character of many of the provisions enshrined in the Blind Persons Act of 1920, it became very skilful in exploiting them so that it actually had to work hard to have a non-detriment provision applied to the 1948 National Assistance Act.

In short, the League was successful by working from both inside as well as outside of the political system and by gaining access to the superior resources of the labour movement. By the 1960s, however, its productivist ideology, male-dominated leadership and faith in the state began to look outdated and the decline of the British labour movement from the 1980s onwards also reduced its standing as well as its ability to act. The League again adapted, but was unable to maintain its status, prestige and influence against a growing number of more dynamic and inclusive organisations which did emerge since the 1960s.

Nevertheless, the League can claim with some justification that it helped to shape the welfare state in Britain. It had fought hard to make the state responsible for all visually impaired people and the fact that they had a relatively privileged position compared to other disabled groups at the start of the Second World War was also due to the League's unrelenting agitation.[81] The services, payments and opportunities provided for blind and partially sighted people then furnished the model for how to treat other disabled groups in society when the welfare state was consolidated after the Second World War. As demonstrated in this book, the League was actively involved in this process. It is still involved in the fight to preserve state services for disabled people in Britain, but the leadership in this campaign has passed to other organisations.

Appendix A: Past Officers of the National League

Presidents

Benjamin O. Purse	1905–1916
R. D. Smith	1916–1917
Benjamin O. Purse	1918–1920
David B. Lawley	1920–1921
Alec Henderson	1922–1924
R. Hughes	1925–1933
James Grierson	1933–1941
J. Wittham	1942–1946
James Grierson	1947
Thomas Smith	1948–1961
Fred Mears	1962–1964
Dan West	1965–1979
C. Hynes	1979–1988
Neil Reid	1988–1991
W. McCready	1991–1997
Jimmy O'Rourke	1997–2000
Gareth Davis	2000–2013
Robert Mooney	2013–

General Secretaries

Benjamin O. Purse	1897–1899 (Northern Section of the League)
Peter Miller	1899
William Banham	1900–1902
John E. Gregory	1903–1925
G. E. Glister	1926–1927
Alec Henderson	1928–1948
Thomas H. Smith	1949–1969
Thomas J. Parker	1969–1979
Michael A. Barrett	1979–1994
Joe Mann	1995–2013
John Park	2013–

Appendix B: Songs

The Song of the National League
Lyrics by J. Lynch.

All hail to thee, Spirit of Brotherly Love,
Thy influence here is supreme;
Do thou from our counsels all discord remove,
And flowing keep harmony's stream.

Chorus.
To sing we success to the National League
Unite hearts and voices round,
Resolving to yield to no sense of fatigue
Till vict'ry our efforts have crowned.

We hail thee, great spirit of unity strong,
And pray thee amongst us to dwell;
We know that without thee, though countless our throng,
We cannot act wisely or well.

We hail thee, mild spirit of wisdom, and ask
That thou o'er our counsels preside,
Deciding how each may essay his own task,
And acting to all as a guide.

Source: *Blind Advocate* 10 (June 1899), p. 94.

The Marcher of the Blind
Lyrics by D. B. Lawley.
Tune: 'England Arise'.

Citizens! Behold ye all the cruel wrongs,
The blame for which to Government belongs.
The Blind from mill and mine and shop and womb,
Whose poverty bespeaks a living tomb,
We march with hearts aflame, we seek no idle fame,
Demanding simply Justice in the People's Name.

Workers! all ye who toil to enrich the State,
Yet live in poverty so desolate.
Fooled and plundered ye by despots so are we,
Remember! He must strike the blow who would be free,
Then rise in all your might, your hearts with ours unite,
With us forth to glory and the People's Right.

168

Though we seem few, the thraldom we deplore,
Is suffered by our thousands thirty-four.
Who, sightless to the Mill of Life must turn,
To find the cause for pain and smart and burn.
Though lordly be our foes, in the toilers we repose,
Our Faith is planted in the People's Cause.

Then, like the needle swings towards the pole,
Resenting beggars' doles and grubber hole.
We seek fair play of which you're ne'er afraid:
Which to the Blind must mean complete State Aid.
For this cause we march, with all our hearts aflame
In quest of Justice in the People's Name.

Source: *Blind Advocate* (April 1920), p. 8.

Notes

Introduction

1. B. Purse, 'The Blind of Great Britain'. Chapter IV. *BA* (January 1899), p. 34.
2. In 2014 Queen Elizabeth II alone acted as patron of over 600 voluntary organisations. http://www.royal.gov.uk/HMTheQueen/QueenCharities/ Overview.aspx [last accessed 28 May 2014].
3. C. Braithwaite, *The Voluntary Citizen* (London, 1938), p. 171, quoted in Nicholas Deakin and Justin Davis Smith, 'Labour, Charity and Voluntary Action: The Myth of Hostility', in Matthew Hilton and James McKay (eds), *The Ages of Voluntarism: How We Got to the Big Society* (Oxford, 2011), p. 75.
4. Justin Davis Smith, 'The Voluntary Tradition: Philanthropy and Self-Help in Britain 1500–1945', in Justin Davis Smith, Colin Rochester and Rodney Hedley (eds), *An Introduction to the Voluntary Sector* (London, 1995), pp. 9–39; Matthew Hilton and James McKay, 'The Ages of Voluntarism: An Introduction', in Hilton and McKay (eds), *The Ages of Voluntarism*, pp. 1–26.
5. Rodney Lowe, *The Welfare State in Britain since 1945* (3rd edn., Basingstoke, 2005), pp. 284–91; Virginia Berridge and Alex Mold, 'Professionalisation, New Social Movements and Voluntary Action in the 1960s and 1970s', in Hilton and McKay (eds), *The Ages of Voluntarism*, pp. 114–16.
6. Matthew Hilton et al., *A Historical Guide to NGOs in Britain: Charities, Civil Society and the Voluntary Sector since 1945* (Basingstoke, 2012), pp. 303–8.
7. *Ibid.*, pp. 326–7.
8. A useful overview of the terminology and categories employed is provided by Jeremy Kendall and Martin Knapp, 'A Loose and Baggy Monster: Boundaries, Definitions and Typologies', in Smith, Rochester and Hedley (eds), *An Introduction to the Voluntary Sector*, pp. 66–95.
9. William Beveridge, *Voluntary Action: A Report on the Methods of Social Advance* (London, 1948), p. 10; Justin Davis Smith, 'The Voluntary Tradition: Philanthropy and Self-Help in Britain 1500–1945', in Smith, Rochester and Hedley (eds), *An Introduction to the Voluntary Sector*, pp. 9–39; Helen McCarthy, 'Associational Voluntarism in Interwar Britain', in Hilton and McKay (eds), *The Ages of Voluntarism*, pp. 53–7; Nicholas Deakin, 'Civil Society', in Paul Addison and Harriet Jones (eds), *A Companion to Contemporary Britain 1939–2000* (Malden, MA, 2007), pp. 407–26; James McKay, 'Voluntary Politics: The Sector's Political Function from Beveridge to Deakin', in Melanie Oppenheimer and Nicholas Deakin (eds), *Beveridge and Voluntary Action in Britain and the Wider British World* (Manchester, 2011), p. 83; Hilton et al., *A Historical Guide to NGOs in Britain*, pp. 1–11 and 284–6.
10. Deakin and Smith, 'Labour, Charity and Voluntary Action', p. 93.
11. Hilton et al., *A Historical Guide to NGOs in Britain*, p. 39.
12. 'Speech by TUC Deputy Gen. Sec. Brendan Barber to Centenary Conference of the National League of the Blind and Disabled, Friday, 11 June 1999', p. 1. TUCL, HD6661z.

13. *Ibid.*, p. 2.
14. Madeline Rooff, *Voluntary Societies and Social Policy* (London, 1957), p. 178.
15. R. Ann Abel, 'Visually Impaired People, the Identification of the Need for Specialist Provision: A Historical Perspective', *British Journal of Visual Impairment* Vol. 7(2) (1989): 47–51.
16. Brian Grant, *The Deaf Advance: A History of The British Deaf Association 1890–1990* (Edinburgh, 1990); Peter W. Jackson and Raymond Lee, *The Origins of the British Deaf Association* (Feltham, 2010); Hilton et al., *A Historical Guide to NGOs in Britain*, pp. 104–7.
17. Thomas H. Smith (ed.), *National League of the Blind 1899–1949: Golden Jubilee Souvenir Brochure* (Glasgow, no date), pp. 8–10; Tom J. Parker, *The National League of the Blind and Disabled 1899–1974: Years of Excitement... and Disappointment* (Glasgow, no date), pp. 3–8.
18. The League's own narrative claims that it affiliated with the Labour Party in 1909, but this is not correct. Michael A. Barrett, 'Justice not Charity: Campaigning for the Blind and Disabled', *Scottish Trade Union Review* (April–June 1991), p. 22; NLB, Report and Balance Sheet 1905, p. 15 and Report and Balance Sheet 1906, p. 5, both in WCML, WRep.
19. Colin Rochester, 'Voluntary Agencies and Accountability', in Smith, Rochester and Hedley (eds), *An Introduction to the Voluntary Sector*, pp. 201–2.
20. Conference Report, Manchester, 7–9 February 1925. WCML, CRP. Minutes, EC Meetings, London, 27–9 June 1925, p. 1 and London, 19–23 June 1937, p. 5, both in WCML, NEC Minutes 1920–37.
21. Tom J. Parker, 'Editorial', *BA* (January 1969), p. 1.
22. On poor people's movements, see Frances Fox Piven and Richard A. Cloward, *Poor People's Movements: Why they Succeed, How they Fail* (New York, 1979).
23. The League's Cork branch had become defunct in the early 1920s and the Belfast branch remained with the parent organisation. Pat Lyons, *A Place in the Sun: A Brief History of the National League of the Blind in Ireland* (Blackrock, Co. Dublin, 1999), pp. 7–8.
24. The ISTC had also merged with the Power Loom Carpet Weaver and Textile Union before forming Community in July 2004 by joining forces with the National Union of Knitwear, Footwear and Apparel Trades, http://www.community-tu.org/information/100308/100310/history/ [last accessed 17 September 2012].
25. http://www.community-tu.org/who-we-represent/nlbd-sector.aspx [last accessed 9 July 2013]; http://www.community-tu.org/information/100308/100310/history/ [last accessed 8 November 2012]; http://nlbit.wordpress.com/ [last accessed 9 July 2013].
26. See, for example, 'Wigan Blind on Holiday', *BA* (October 1909), p. 1; 'London Notes', *BA* (September 1944), p. 3; 'Report of Social of the West London Branch', *BA* (March 1947), p. 4.
27. NLB, Report and Balance Sheet 1914, pp. 11–12; WCML, WRep. 'Why Travelling Concessions for Blind Persons?', *BA* (October 1950), pp. 6–7.
28. 'Editorial', *BA* (January 1951), p. 4; 'The First Museum for the Blind', *BA* (January 1962), p. 7.
29. 'Quarterly Notes', *BA* (July 1951), p. 2.

30. Res. No. 7, Report, 1967 Triennial Conference, 20–2 May 1967, p. 3, WCML, CRP. Res. No. 37, Report, 1988 Triennial Conference, 14–16 May 1988, p. 22, TUCL, HD6661z.

31. There are far too many articles on medical procedures in the *Blind Advocate* to list them all. For just two examples, see 'American Ophthalmic: A Disappointing Operation', *BA* (February 1899), p. 48; 'New Eye Operation', *BA* (October 1956), p. 8.

32. The League argued that he was in fact victimised for being a member of the League. 'A Blind Workman Victimised by Henshaw's Charity, Manchester!', *BA* (February 1901), pp. 1–3.

33. Minutes, EC Meeting, Manchester, 13–15 December 1930, p. 5 and Special EC Meeting, London, 16–19 February 1935, p. 8, both in WCML, NEC Minutes 1920–37.

34. 'City Workshop Allegations are Denied', *Carlisle Evening News*, 2 October 1973; 'Move to End Charges Storm', *Carlisle Evening News*, 3 October 1973; 'Blind Workshop Strike is on', *Cumberland News*, 4 October 1973. Clippings in MRC, MSS349/3/1/2.

35. Smith (ed.), *Golden Jubilee Brochure*, pp. 21–2.

36. See, for example, 'Short Strike at Norwich Blind Institution', *BA* (July 1947), p. 8.

37. 'Midland Notes', *BA* (July 1951), p. 6.

38. Simon Duffy, 'It's Clear Who Is the Hardest Hit – Disabled People', posted 9 May 2013, HuffPost Politics UK, http://www.huffingtonpost.co.uk/dr-simon-duffy/austerity-cuts-disabled-people_b_3248615.html [last accessed 10 July 2013].

39. For an overview of the development of trade union membership in Britain see Duncan Gallie, 'The Labour Force', in A. H. Halsey and Josephine Webb (eds), *Twentieth-Century British Social Trends* (New York, 2000), pp. 308–11 and Chris Wrigley, 'Trade Unions: Rise and Decline', in Francesca Carnevali and Julie-Marie Strange (eds), *Twentieth-Century Britain: Economic, Cultural and Social Change* (2nd edn., Harlow, 2007), pp. 281–92.

40. Steve Humphries and Pamela Gordon, *Out of Sight: The Experience of Disability 1900–1950* (Plymouth, 1992), p. 118.

41. Although the term 'disability' carries a negative connotation it will be used in this study together with 'visual impairment' in reference to the blind and partially sighted. This will be done partly for stylistic reasons but also because these terms reflect the fact that the League did indeed regard its members as disadvantaged in comparison with sighted workers.

42. Minutes, EC Meeting, Manchester, 28–31 March 1931, p. 5. WCML, NEC Minutes 1920–37.

43. Letter, Asst. Gen. Sec. to R. W. Hanlan, North East District Council, NLB, 3 June 1965. MRC, MSS292/91/24.

44. 'Editorial', *BA* (October 1971), pp. 1–2.

45. Interview with Joe Mann, retired Gen. Sec., NLB, Tipton St John, Devon, 10 June 2014.

46. These files are in group 801 and the last deposit for it was only received in July 2011.

47. http://hansard.millbanksystems.com/.

48. The Royal National Institute for the Blind (now Royal National Institute of Blind People) holds the copyright to the book. June Rose, *Changing Focus: The Development of Blind Welfare in Britain* (London, 1970), pp. 57–8. See also John Coles, *Blindness and the Visionary: The Life and Work of John Wilson* (London, 2006) and Andrew Norman, *Father of the Blind: A Portrait of Sir Arthur Pearson* (Stroud, 2009).

49. Ardha Danieli and Peter Wheeler, 'Employment Policy and Disabled People: Old Wine in New Glasses', *Disability & Society* Vol. 21(5) (2006): 487. For examples see, among others, Patrick Phelan, 'Are We Producing the Goods?', *British Journal of Visual Impairment* Vol. 2(3) (Autumn 1984): 70; Mark Priestley, 'Commonality and Difference in the Movement: An "Association of Blind Asians" in Leeds', *Disability & Society* Vol. 10(2) (1995): 158.

50. Smith (ed.), *Golden Jubilee Brochure* (Glasgow, no date); Parker, *The National League of the Blind and Disabled 1899–1974* (Glasgow, no date). The brochures were written and edited by high-ranking officials of the League. A similar publication exists for the League's sister organisation in Ireland. Written by Pat Lyons, who was the General Secretary of the National League of the Blind of Ireland for over seventeen years, the book also fails to meet academic standards. In the foreword Lyons states: 'One of the principles I set down in writing this history was to engage in no personal criticism of any other organisation working in the field of blind welfare, or of any individual, whether members of the League or not.' Lyons, *A Place in the Sun*, no page number.

51. To name but a few: Moshe Barasch, *Blindness: The History of a Mental Image in Western Thought* (New York, 2001); Ronald J. Ferguson, *We Know Who We Are: A History of the Blind in Challenging Educational and Socially-Constructed Policies. A Study in Policy Archaeology* (San Francisco, CA, 2001); Catherine J. Kudlick, 'Disability History: Why We Need Another "Other" ', *American Historical Review* Vol. 108(3) (June 2003): 763–93; Simon Hayhoe, *God, Money, and Politics: English Attitudes to Blindness and Touch, from the Enlightenment to Integration* (Charlotte, NC, 2008); Zina Weygand, *The Blind in French Society from the Middle Ages to the Century of Louis Braille* (Stanford, CA, 2009); Susan Schweik, *The Ugly Laws: Disability in Public* (New York, 2010); Julie Anderson, *War, Disability and Rehabilitation in Britain: 'Soul of a Nation'* (Manchester, 2011); Selina Mills, *Life Unseen: The Story of Blindness* (London, forthcoming).

52. Selina Mills, 'Darkness, Visible: The History of Blindness', *History Today* Vol. 63(9) (2013), http://www.historytoday.com/selina-mills/darkness-visible-history-blindness [last accessed 18 October 2014].

53. Amanda Nichola Bergen, 'The Blind, the Deaf and the Halt: Physical Disability, the Poor Law and Charity c.1830–1890, with particular reference to the County of Yorkshire (PhD thesis, University of Leeds, School of History, November 2004), pp. 402 and 409; John Oliphant, 'Empowerment and Debilitation in the Educational Experience of the Blind in Nineteenth-century England and Scotland', *History of Education* Vol. 35(1) (January 2006): 47–68; John Oliphant, *The Early Education of the Blind in Britain, c.1790–1900: Institutional Experience in England and Scotland* (Lewiston, NY, 2007); Julie Anderson and Neil Pemberton, 'Walking Alone: Aiding the

War and Civilian Blind in the Inter-War Period', *European Review of History* Vol. 14(4) (2007): 459–79; John Oliphant, ' "Touching the Light": The Invention of Literacy for the Blind', *Paedagogica Historica* Vol. 44(1–2) (February–April 2008): 67–82. For more general works see, for example, Humphries and Gordon, *Out of Sight*; Anne Borsay, *Disability and Social Policy in Britain since 1750* (Basingstoke, 2005).

54. Gordon Phillips, *The Blind in British Society: Charity, State, and Community, c.1780–1930* (Aldershot, 2004).

55. Phillips presents the 1905 conference of voluntary agencies in Edinburgh as the watershed event, although he admits that the NLB 'recovered some of its earlier militancy' after the First World War. Phillips, *The Blind in British Society*, pp. 312–13 and 390; Rooff, *Voluntary Societies and Social Policy*, p. 218.

56. C. Kenneth Lysons, 'The Development of Social Legislation for Blind or Deaf Persons in England, 1834–1939' (PhD thesis, University of Brunel, 1973).

57. 'Editorial', *BA* (October 1971), pp. 1–2.

58. Peter Carter, 'State Aid – Direct and Complete: The Blind Workers March 1920', *Working Class Movement Library Bulletin* 7 (1997), pp. 11–19; Matthias Reiss, 'Forgotten Pioneers of the National Protest March: The National League of the Blind Marches to London, 1920 & 1936', *Labour History Review* Vol. 70(2) (2005): 131–65. Carter also produced a paper on the League's badges. Peter Carter, 'The National League of the Blind and Disabled', MS, July 1996. TUCL, HD6661z.

59. Gerry Northam, 'Before Jarrow', BBC Radio 4 FM, Friday, 8 April 2005, 11:00–11:30 a.m.; Tony Baldwinson, *Unacknowledged Traces: Exploring through Photographic Records the Self-Organisation of Disabled People in England from the 1920s to the 1970s* (Manchester, 2012).

60. Floyd Matson, *Walking Alone and Marching Together: A History of the Organized Blind Movement in the United States, 1940–1990* (Baltimore, MD, 1990). See also Felicia Kornbluh, 'Disability, Antiprofessionalism, and Civil Rights: The National Federation of the Blind and the "Right to Organize" in the 1950s', *Journal of American History* Vol. 97(4) (March 2011): 1023–47.

1   New Union or Poor People's Movement? Building the National League of the Blind

1. Clare Griffiths, 'Remembering Tolpuddle: Rural History and Commemoration in the Inter-War Labour Movement', *History Workshop Journal* Vol. 44 (Autumn 1997): 144–69.

2. W. H. Oliver, 'Tolpuddle Martyrs and Trade Union Oaths', *Labour History* 10 (May 1966), p. 5; http://www.tuc.org.uk/the_tuc/index.cfm?mins=49&minors=45&majorsubjectID=19 [last accessed 17 April 2013]. In a similar fashion, the Cooperative Movement kept the memory of the 'Rochdale Pioneers' alive to remind its members what their movement was all about.

3. Griffiths, 'Remembering Tolpuddle', p. 164. The League provided a small donation of £1 to support the TUC's 'Pageant of Labour' at the Crystal

Palace in May 1934 which celebrated the Tolpuddle Martyrs. Minutes, EC Meeting, London, 2–7 December 1933, p. 6. WCML, NEC Minutes 1920–37.

4. Smith (ed.), *Golden Jubilee Brochure*, p. 3.
5. Parker, 'Editorial', *BA* (January 1969), p. 1.
6. Minutes, EC Meeting, Manchester, 17–20 September 1927, p. 3. WCML, NEC Minutes 1920–37.
7. NLB, *Handbook* (London, 1932), p. 2. TUCL, HV1744.
8. Minutes, EC Meeting, Manchester, 20–3 June 1931, p. 3. WCML, NEC Minutes 1920–37.
9. The Honorary Secretary of the Derby Branch also collected material on the League's history but apparently failed to publish the results of his research. Letter J. L. Batchelor, Hon. Sec., Derby branch, NLB, to W. Citrine, Gen. Sec., TUC, 16 July 1935. MRC, MSS292/91/25.
10. Golden Jubilee Celebrations, Blackpool, 20th May 1949. Leaflet from T. H. Smith, Gen. Sec., NLB, undated, WCML, WCir. Only in the 1990s did the League produce a badge which read 'Est. 1893'. Carter, 'The National League of the Blind and Disabled', p. 1.TUCL, HD6661z. See also 'Speech by TUC Deputy Gen. Sec. Brendan Barber to Centenary Conference of the National League of the Blind and Disabled, Friday, 11 June 1999', p. 1. TUCL, HD6661z.
11. The *Golden Jubilee Brochure* was written by an elected committee (J. Grierson, A. McAlpine and J. Clydesdale) to which the League's President and General Secretary were added ex officio. Minutes, EC Meeting, London, 18–21 September 1948, p. 2. WCML, NEC Minutes 1938–50.
12. See also Ben Purse, 'A Few Interesting Facts', leaflet, undated (*c.*1920), MRC, MSS292/91/27.
13. Smith (ed.), *Golden Jubilee Brochure*, pp. 6–8.
14. *Ibid.*, p. 6. See also Parker, *1899–1974*, p. 3.
15. Hamish W. Fraser, *A History of British Trade Unionism 1700–1998* (Basingstoke, 1999), p. 79; Hugh Clegg, A *History of British Trade Unions since 1889*, Vol. I: 1889–1910 (Oxford, 1964), pp. 66–87.
16. Smith (ed.), *Golden Jubilee Brochure*, p. 6.
17. When Tillett died in 1943, the Tunbridge Wells branch of the National Amalgamated Union of Life Assurance Workers decided that the best way to honour his memory was to make a donation to a fund for the blind. Postcard C. E. Dumbleton, NAULAW, to W. Citrine, Gen. Sec., TUC, 17 February 1943. Letter Asst. Sec., TUC, to C. E. Dumbleton, 19 February 1943, both in MRC, MSS292/91/27.
18. *Report of the Royal Commission on the Blind, the Deaf and Dumb, &c., of the United Kingdom* (London: HMSO, 1889). Hereafter quoted as RCBDD.
19. 'History of the League, 1893–1921', anonymous typescript manuscript (probably by Ben Purse), 19 December 1947, p. 1. British Library, YA.1992.C48. No copy of the Charter has survived, but another '*Blind Persons Charter*' was issued in 1935 (see Chapter 4).
20. *Ibid.*
21. Smith (ed.), *Golden Jubilee Brochure*, p. 8.
22. Lyons, *A Place in the Sun*, p. 7.
23. 'Editorial Notes', *BA* (September 1898), p. 4

24. 'Editorial Notes', *BA* (December 1898), p. 28; 'Help for the Blind', *BA* (December 1898), p. 31.
25. The other members came from Dublin, Liverpool, Hull, Oldham and Manchester. 'Editorial Notes', *BA* (February 1899), p. 54.
26. According to the anonymous manuscript in the British Library, a national conference was also held at the initiative of Ben Purse in 1898. 'History of the League, 1893–1921', p. 1. British Library, YA.1992.C48.
27. Despite the significance the League attached to its relationship with the TUC in hindsight, no one kept a record of the exact date of the League's affiliation, which probably took place sometime between the 1901 and 1902 Congresses. Letter, Asst. Gen. Sec., TUC, to A. Henderson, Gen. Sec., NLB, 14 May 1931. MRC, MSS292/91/27.
28. Smith (ed.), *Golden Jubilee Brochure*, p. 4.
29. Phillips, *The Blind in British Society*, pp. 305–6.
30. The Union later merged into the League. Lyons, *A Place in the Sun*, p. 7.
31. 'Sunderland School Board and the Education of the Blind', *North-Eastern Daily Gazette*, 30 December 1884, no page number.
32. RCBDD, Appendix I, p. 3 and Minutes of Evidence, pp. 577–86 (16, 114–16, 317), quotation p. 577 (16, 117).
33. Phillips, *The Blind in British Society*, pp. 305–6.
34. *BA* (June 1907), p. 5. For a photo see 'Editorial Notes', *BA* (November 1898), pp. 4–5.
35. A British Blind Association for Promoting the Education and Employment of the Blind was founded in 1868, but its scope of activities suggests that it was a different society. It printed books and music in Braille, tried to find work for blind people and published an embossed magazine entitled *Progress* produced from 'stereotype plates prepared by the blind themselves'. None of the other newspaper articles on the British Blind Association in Scotland mentions any of these activities. 'Literature', *Lloyd's Weekly Newspaper*, 15 January 1882, p. 5.
36. The year suggested that it might have been created in reaction to the 1870 Education Act for England and Wales. An Elementary Education Act for Scotland was passed in 1872. Borsay, *Disability*, p. 106. The *Glasgow Herald* reported on the meeting: 'Notwithstanding the stormy weather, which is very unfavourable for the blind being abroad after dark, there was a numerous attendance.' 'British Blind Association', *Glasgow Herald*, 22 October 1870, p. 2.
37. The distribution of the pamphlet was to be followed by an appeal to the public for donations as the funds of the Association 'were almost exhausted'. *Ibid.*
38. *Ibid.* 'Aberdeen Branch of the British Blind Association', *Aberdeen Journal*, 11 December 1891, p. 2.
39. These institutions were called 'asylums' in the language of the time. 'Aberdeen Branch of the British Blind Association', *Aberdeen Journal*, 11 December 1891, p. 2.
40. Phillips, *The Blind in British Society*, pp. 60–7.
41. RCBDD, Appendix I, pp. 3–5. The memorial was prepared at a conference in Edinburgh, thereby establishing a template for the conference held in March 1890. 'Letters to Editor', *Dundee Courier & Argus and Northern Warder*,

12 February 1886, p. 2. See also Phillips, *The Blind in British Society*, p. 305, note 184.

42. Fraser, *A History of British Trade Unionism*, pp. 74 and 76.

43. Keir is referred to as the Association's President in 'Aberdeen – Lecture by Rev. John Duncan', *Aberdeen Weekly Journal*, 13 April 1887, p. 4. He was elected branch Secretary and Trades Council delegate in 1888, although it is not clear whether this was the first time and apparently retained these positions for many years. He was unanimously reappointed as President of the Aberdeen United Trades Council in 1895. 'Aberdeen Branch of the British Blind Association', *Aberdeen Weekly Journal*, 15 December 1888, p. 5; 'Aberdeen Trades Council', *Aberdeen Weekly Journal*, 17 January 1895, p. 3. From 1894 to 1903 he was also a member of the Aberdeen School Board. Phillips, *The Blind in British Society*, p. 305, note 184.

44. 'Rev. C. C. MacDonald on the Reconstruction of the Blind Asylum', *Aberdeen Weekly Journal*, 16 December 1887, p. 4.

45. Phillips states incorrectly that Keir attended as 'a delegate on behalf of the Aberdeen blind workers'. Phillips, *The Blind in British Society*, p. 305, note 184. 22nd Annual Trades Union Congress, Report of Proceedings, 2 September 1889, p. 5. TUCL.

46. 22nd Annual Trades Union Congress, Report of Proceedings, 2 September 1889, p. 60. TUCL. Smith and Phillips both claim incorrectly that this took place in 1899. Smith (ed.), *Golden Jubilee Brochure*, p. 12; Phillips, *The Blind in British Society*, p. 305, note 184.

47. In reply to a question in the Commons, W. H. Smith announced in February 1890 that the government was hoping to 'introduce a Bill during the present Session' which would by and large 'follow the recommendations of the Report of the Royal Commission'. Hansard 341 HC Deb., 21 February 1890, cols. 893–4.

48. 'Conference of Blind Persons in Edinburgh', *Aberdeen Journal*, 1 April 1890, p. 4.

49. *Ibid.*

50. According to Smith, the first Scottish branch was formed in Edinburgh, while Phillips states that it was located in Glasgow. Smith (ed.), *Golden Jubilee Brochure*, p. 10. Phillips, *The Blind in British Society*, pp. 305, note 184 and 309–10. 'National League of the Blind', *BA* (January 1908), p. 8.

51. 'Rev. C. C. MacDonald on the Reconstruction of the Blind Asylum', *Aberdeen Weekly Journal*, 16 December 1887, p. 4.

52. Draft Petition, attachment to letter W. Banham, Gen. Sec., NLB, to K. Hardie, ILP, 15 April 1901. LSE, ILP 4, docs. 7 and 8. For later claims to represent the blind community see, for example, Minutes, EC Meeting, London, 19–22 September 1936, p. 4. WCML, NEC Minutes 1920–37.

53. NLB Rules 1901, p. 4. WCML, NLB Rule Books.

54. NLB Rules 1905, p. 1. TNA, FS28/97. NLB Rules 1915, p. 1. WCML, NLB Rule Books. The League defined 'partially blind' as having 'less than 6/60 of sight'. All partially blind members had to provide 'a certificate signed by an opthalmic [*sic*] surgeon stating the percentage of sight they possess'. Minutes, EC Meeting, Manchester, 15–18 September 1928, pp. 6–7. WCML, NEC Minutes 1920–37.

55. NLB Rules 1924, p. 2. WCML, NLB Rule Books. See also Chapter 3.

56. 'Printing and Kindred Trades', Blind Aid Committee: 'Transcription of a discussion which took place on Saturday, November 24th 1923, between Messrs. Lothian and Turner of the National League of the Blind, and Mr. H. C. Preece and Mr. Ben Purse, Greater London Fund for the Blind', H. S. Weeden, Hon. Sec., November 1923, p. 5. WCML, WCir.

57. NLB Rules 1901, p. 5. WCML, NLB Rule Books.

58. Initially, Associates had to pay a minimum of one shilling per year. This rose to two shillings in 1924 but dropped back to one shilling in 1929. NLB Rules 1901, p. 4; NLB Rules 1924, p. 3; NLB Rules 1929, p. 10; all in WCML, NLB Rule Books.

59. This question triggered a lengthy debate but was ultimately rejected with a two-thirds majority. 'National League for the Blind, Minutes of E.C. Meetings, Liverpool, Nov. 13 & 14, 1898', *BA* (January 1899), p. 37.

60. NLB Rules 1901, p. 4; NLB Rules 1905, pp. 1–2, both in WCML, NLB Rule Books.

61. NLB Rules 1901, p. 4; NLB Rules 1924, p. 3; NLB Rules 1929, p. 10; all in WCML, NLB Rule Books.

62. NLB Rules 1924, p. 5. WCML, NLB Rule Books.

63. Minutes, EC Meetings, Manchester, 15–18 September 1928, p. 1 and London, 12–15 December 1931, p. 10, both in WCML, NEC Minutes 1920–37.

64. Minutes, EC Meeting, Manchester, 3–5 December 1932, p. 3. WCML, NEC Minutes 1920–37.

65. Minutes, EC Meetings, London, 17–22 June 1933, p. 9 and London, 2–7 December 1933, p. 10, both in WCML, NEC Minutes 1920–37.

66. Minutes, EC Meetings, London, 17–22 June 1933, p. 9 and London, 9–13 September 1933, p. 8, both in WCML, NEC Minutes 1920–37.

67. Minutes, Special EC Meeting, London, 13–16 October 1934, p. 9. WCML, NEC Minutes 1920–37.

68. Significantly, two of the nine EC members voted to allow the creation of a separate branch. One hundred employees of the Blind Asylum in Glasgow had supported the proposal, while sixty had voted 'for the formation of a workers' committee in conjunction with the existing Branch'. Minutes, EC Meeting, Manchester, 12–14 April 1924, p. 2. WCML, WCir.

69. Minutes, EC Meeting, London, 27–9 June 1925, p. 1. WCML, NEC Minutes 1920–37.

70. Minutes, EC Meeting, London, 20–3 March 1937, p. 9. WCML, NEC Minutes 1920–37.

71. 'History of the League, 1893–1921', p. 2.

72. *Ibid.*

73. Letter C. S. Loch, COS, to Sec., Manchester COS, 9 May 1906. London Metropolitan Archives, Charity Organisation Society, Enquiries Department II, National League for the Blind, A/FWA/C/D/285/1. I would like to thank Dr Julie-Marie Strange for providing me with this source.

74. *Barber v. Chudley*, Judgement, Royal Courts of Justice, 19 December 1922. WCML, WCir.

75. See, for example, the correspondence in MRC, MSS292/91/27.

76. Letter Sec., Mansfield, Sutton & District Co-operative Society, to W. Citrine, Gen. Sec., TUC, 18 June 1940. Letter Asst. Sec., TUC, to Sec., Mansfield,

Sutton & District Cooperative Society, 20 June 1940, both in MRC, MSS292/91/27.

77. Copy of Report from Mr. Farrow, Minute Sheet, MoH, 25 September 1936, p. 1. TNA, MH55/607.

78. 'History of the League, 1893–1921', p. 2.

79. 'An Appeal to and for the Blind', *BA* (September 1898), p. 8.

80. NLB, Report and Balance Sheet 1917, p. 3. WCML, WRep.

81. See, for example, 'What do we mean by "Direct State Aid for the Blind"?', *BA* (April 1899), p. 65.

82. Joseph Slater, 'The Gossip's Bowl', *BA* (April 1899), p. 67.

83. Kenneth D. Brown, *Labour and Unemployment 1900–1914* (Newton Abbot, 1971), especially pp. 18–19 and 62–7.

84. Joseph Slater, 'The Gossip's Bowl', *BA* (April 1899), p. 67.

85. *Ibid.*

86. Ross M. Martin, *TUC: The Growth of a Pressure Group 1868–1976* (Oxford, 1980), pp. 75–6.

87. Oliphant, 'Empowerment and Debilitation', pp. 55–60.

88. Phillips, *The Blind in British Society*, pp. 114–17; Oliphant, 'Empowerment and Debilitation', pp. 60 and 66.

89. According to Phillips there is no evidence that either Gilbert or Levy were familiar with the workshops of the Scottish asylums or that they were trying to copy them. Phillips, *The Blind in British Society*, pp. 117–19.

90. *Ibid.*, pp. 123–6.

91. *Ibid.*, pp. 288–90.

92. NLB Rules 1905, p. 1. TNA, FS28/97.

93. This definition was given by the League's conference in August 1917. NLB, Report and Balance Sheet 1917, p. 7. WCML, WRep.

94. As already mentioned in the introduction, the League provided strike, lock-out and victimisation pay, distress grants, legal assistance and funeral benefits. NLB Rules 1901, pp. 3 and 6. WCML, NLB Rule Books. NLB Rules 1905, pp. 5–6. TNA, FS28/97.

95. NLB, Annual Report and Balance Sheet 1907, p. 5. WCML, WRep.

96. NLB Rules 1915, p. 1. WCML, NLB Rule Books.

97. NLB Rules 1901, p. 1. WCML, NLB Rule Books.

98. Those who were capable were to be given 'training in agricultural pursuits, such as gardening and poultry-rearing, to be followed by settlements upon suitable land, rent for a period of not less than three years, together with other special facilities guaranteed by the State, such as supplies of tools, seeds, fowls, food, and other requisites at cost price and easy terms of repayment'. NLB Rules 1924, p. 2; NLB Rules 1929, pp. 3–4, both in WCML, NLB Rule Books.

99. Ben Purse, 'The Blind of Greater Britain', *BA* (September 1898), p. 1; J. E. Gregory, *NLB Manifesto*, 1925, p. 1. MRC, MSS292/91/27.

100. NLB, Annual Report and Balance Sheets 1909, p. 8 and 1910, pp. 8–9, both in WCML, WRep.

101. See, for example, 'Miss Mona Wilson on Blindness', *BA* (September 1899), pp. 1–2; 'The Prevention of Blindness', *BA* (October 1930), p. 7; 'Workers' Welfare: Protective Goggles', *BA* (October 1941), p. 6; 'Prevention of Blindness', *BA* (June 1944), p. 3; 'World Blindness', *BA* (July 1962), p. 7; 'The

Prevention and Alleviation of Blindness', *BA* (January 1963), p. 7; Smith (ed.), *Golden Jubilee Brochure*, pp. 18–20.

102. 'Editorial Notes', *BA* (November 1898), p. 5.
103. If they were unable to attend the Annual Conference due to workhouse regulations they could appoint a proxy from their peers to vote in their name. Peter Miller, 'Suggestions for the Constitution of the N.L.B.', *BA* (September 1898), p. 6.
104. 'Editorial Notes', *BA* (November 1898), p. 5.
105. 'Editorial Notes', *BA* (February 1899), p. 43.
106. *Ibid.*
107. They were allowed to add to that number 'as occasion may demand' or 'should occasion arise'. NLB Rules 1901, p. 5. WCML, NLB Rule Books. NLB Rules 1905, p. 2. TNA, FS28/97. This was reaffirmed in 1914. NLB Rules 1914, p. 4. WCML, NLB Rule Books.
108. NLB Rules 1901, p. 5. WCML, NLB Rule Books.
109. NLB Rules 1924, p. 4. WCML, NLB Rule Books.
110. NLB Rules 1901, p. 5. WCML, NLB Rule Books. From 1905 onwards meetings were to be held at Easter and in September. NLB Rules 1905, p. 4. TNA, FS28/97.
111. NLB Rules 1905, pp. 2 and 4. TNA, FS28/97.
112. *Ibid.*, p. 7.
113. NLB Rules 1901, p. 5. WCML, NLB Rule Books.
114. NLB Rules 1946, p. 9. WCML, NLB Rule Books.
115. NLB Rules 1901, pp. 5–6. WCML, NLB Rule Books. Until 1952 the maximum number of delegates per branch was two. From then on, branches with more than 350 members were entitled to four delegates. NLB Rules 1952, p. 20. WCML, NLB Rule Books.
116. NLB Rules 1905, pp. 4–5. TNA, FS28/97. NLB Rules 1915, p. 5. WCML, NLB Rule Books.
117. NLB Rules 1901, p. 7. WCML, NLB Rule Books.
118. NLB Rules 1905, p. 6. TNA, FS28/97.
119. The areas were: North-Western, South-Western, Midland, North-Eastern, London and Home Counties, and Scottish and Irish. NLB Rules 1915, p. 4 and NLB Rules 1924, p. 5, both in WCML, NLB Rule Books.
120. NLB Rules 1952, p. 12. WCML, NLB Rule Books.
121. The Executive Council would meet in March, June, September and December. NLB Rules 1924, p. 5. WCML, NLB Rule Books.
122. The Committee consisted of three members of the Executive, the President and General Secretary and could be convened at the discretion of the latter two. Minutes, EC Meeting, Manchester, 25–9 March 1933, p. 4. WCML, NEC Minutes 1920–37.
123. 'A Northern Federation of the National League of the Blind', *BA* (April 1902), p. 3.
124. NLB, Records of Resolutions Passed at the Conference held at the Club House, Manchester, 29 November 1914, p. 1. WCML, CRP.
125. *Ibid.*, p. 2.
126. Minutes, EC Meeting, London, 19–21 June 1920, p. 5. WCML, WCir.
127. Minutes, EC Meeting, London, 3–5 March 1923, p. 3. WCML, NEC Minutes 1920–37.

128. Conference of Delegates from the Branches of the League in the N.W. Area, J. E. Gregory, Gen. Sec., NLB, 11 October 1924. WCML, WCir.
129. The ban was only lifted in March 1931. Minutes, EC Meetings, Manchester, 16–18 March 1929, pp. 6–8 and Manchester, 28–31 March 1931, p. 9, both in WCML, NEC Minutes 1920–37.
130. Minutes, EC Meetings, Manchester, 29 March–1 April 1930, p. 9; Manchester, 21–3 June 1930, p. 4 and Manchester, 13–15 December 1930, pp. 1 and 8, all in WCML, NEC Minutes 1920–37.
131. It is not clear what exactly happened at the conference, but Whittam argued that 'the action of the President and Secretary [...] at Leeds was tantamount to resignation'. Minutes, EC Meetings, Manchester, 20–3 June 1931, p. 1; London, 12–15 September 1931, p. 9 and London, 12–15 December 1931, pp. 9–10, all in WCML, NEC Minutes 1920–37.
132. Minutes, EC Meeting, London, 12–15 September 1931, p. 10. The Birkenhead branch also accused the General Secretary of illegal actions and even asked that 'proceedings shall be immediately instituted against Mr. Henderson for the recovery of Funds' he had allegedly misused. Minutes, EC Meeting, London, 19–22 March 1932, p. 7, both in WCML, NEC Minutes 1920–37.
133. Minutes, EC Meeting, London, 12–15 September 1931, pp. 9–10. WCML, NEC Minutes 1920–37.
134. Minutes, EC Meeting, London, 19–22 March 1932, pp. 8 and 10. WCML, NEC Minutes 1920–37.
135. Minutes, EC Meeting, Manchester, 25–9 March 1933, p. 1. WCML, NEC Minutes 1920–37.
136. The South London branch, for example, argued in 1932 that it was 'suffering grave injustice consequent upon the mal administration [*sic*] of the Central Office'. Letter A. Healy, Hon. Sec., South London Branch, NLB, to W. Citrine, Gen. Sec., TUC, 9 May 1932. MRC, MSS292/91/27.
137. NLB Rules 1905, p. 3. TNA, FS28/97.
138. Minutes, EC Meeting, Manchester, 15–18 September 1928, p. 5. WCML, NEC Minutes 1920–37. Letter Pattinson & Brewer, Solicitors, to A. Henderson, Gen. Sec., NLB, 18 June 1930. WCML, WCir.
139. NLB Rules 1946, p. 6. WCML, NLB Rule Books.
140. Minutes, EC Meeting, Manchester, 22 October 1932, p. 3. WCML, NEC Minutes 1920–37.
141. Minutes, EC Meetings, London, 12–15 September 1931, p. 4; Manchester, 3–5 December 1932, p. 3; London, 19–22 March 1934, p. 2; London, 7–12 December 1935, p. 7 and London, 19–22 September 1936, all in WCML, NEC Minutes 1920–37.
142. Minutes, EC Meeting, London, 19–22 September 1936, p. 7. WCML, NEC Minutes 1920–37.
143. Minutes, EC Meeting, London, 19–23 June 1937, p. 9. WCML, NEC Minutes 1920–37.
144. Minutes, EC Meetings, London, 19–22 March 1934, pp. 1–3; London, 8–11 December 1934, p. 2; London, 19–22 September 1936 and London, 5–9 December 1936, p. 7, all in WCML, NEC Minutes 1920–37.
145. Letter R. W. Hanlon, President, AUBB, and T. P. Reed, Sec. pro tem, AUBB, to W. Citrine, Gen. Sec., TUC, 30 October 1933. MRC, MSS292/91/27.

146. NLB Rules 1901, pp. 5–6; NLB Rules 1924, p. 4, both in WCML, NLB Rule Books. The Rules at first limited the amount of money the Executive was allowed to spend without first consulting all members of the League, but this restriction was quickly dropped. NLB Rules 1901, p. 5. WCML, NLB Rule Books.
147. Memo, A. Henderson, T. Rainbird and C. Hird, NLB, January 1925. WCML, WCir.
148. Minutes, EC Meeting, London, 3–5 March 1923, p. 2. WCML, NEC Minutes 1920–37.
149. Peter Grant, 'Voluntarism and the Impact of the First World War', in Matthew Hilton and James McKay (eds), *The Ages of Voluntarism: How We Got to the Big Society* (Oxford, 2011), pp. 27–46.
150. The *Barber v. Chudley* case cost the League around £210. Minutes, EC Meeting, London, 3–5 March 1923, p. 3. WCML, NEC Minutes 1920–37.
151. Minutes, EC Meetings, London, 3–5 March 1923, p. 3 and Manchester, 12–14 January 1924, p. 2, both in WCML, NEC Minutes 1920–37. Memo, A. Henderson, T. Rainbird and C. Hird, NLB, January 1925. WCML, WCir.
152. Memo, A. Henderson, T. Rainbird and C. Hird, NLB, January 1925. WCML, WCir. North-Eastern Area: Minutes, EC Meeting, Manchester, 12–14 April 1924, p. 2. WCML, WCir. Northern Ireland: Minutes, EC Meeting, Manchester, 16–18 June 1928, p. 4. WCML, NEC Minutes 1920–37.
153. Branches who had not signed up to the scheme were allowed to keep one-third of the membership fees and to raise additional funds locally in order to promote the goals of the League. NLB Rules 1924, pp. 4 and 8. WCML, NLB Rule Books. District Councils which signed up for the scheme would receive a proportion of the funds raised by the Organisers. Minutes, EC Meeting, Manchester, 17–19 December 1927, p. 4. WCML, NEC Minutes 1920–37.
154. Conference of Delegates of the League in the N.W. Area, J. E. Gregory, Gen. Sec., NLB, 11 October 1924. WCML, WCir.
155. Memo, A. Henderson, T. Rainbird and C. Hird, NLB, January 1925. WCML, WCir. Minutes, EC Meeting, London, 27–9 June 1925. WCML, NEC Minutes 1920–37.
156. Minutes, EC Meeting, Manchester, 26–8 September 1925. WCML, NEC Minutes 1920–37.
157. Conference of Delegates of the League in the N.W. Area, J. E. Gregory, Gen. Sec., NLB, 11 October 1924. WCML, WCir. Minutes, EC Meeting, Manchester, 26–8 September 1925. WCML, NEC Minutes 1920–37.
158. Minutes, EC Meeting, Manchester, 31 March–2 April 1926. WCML, NEC Minutes 1920–37.
159. Minutes, EC Meeting, Manchester, 17–19 December 1927, p. 4. WCML, NEC Minutes 1920–37.
160. *Ibid.*, p. 2.
161. *Ibid.*, p. 4.
162. Letter C. Chamberlain, Sec., North-Western District, NLB, to W. Citrine, Sec Gen., TUC, 23 January 1928. MRC, MSS292/91/27.
163. After the meeting the Executive sent a statement documenting the history of conflict to all branches. Minutes, EC Meeting, Swansea, 17–19 March 1928, p. 5. WCML, NEC Minutes 1920–37.

164. *Ibid.*, p. 6.
165. *Ibid.* Minutes, EC Meeting, Manchester, 16–18 June 1928. Efforts to re-unify the North-Western District started in March 1931. Minutes, EC Meetings, Manchester, 28–31 March 1931, p. 3 and Manchester, 20–3 June 1931, pp. 4–5, all in WCML, NEC Minutes 1920–37.
166. Minutes, EC Meeting, Manchester, 16–18 June 1928, pp. 7–8. WCML, NEC Minutes 1920–37.
167. The Executive Council argued that the Rules did not allow it to transfer its authority to another body. The Scottish District Council also asked the Executive to publish a statement outlining the cost of the dispute with the North-Western area. Minutes, EC Meeting, Manchester, 16–18 March 1929, pp. 4–5. WCML, NEC Minutes 1920–37.
168. The General Secretary's letter created so many rumours within the League that the Executive felt compelled to re-print it in the minutes of their June meeting. Minutes, EC Meeting, Manchester, 11–15 June 1932, pp. 7–8. WCML, NEC Minutes 1920–37.
169. *Ibid.*, p. 6.
170. Minutes, EC Meetings, Manchester, 25–9 March 1933, pp. 4–5 and London, 17–22 June 1933, pp. 8–9, both in WCML, NEC Minutes 1920–37.
171. Minutes, EC Meetings, Manchester, 8–10 June 1929, p. 2 and Manchester, 29 March–1 April 1930, p. 3, both in WCML, NEC Minutes 1920–37.
172. Minutes, EC Meeting, Manchester, 29 March–1 April 1930, p. 5. WCML, NEC Minutes 1920–37.
173. Somewhat bizarrely, Midland District Council's choice for the position was J. Perry, the old Organiser for the District who had just been made redundant by the Executive for not being successful enough in his job. Minutes, EC Meeting, Manchester, 8–10 December 1928, p. 5. For the EC's response, see Minutes, EC Meeting, Manchester, 8–10 June 1929, p. 3. A request in March 1931 to reinstate Perry as Midland Organiser was not debated by the Executive. Minutes, EC Meeting, Manchester, 28–31 March 1931, p. 8. All in WCML, NEC Minutes 1920–37.
174. Minutes, EC Meeting, Manchester, 29 March–1 April 1930, p. 8. WCML, NEC Minutes 1920–37. Circular letter, from R. Hughes, President, NLB and A. Henderson, Gen. Sec., NLB, 15 June 1930. WCML, WCir.
175. The Executive's Finance Committee voted unanimously to introduce a new allocation scheme in April 1929 and the Executive Council accepted this recommendation at its next meeting in June. Minutes, EC Meeting, Manchester, 8–10 June 1929, p. 1. The branch vote was 25 against and 8 in favour of the new scheme. Minutes, EC Meeting, Manchester, 29 March–1 April 1930, p. 9. Both in WCML, NEC Minutes 1920–37.
176. Minutes, EC Meetings, Manchester, 21–3 June 1930, p. 2 and Manchester, 13–15 September 1930, p. 3. However, by early 1932 the North-Eastern District Council once again requested permission to opt out of the centralisation scheme 'as the scheme was unworkable'. Minutes, EC Meeting, London, 19–22 March 1932, p. 6. All in WCML, NEC Minutes 1920–37.
177. Minutes, EC Meeting, Manchester, 13–15 December 1930, p. 4. Belfast No. 1 branch, for example, was refused financial assistance as it tried to raise funds by organising a lottery. Minutes, EC Meeting, London, 19–22 March

1932, p. 4. See also Minutes, EC Meeting, London, 19–22 March 1932, p. 6. All in WCML, NEC Minutes 1920–37.

178. Minutes, EC Meeting, London, 12–15 December 1931, p. 3. WCML, NEC Minutes 1920–37.

179. Circular to all branches, R. Hughes, President and A. Henderson, Gen. Sec., NLB, undated. WCML, WCir. Minutes, EC Meeting, London, 12–15 December 1931, pp. 2–3. WCML, NEC Minutes 1920–37.

180. Minutes, EC Meeting, London, 19–22 March 1932, p. 5. WCML, NEC Minutes 1920–37.

181. Circular to all branches, R. Hughes, President and A. Henderson, Gen. Sec., NLB, 30 September 1930. WCML, WCir. Minutes, EC Meetings, Manchester, 17–20 September 1932, p. 1 and Manchester, 3–5 December 1932, p. 1, both in WCML, NEC Minutes 1920–37.

182. One of them was Plymouth. Minutes, Special EC Meeting, London, 14–19 July 1934, p. 15. WCML, NEC Minutes 1920–37.

183. Minutes, EC Meetings, Manchester, 25–9 March 1933, p. 9; London, 2–7 December 1933, p. 10; London, 19–22 March 1934, pp. 3–4 and Special EC Meeting, London, 14–19 July 1934, pp. 8–10, all in WCML, NEC Minutes 1920–37.

184. Minutes, Special EC Meeting, London, 16–19 February 1935, pp. 1–3 and EC Meeting, London, 22–6 June 1935, pp. 5–6, both in WCML, NEC Minutes 1920–37.

185. Of the 46 branches which responded, 26 favoured the scheme. If a District Council decided to not participate its share fell to the Central Office. The share allotted to branches was distributed among those which had opted in. Minutes, EC Meetings, London, 14–18 September 1935, p. 9 and London, 7–12 December 1935, p. 10, both in WCML, NEC Minutes 1920–37.

186. Minutes, EC Meetings, London, 19–23 June 1937, p. 6; London, 11–15 September 1937, pp. 2–3 and London, 4–7 December 1937. All in WCML, NEC Minutes 1920–37.

187. Email G. Davies, NLB, to author, 21 July 2014.

188. Report, 1994 Triennial Conference, 4–6 June 1994, pp. 19–20. MRC, MSS349/2/3.

189. *Ibid.*, pp. 3 and 19.

190. *Ibid.*, p. 19.

191. Fraser, *A History of British Trade Unionism*, pp. 152–76; Hugh Clegg, *A History of British Trade Unions since 1889*, Vol. II: 1911–1933 (Oxford, 1985), pp. 449–51.

192. See, for example, Minutes, 1934 Triennial Conference, 22–4 September 1934, p. 5. WCML, CRP.

193. J. Lynch, 'Song of the National League', *BA* (June 1899), p. 94. For the lyrics see Appendix B.

194. The boxes also included a Christmas pudding specially made for the League by Peak, Frean & Co.; '10,000 Xmas Puddings Free: Send for this Box of Toys and Help the Poor Blind', Advertisement, *Daily Mail*, 29 November 1911, p. 3.

195. NLB, Report and Balance Sheet 1905, pp. 5 and 14. WCML, WRep.

196. NLB, Report and Balance Sheet 1906, p. 10. WCML, WRep.

197. NLB, Reports and Balance Sheets 1907, p. 12 and 1912, p. 10. WCML, WRep.
198. NLB, Report and Balance Sheet 1916, p. 15. WCML, WRep.
199. Until 1916 the levy had raised around £20,000 for what the Society called 'the needy blind'. 'Far and Near', *Daily Mail*, 18 September 1916, p. 3. In 1937 the League also tried to convince the AEU to arrange a national levy from its members for the NLB. Minutes, EC Meeting, London, 11–15 September 1937, p. 5. WCML, NEC Minutes 1920–37.
200. NLB, Report and Balance Sheet 1916, p. 13. WCML, WRep.
201. *Ibid.*, p. 20.
202. NLB, Report and Balance Sheet 1920, p. 10. WCML, WRep. NLB, 'List of Donations 1920', undated pamphlet, p. 18.
203. NLB, Statement of Income and Expenditure for the Year ending 31 December 1921. WCML, NLB Statements of Income 1921–52.
204. Minutes, EC Meeting, London, 9–13 September 1933, p. 5. WCML, NEC Minutes 1920–37.
205. Conference Report, Manchester, 7–9 February 1925. WCML, CRP. Minutes, EC Meetings, London, 27–9 June 1925, p. 1 and Manchester, 31 March–2 April 1926, p. 1, both in WCML, NEC Minutes 1920–37.
206. Minutes, EC Meetings, Manchester, 25–9 March 1933, p. 2 and London, 17–22 June 1933, pp. 1–2 and 10, both in WCML, NEC Minutes 1920–37. Letter A. Henderson, Gen. Sec., NLB, to branch Secretaries, July 1933. WCML, WCir.
207. Smith (ed.), *Golden Jubilee Brochure*, p. 10.
208. J. de la Mare Rowley, 'Purse, Benjamin Ormond (1874–1950)', rev. Patrick Wallis, *Oxford Dictionary of National Biography* (*ODNB*) Oxford University Press, 2004, http://0-www.oxforddnb.com.lib.exeter.ac.uk/view/article/35633 [last accessed 20 September 2012].
209. 'Obituary: Mr. Ben Purse', *The Times*, 12 April 1950, p. 8.
210. Ben Purse, *The British Blind: A Revolution in Thought and Action* (London, 1928), p. 1; Smith (ed.), *Golden Jubilee Brochure*, p. 8.
211. Purse, 'Manchester Guardians' Election', *BA* (April 1899), p. 64.
212. de la Mare Rowley, 'Purse', *ODNB*. NLB, Reports and Balance Sheets 1914, pp. 8–9 and 1917, p. 6 , both in WCML, WRep.
213. Hansard 59 HC Deb., 11 March 1914, col. 1315.
214. Letter B. Purse, President, NLB, to K. Hardie, ILP, 12 July 1906. LSE, ILP 4. Phillips, *The Blind in British Society*, p. 314.
215. Mary G. Thomas, *The Royal National Institute for the Blind, 1868–1956* (Brighton, 1957), pp. 112–13.
216. 'Care of the Blind', *The Times*, 27 May 1914, p. 8.
217. The League only paid Purse a weekly salary of £2 5*s* 0*d* in 1916, although it offered him a pay rise in order to keep him. 'Printing and Kindred Trades' Blind Aid Committee, 24 November 1923, p. 8. WCML, WCir. Resolution passed by the Birmingham Branch of the National League of the Blind, sent 27 January 1927, pp. 2–3. MRC, MSS292/74/4/1.
218. Purse's letter is reprinted in NLB, Report and Balance Sheet 1916, p. 7. WCML, WRep. Purse subsequently argued that his new employers had ordered him to write the letter. 'Printing and Kindred Trades' Blind Aid Committee, November 1923, pp. 2 and 8. WCML, WCir.

219. 'The Blind in Conference', *Manchester Guardian*, 28 August 1917, p. 3.
220. Minutes, EC Meeting, London, 19–21 June 1920, p. 3. WCML, WCir.
221. 'Obituary: Mr. Ben Purse', *The Times*, 12 April 1950, p. 8.
222. Thomas, *The Royal National Institute*, p. 113.
223. Extract from 'The Tribune', September 1926. MRC, MSS292/91/26. Purse, for example, attacked the Blind Persons Bill introduced by the Labour Party in Parliament in 1925 in a letter to *The Times*. 'Help for the Blind: A Labour Bill', letter Ben Purse to the Editor, *The Times*, 8 May 1925, p. 10.
224. The typed manuscript 'History of the League, 1893–1921' in the British Library dated 19 December 1947 is almost certainly written by Purse. BL, YA.1992.C.48. After his departure the organisation was not even able to reconstruct when it had been affiliated to the TUC. Smith (ed.), *Golden Jubilee Brochure*, p. 4. Letter from A. Henderson, Gen. Sec., NLB, to W. Citrine, Gen. Sec., TUC, 13 May 1931. MRC, MSS292/91/27.
225. de la Mare Rowley, 'Purse', *ODNB*. *The Times*, 22 April 1944, p. 2.
226. Letter Dorothy Cleaver, Gen. Sec. pro tem to Registrar of Friendly Societies, 17 August 1942. TNA, FS 27/232.
227. *The Times*, 22 April 1944, p. 2. Thomas, *The Royal National Institute*, p. 13.
228. Minutes of a Meeting with the Minister of National Insurance, 6 November 1947, p. 5. TNA, AST 7/977.
229. Minutes, EC Sub-Committee, Glasgow, 3–4 July 1948, p. 2; Minutes, EC Meeting, London, 18–21 September 1948, p. 2, both in WCML, NEC Minutes 1938–50. The Glasgow branch protested in vain against this decision. Minutes, EC Meeting, London, 11–14 December 1948, p. 10. WCML, NEC Minutes 1938–50. J. Perry, 'Our Right to Celebrate', *BA* (April 1948), p. 6.
230. Ben Purse, *Moods and Melodies: A Book of Verse* (London, 1931).
231. 'Correspondence', *BA* (May 1899) p. 82.
232. de la Mare Rowley, 'Purse', *ODNB*.
233. 'Quarterly Notes', *BA* (July 1950), p. 2.

2   'Justice not Charity': Framing the Message

1. Ben Purse, *The Social and Industrial Conditions of the Blind* (Manchester, 1908), p. 1.
2. 'Framing' describes the process of highlighting selected aspects of a specific grievance in order to convince people that an injustice exists which can be removed by a specific path of action. For an introduction on Frame Theory, see David A. Snow, 'Framing Processes, Ideology, and Discursive Fields', in David A. Snow, Sarah A. Soule and Hanspeter Kriesi (eds), *The Blackwell Companion to Social Movements* (Malden, MA, 2004), pp. 380–412.
3. 'Freedom has been the battle-cry of the pioneers of the Blind cause. My sightless friends have struggled for that one solitary thing. Freedom!' George Chamberlain, 'Out of the Darkness comes the Light', *BA* (April 1918), p. 5.
4. Joseph Slater, 'The Gossip's Bowl', *BA* (April 1899), p. 67.
5. *Ibid.*
6. C. G. Lothian, 'Justice or Charity? Which?', *BA* (January 1920), p. 8.

7. Phillips, *The Blind in British Society*, p. 312. For a discussion of the concept of 'social citizenship' and how it evolved since it was first proposed by T. H. Marshall, see Martin Powell, 'The Hidden History of Social Citizenship', *Citizenship Studies* Vol. 6(3) (2002): 229–44.

8. Labour Publications Department, *The Blind Persons Charter* (London, September 1935), p. 8 (in the original this was printed in bold type).

9. Dickensonian, 'A Blind Man's Triumph over Affliction', *BA* (February 1909), p. 6.

10. *Royal Commission on the Poor Laws and Relief of Distress* (London, 1909), Appendix Vol. III: 55th Day, 22 October 1906, 28168, p. 161. In his opening statement Purse even claimed that 'more than one half' had become blind after their thirty-fifth birthday. *Ibid.*, 28165 (2), p. 160.

11. 'Lest You Forget!' leaflet, NLB, undated (1918–19). MRC, MSS292/91/27.

12. 'Justice or Charity? Which?' leaflet, NLB, undated (1918–19). MRC, MSS292/91/27.

13. The slogan began to appear around 1918. See, for example, C. G. Lothian, 'Charity or Justice', *BA* (November 1918), p. 6.

14. 'Justice or Charity? Which?' leaflet, NLB, undated (1918–19). MRC, MSS292/91/27.

15. See, for example, 'In support of that position we submit two reasons, the first of which is: That the various charity organisations and institutions, which are supposed to exist primarily for the relief of the blind, are so disunited and fenced round with anomalies that they are wholly incapable of united action for any given object of material progress. In the second place, the limitation of their resources prevents them from discovering and developing those spheres of industry which might be opened out to the blind with advantages to themselves and to the community at large.' Ben Purse, 'The Blind of Greater Britain, chapter VII', *BA* (June 1899), p. 85.

16. 'Reports of Propaganda', *BA* (September 1898), p. 6.

17. See, for example, 'The Bitter Cry of the Blind!', *BA* (April 1918), p. 1; Andrew Mearns, *The Bitter Cry of Outcast London: An Inquiry into the Condition of the Abject Poor* (London, 1883); Peter J. Keating (ed.), *Into Unknown England, 1866–1913: Selections from the Social Explorers* (Manchester, 1976), p. 91.

18. 'State Aid for the Blind: The Plea for a Wider Opportunity', *Manchester Guardian*, 11 August 1919, p. 11.

19. Phillips, *The Blind in British Society*, pp. 313–20.

20. *Ibid.*, p. 311.

21. Borsay, *Disability*, pp. 106–7.

22. Purse, *The Social and Industrial Conditions of the Blind*, p. 13.

23. Purse, 'The Blind of Greater Britain', *BA* (June 1899), p. 85.

24. Letter W. Banham, Gen. Sec., NLB, to K. Hardie, ILP, 15 May 1901. LSE, ILP 4, doc. 9.

25. 'Notes regarding the Petition to Parliament', undated. LSE, ILP 4, doc. 10.

26. *Ibid.*

27. The ILP continued to support the League. In January 1902 Will Crooks persuaded the London County Council to adopt both a resolution in favour of more workshops and a public inquiry into the administration of charitable organisations for blind people in the metropolis and the ILP's 20th Annual Conference in 1912 unanimously adopted a resolution in support of the

League's core demands. Phillips, *The Blind in British Society*, p. 310. *Report of the 20th Annual Conference held at Merthyr 27th and 28th May, 1912* (ILP: London, June 1912), p. 96. LSE, ILP 5.

28. Ben Purse, 'Editorial Notes', *BA* (February 1899), p. 44.
29. The meeting was also attended by two Councillors, an Alderman and other local dignitaries. 'Help for the Blind', *BA* (May 1899), p. 75.
30. 'Grand Demonstration in Hull', *BA* (May 1899), p. 76.
31. 'State Aid for the Blind', *BA* (July 1899), pp. 104–5.
32. 'The Gardner Trust Conference', *BA* (May 1902), p. 1.
33. 'Blind Men's Protest', *Daily Mail*, 28 April 1902, p. 3.
34. The contingents had started at Mile End Waste, St Pancras Arches and St George's Circus. 'State Aid for the Blind', *The Times*, 13 July 1909, p. 9; 'March of Blind', *Daily Mail*, 10 July 1909, p. 3.
35. 'March of Blind', *Daily Mail*, 10 July 1909, p. 3.
36. Temple Bar, 'March of the Blind Proletariat', *BA* (August 1909), p. 7.
37. 'The Trafalgar Square Demonstration', *BA* (September 1909), p. 4.
38. It was unsuccessfully reintroduced in 1908, 1909 and 1910. Lysons, 'The Development of Social Legislation', p. 116; Phillips, *The Blind in British Society*, p. 311; E. Martin, 'Steadman, William Charles (1851–1911)', *ODNB*, 2004, online edn., May 2008 [last accessed 19 October 2012].
39. Letter B. Purse, Pres., NLB, to K. Hardie, ILP, 12 July 1906. LSE, ILP 4.
40. 'Conferences held between Representatives of Blind Organisations and the Parliamentary Committee', Memo, Research and Economics Dept., TUC, 18 July 1935. MRC, MSS292/91/25. According to Phillips negotiations started in late 1910. Phillips, *The Blind in British Society*, p. 315.
41. Lysons, 'The Development of Social Legislation', p. 120.
42. Hansard 59 HC Deb., 11 March 1914, cols. 1318–32; Rooff, *Voluntary Societies and Social Policy*, p. 200; Lysons, 'The Development of Social Legislation', pp. 116–27.
43. Lysons, 'The Development of Social Legislation', pp. 127–31.
44. Hansard 59 HC Deb., 11 March 1914, col. 1355.
45. Phillips, *The Blind in British Society*, p. 315; Hansard 59 HC Deb., 11 March 1914, col. 1352; NLB, Report and Balance Sheet 1914, pp. 8–9, WCML, WRep.; Lysons, 'The Development of Social Legislation', pp. 132–3.
46. Lewis was Parliamentary Secretary to the Local Government Board. Hansard 59 HC Deb., 11 March 1914, col. 1353.
47. Blindness was defined as 'too blind to perform work for which eyesight is essential', National Joint Council, *The Blind Persons Act 1920* (London, no date), pp. 2–3; 'Care of the Blind', *British Medical Journal* Vol. 2(2955) (18 August 1917): 227–8; Phillips, *The Blind in British Society*, pp. 381–2.
48. 'Conference of the Blind', *Manchester Guardian*, 27 August 1917, p. 8; 'The Blind in Conference', *Manchester Guardian*, 28 August 1917, p. 3.
49. Among the MPs who attended were Henry Norman, Alfred Bigland, Neville Chamberlain, G. Thorne, R. Tootill, W. H. Sugden and J. Jones. 'Blind Men at the House', *Manchester Guardian*, 1 August 1919, p. 6; 'The Unemployed Blind', *The Times*, 1 August 1919, p. 17; Lysons, 'The Development of Social Legislation', pp. 187–8.
50. 'Blind Men at the House' and 'Higher Pensions', *Manchester Guardian*, 1 August 1919, pp. 6 and 7; 'State Aid for the Blind', *Manchester Guardian*, 11 August 1919, p. 11.

51. The protestors were removed from the galleries. 'Higher Pensions', *Manchester Guardian*, 1 August 1919, p. 7.
52. 'Champions of the Blind', *The Times*, 18 August 1919, p. 7.
53. Resolution adopted at a League meeting at Plymouth, 14 December 1919; 'League Meeting at Plymouth', *BA* (January 1920), p. 1.
54. Hansard 122 HC Deb., 11 December 1919, cols. 1600–1.
55. Hansard 121 HC Deb., 25 November 1919, cols. 1635–9.
56. Hansard 125 HC Deb., 13 February 1920, col. 389.
57. Jonathan Schneer, *Ben Tillett: Portrait of a Labour Leader* (London, 1982), p. 206.
58. The TUC's General Council referred them to the National League of the Blind. Letter Asst. Sec., TUC, to C. E. Dumbleton, Branch Sec., National Amalgamated Union of Life Assurance Workers, Manchester, 19 February 1943. MRC, MSS292/91/27.
59. The only exception was Sir F. Banbury, Member for the City of London, who had already opposed the 1914 Bill. Hansard 126 HC Deb., 12 March 1920, cols. 1712–18.
60. *Ibid.*, col. 1696.
61. *Ibid.*, col. 1712.
62. *Ibid.*, cols. 1727–30.
63. Lothian, 'Justice or Charity? Which?', *BA* (January 1920), p. 8.
64. 'Notable League Conference. North West Council', *BA* (February 1920), pp. 2–3; 'North-Western Notes', *BA* (January 1939), p. 6.
65. Jess Jenkins, *Leicester's Unemployed March to London 1905* (Friends of the Record Office for Leicestershire, Leicester & Rutland, 2005); Lisa Tickner, *The Spectacle of Women: Imagery of the Suffrage Campaign 1907–14* (London, 1989), pp. 141–8.
66. Matthias Reiss, 'Marching on the Capital: National Protest Marches of the British Unemployed in the 1920s and 1930s', in Matthias Reiss (ed.), *The Street as Stage: Protest Marches and Public Rallies since the Nineteenth Century* (Oxford, 2007), pp. 147–68.
67. 'Notable League Conference. North West Council', *BA* (February 1920), p. 3.
68. D. B. Lawley, 'The Iron Heel', *BA* (January 1920), p. 5.
69. 'Notable League Conference. North West Council', *BA* (February 1920), p. 3.
70. For a list of the march's objectives see 'Souvenir Programme of the Great March by the Blind from Leeds, Manchester, & Newport, to London, commencing April 5, 1920' (Warrington, 1920), p. 3. Copy provided by Robert Mooney.
71. A new branch was subsequently organised. Minutes, EC Meeting at Central Office, London, 19–21 June 1920, p. 5. WCML, WCir.
72. 'Blind Men's March', *Leeds Mercury*, 6 April 1920, p. 7; 'The March of the Blind', *Manchester Guardian*, 6 April 1920, p. 12; 'The March of the Blind', *Macclesfield Courier and Herald*, 10 April 1920, p. 8; 'March of the Blind', *West Herts Post & Watford Echo*, 27 April 1920, p. 5; 'The March of the Blind', *Worcestershire Echo*, 9 April 1920, p. 3.
73. 'Blind Women Held Back', *Daily Herald*, 12 April 1920, p. 3. A picture of the Leeds contingent in the *Golden Jubilee Brochure* shows two women. They are looking straight at the camera and are probably guides. Smith, *Golden Jubilee Brochure*, p. 15. In 1920, the League had 4,284 male and 564 female

members. National League of the Blind of Great Britain and Ireland, Annual Returns 1912–50, TNA, FS 12/141.

74. The first march to London to include a female contingent was the 1930 Hunger Marchers of the National Unemployed Workers Movement. Peter Kingsford, *The Hunger Marchers in Britain 1920–1939* (London, 1982), p. 109.

75. 'Blind Men's March', *Yorkshire Weekly Post*, 10 April 1920, p. 19; 'The March of the Blind', *Macclesfield Courier and Herald*, 10 April 1920, p. 8.

76. 'Blind Men's March', *Leeds Mercury*, 6 April 1920, p. 7.

77. *Ibid.*

78. 'The March of the Blind', *Manchester Guardian*, 6 April 1920, p. 12; the *South Wales Echo*, 6 April 1920, p. 5, however, was more positive.

79. 'March of the Blind', *Cheshire Daily Echo*, 6 April 1920, p. 2; 'The March of the Blind', *Manchester Guardian*, 6 April 1920, p. 12.

80. 'Blind Men's March', *The Times*, 6 April 1920, p. 7.

81. 'Blind Men's March', *Leeds Mercury*, 6 April 1920, p. 7; 'Blind Men's March', *The Times*, 6 April 1920, p. 7.

82. 'Blind Wayfarers', *Daily Herald*, 21 April 1920, p. 1.

83. 'Tragic Country of the Blind', *Daily Herald*, 23 April 1920, p. 1.

84. 'The March of the Blind', *Macclesfield Courier and Herald*, 10 April 1920, p. 8; 'Blind Marchers in the Potteries', *Staffordshire Sentinel*, 8 April 1920, p. 3.

85. 'Blind Men's March', *Yorkshire Weekly Post*, 10 April 1920, p. 19.

86. First quotation: 'March with the Blind', *Daily Herald*, 20 April 1920, p. 1; second quotation: 'Sightless Pilgrims to the Capital', *Yorkshire Evening Post*, 6 April 1920, p. 5.

87. 'Sightless Pilgrims to the Capital', *Yorkshire Evening Post*, 6 April 1920, p. 5.

88. 'The Blind Marchers', *Leicester Mercury*, 15 April 1920, p. 4.

89. 'Blind Marchers at Derby', *Derby Daily Telegraph*, 13 April 1920, p. 2.

90. 'March of the Blind', *Sheffield Daily Telegraph*, 8 April 1920, p. 5.

91. 'On to London', *Birmingham Gazette*, 12 April 1920, p. 3.

92. 'March of the Blind', *Sheffield Daily Telegraph*, 8 April 1920, p. 5.

93. First quotation: 'Blind Marchers at Derby', *Derby and Chesterfield Reporter*, 16 April 1920, p. 5; second quotation: 'Luton's Sympathy Aroused', *Luton News & Bedfordshire Advertiser*, 22 April 1920, p. 11.

94. 'March of the Blind ended', *Manchester Guardian*, 26 April 1920, p. 8.

95. 'Blind Men's March to London', *Leicester Daily Mercury*, 14 April 1920, p. 9. It seems that there were always two resolutions. One read 'This mass meeting of the citizens of [name of the city] deeply deplores the unsatisfactory social and industrial condition of the blind, and demands that the Government shall, without further delay, redeem its promises by providing the necessary financial arrangements with which to give effect to the proposals embodied in the Technical Education, Employment, and Maintenance of the Blind Bill. This meeting directs that copies of the resolution should be forwarded to the Prime Minister and Chancellor of the Exchequer, and the Minister of Health (Dr. Addison).' Quoted in 'The March of the Blind', *Worcestershire Echo*, 9 April 1920, p. 3. The other resolution dealt with the request that the Prime Minister should receive a deputation of marchers on their arrival in London. 'Luton's Sympathy Aroused', *Luton News & Bedfordshire Advertiser*, 22 April 1920, p. 11.

96. For example, at Wolverhampton, Leicester and Luton. 'Blind Marchers', *Birmingham Gazette*, 10 April 1920, p. 3; 'The Blind Marchers', *Leicester Daily Mercury*, 15 April 1920, p. 4; 'Blind Wayfarers', *Daily Herald*, 21 April 1920, p. 1. See also 'March of the Blind Ended', *Manchester Guardian*, 26 April 1920, p. 8.

97. See, for example, 'March of the Blind', *Mansfield and North Notts. Advertiser*, 16 April 1920, p. 7; 'March of the Blind', *West Herts Post & Watford Echo*, 27 April 1920, p. 5.

98. 'Blind Men's March', *Yorkshire Post*, 7 April 1920, p. 3.

99. 'March of the Blind', *Cheshire Daily Echo*, 7 April 1920, p. 3.

100. 'Blind Marchers in the Potteries', *Staffordshire Sentinel*, 8 April 1920, p. 3. See also, for example, 'March of the Blind', *Sheffield Daily Telegraph*, 8 April 1920, p. 5; 'The March of the Blind', *Macclesfield Courier and Herald*, 10 April 1920, p. 8; 'The March of the Blind', *Leicester Mercury*, 13 April 1920, p. 6; 'The Blind Marchers at Market Harborough', *Market Harborough Advertiser*, 20 April 1920, p. 5; 'My March for the Blind: A Partially-Sighted Pensioner Recalls a Great Walk 61 Years Ago', *BA* (July/August 1981), pp. 2–3.

101. The tramwaymen at Stoke, for example, collected on behalf of the marchers at every tram depot. According to the United Vehicle Workers' Union's National Organiser, 'they felt the least they could do was to help those who were trying to help themselves'. 'Blind Marchers in the Potteries', *Staffordshire Sentinel*, 8 April 1920, p. 3. See also D. B. Lawley, 'The March Against Addison', *BA* (April 1920), p. 2.

102. Figure for Stockport in 'March of the Blind', *Advertiser*, 9 April 1920, p. 4; for Macclesfield in 'The March of the Blind', *Macclesfield Courier and Herald*, 10 April 1920, p. 8; for Barnsley in 'Walking with the Blind Men to London', *Yorkshire Evening Post*, 8 April 1920, p. 6; for Leicester in 'Blind Men's March to London', *Leicester Daily Mercury*, 14 April 1920, p. 9; for Northampton in 'Blind Marchers', *Northampton Mercury*, 23 April 1920, p. 8. Conversion according to http://www.measuringworth.com/ukcompare/ [last accessed 27 May 2014]. The League's annual return showed an income of £4,294 16s. 9½d. from collections and donations for 1920. In addition, £10,634 5s. 7¼d. was received from the League's branches. NLB, Annual Returns, TNA, FS 12/141.

103. See, for example, 'Blind Pilgrims', *Derby Mercury*, 16 April 1920, p. 9; 'The Blind Marchers at Market Harborough', *Market Harborough Advertiser*, 20 April 1920, p. 5; 'Blind Wayfarers', *Daily Herald*, 21 April 1920, p. 1.

104. Knots were tied into the rope to indicate the places for the marchers. Those who were completely sightless marched in the centre while the partially sighted took the outer and inner sides. 'My March for the Blind: A Partially-Sighted Pensioner Recalls a Great Walk 61 Years Ago', *BA* (July/August 1981), p. 3.

105. D. B. Lawley, 'The March of the Blind', *BA* (April 1920), p. 8. See also Appendix B.

106. 'Blind Men's March', *Yorkshire Weekly Post*, 10 April 1920, p. 19; 'Walking with the Blind Men to London', *Yorkshire Evening Post*, 8 April 1920, p. 6; 'March with the Blind', *Daily Herald*, 20 April 1920, p. 1. The number of partially sighted marchers was limited. The North-Eastern contingent, for

example, had only two partially sighted among the more than 70 marchers. 'Blind Pilgrims', *Derby Daily Express*, 13 April 1920, p. 7.

107. 'March of the Blind', *Cheshire Daily Echo*, 6 April 1920, p. 2.
108. Quoted in 'Blind Marchers in the Potteries', *Staffordshire Sentinel*, 8 April 1920, p. 3.
109. 'The Blind Marchers', *Leicester Daily Mercury*, 15 April 1920, p. 4.
110. 'On to London', *Birmingham Gazette*, 12 April 1920, p. 3.
111. 'Blind Marchers in the Potteries', *Staffordshire Sentinel*, 8 April 1920, p. 3; 'March of the Blind', *Advertiser*, 9 April 1920, p. 4; 'Blind Men's March', *Yorkshire Weekly Post*, 10 April 1920, p. 19; 'The March of the Blind', *Macclesfield Courier and Herald*, 10 April 1920, p. 8.
112. 'Luton's Sympathy Aroused', *Luton News & Bedfordshire Advertiser*, 22 April 1920, p. 11.
113. 'Walking with the Blind Men to London', *Yorkshire Evening Post*, 8 April 1920, p. 6.
114. 'Blind Marchers', *Northampton Mercury*, 23 April 1920, p. 8.
115. 'Blind Marchers at Derby', *Derby and Chesterfield Reporter*, 16 April 1920, p. 5.
116. 'March of the Blind', *Sheffield Daily Telegraph*, 8 April 1920, p. 5.
117. 'Blind Marchers in the Potteries', *Staffordshire Sentinel*, 8 April 1920, p. 3.
118. 'Luton's Sympathy Aroused', *Luton News & Bedfordshire Advertiser*, 22 April 1920, p. 11; 'March of the Blind', *West Herts Post & Watford Echo*, 27 April 1920, p. 5.
119. 'Blind Pilgrims', *Derby Mercury*, 16 April 1920, p. 9; 'Luton's Sympathy Aroused', *Luton News & Bedfordshire Advertiser*, 22 April 1920, p. 11.
120. D. B. Lawley, 'The March of the Blind', *BA* (April 1920), p. 8. See also Appendix B.
121. 'Blind Pilgrims', *Derby Mercury*, 16 April 1920, p. 9. See also, for example, 'The March of the Blind', *Worcestershire Echo*, 9 April 1920, p. 3; 'Tragic Country of the Blind', *Daily Herald*, 23 April 1920, p. 1.
122. 'The March of the Blind', *Macclesfield Courier and Herald*, 10 April 1920, p. 8.
123. 'Blind Marchers at Derby', *Derby and Chesterfield Reporter*, 16 April 1920, p. 5.
124. 'Blind Men's Welcome', *Evening Standard*, 23 April 1920, p. 9; 'Blind Men's March', *Yorkshire Post*, 7 April 1920, p. 3; 'The Blind Marchers', *Evening Standard*, 26 April 1920, p. 7. *The Times*, however, made it clear that the party did not include any ex-soldiers. 'Blind Marchers in London', *The Times*, 26 April 1920, p. 11.
125. 'March with the Blind', *Daily Herald*, 20 April 1920, p. 1; 'Luton's Sympathy Aroused', *Luton News & Bedfordshire Advertiser*, 22 April 1920, p. 11.
126. 'Blind Men's March', *Yorkshire Weekly Post*, 10 April 1920, p. 19.
127. 'Blind Marchers' Arrival', *Daily Herald*, 24 April 1920, p. 1.
128. 'Blind Men's March', *The Times*, 6 April 1920, p. 7.
129. 'On to London', *Birmingham Gazette*, 12 April 1920, p. 3. See also 'The Blind Marchers', *Leicester Daily Mercury*, 15 April 1920, p. 4; Hansard 128 HC Deb., 22 April 1920, col. 554. The League's Executive Council considered meeting Bonar Law at once and insisting on also seeing Lloyd George as soon as he had returned to London. The March Committee, however, was 'unanimous and emphatic in the opinion that we should await the return of Mr. Lloyd George before sending our deputation to Downing Street'. *BA* (June 1920), p. 7.

130. 'The Blind Marchers', *Evening Standard*, 26 April 1920, p. 7.
131. 'Day of the Blind', *Daily Herald*, 26 April 1920, p. 1.
132. Ben Tillett was unable to attend, due to illness. 'Day of the Blind', *Daily Herald*, 26 April 1920, p. 1; 'March of the Blind Ended', *Manchester Guardian*, 26 April 1920, p. 8; 'Blind Marchers in London', *The Times*, 26 April 1920, p. 11.
133. Purse also accused Scotland Yard of having made transcriptions of all speeches delivered on the march. 'Day of the Blind', *Daily Herald*, 26 April 1920, p. 1.
134. Hansard 126 HC Deb., 12 March 1920, cols. 1695–739.
135. 'Day of the Blind', *Daily Herald*, 26 April 1920, p. 1.
136. Hansard 128 HC Deb., 26 April 1920, col. 859.
137. For a transcript of this meeting see Deputation to the Rt. Hon. David Lloyd George, (Prime Minister) from The National League of the Blind of Great Britain and Ireland. 10, Downing Street, Whitehall, S.W.1., Friday, 30th April, 1920. House of Lords Record Office (HLRO), LG/F/230/3, 16 pp.
138. *Ibid.*, p. 11.
139. *Ibid.*, pp. 12–16.
140. 'Disappointed Blind', *Daily Herald*, 1 May 1920, p. 5; 'Blind Marchers at Downing Street', *Manchester Guardian*, 1 May 1920, p. 12. See also *BA* (August 1920), p. 7.
141. Minutes, EC Meeting, London, 19–21 June 1920, p. 1. WCML, WCir.
142. Blind Persons Act, 1920, 10 & 11 Geo. 5 1920–1, Chapter 49. For the discussion in the House of Commons see Hansard 129 HC Deb., 14 May 1920, cols. 968–96; Hansard 131 HC Deb., 25 June 1920, cols. 2590–634 and 28 June 1920, cols. 206–14.
143. Following criticism of the original draft, the Minister of Health included a passage which required local authorities to submit within six months (changed by the Lords to twelve months) plans of how they intended to promote the welfare of the blind in their area. How these plans were assessed by the Ministry of Health is, however, unclear. Blind Persons Act, 1920, 10 & 11 Geo. 5 1920–1, Chapter 49. Phillips, *The Blind in British Society*, p. 391.
144. Smith (ed.), *Golden Jubilee Brochure*, p. 13; Phillips, *The Blind in British Society*, pp. 390–1.
145. Smith (ed.), *Golden Jubilee Brochure*, p. 22; Parker, *Years of Excitement*, pp. 4–5.
146. Annual Report and Balance Sheet, National League of the Blind of Great Britain, North-Western District Council, 16 March 1940. WCML, League for the Blind North-Western District.
147. Smith (ed.), *Golden Jubilee Brochure*, p. 19.
148. Martin Pagel, *'On Our Own Behalf': An Introduction to the Self-Organisation of Disabled People* (Manchester, 1998), p. 10.
149. 'Protest Demonstration. March to London. To the Members; Trades Councils, Labour Parties, Trade Union Branches, Cooperative Societies, Men's and Women's Guilds', A. Henderson, Gen. Sec., NLB, Approved by General Council, TUC on 23 July 1936. TNA, MH 55/607.
150. Annual Report and Balance Sheet, National League of the Blind of Great Britain, North-Western District Council, 16 March 1940. WCML, League for the Blind North-Western District.

151. 'Printing and Kindred Trades Blind Aid Committee: Transcription of a discussion which took place on Saturday, November 24th 1923, between Messrs. Lothian and Turner of the National League of the Blind, and Mr. H. C. Preece and Mr. Ben Purse, Greater London Fund for the Blind', H. S. Weeden, Hon. Sec., November 1923, p. 3. WCML, WCir. For later statements to the same effect see, for example, 'My March for the Blind: A Partially-Sighted Pensioner Recalls a Great Walk 61 Years Ago', *BA* (July/August 1981), pp. 2–3.

152. NLB, *Handbook* (London 1932), pp. 9–10. TUCL, HV1744.

153. Carter, 'State Aid', p. 19; Máirtín Ó Catháin, ' "Blind, but Not to the Hard Facts of Life": The Blind Workers' Struggle in Derry, 1928–1940', *Radical History Review* Vol. 94 (2006): 9–21 (11).

154. http://www.community-tu.org/who-we-represent/nlbd-sector.aspx   [last accessed 18 April 2013].

155. Phelan's claim that the passing of the Act 'can be ascribed to the imaginative and influential leadership of one man, Sir Arthur Pearson' is therefore also questionable. Phelan, 'Are we Producing the Goods?', p. 70.

156. Lysons, 'The Development of Social Legislation', p. 189.

157. Anderson, *War, Disability and Rehabilitation*, p. 42.

158. Phillips, *The Blind in British Society*, pp. 389–91.

159. Carter, 'The National League of the Blind and Disabled', p. 3. TUCL, HD6661z. Carter, 'State Aid', p. 18.

160. S. Dewar, 'Glasgow Notes', *BA* (June 1920), p. 4.

161. The workshop which employed the men dismissed them 'for going on the march without leave' but they were quickly reinstated. C. G. Lothian, 'Paisley's Welcome to the Blind Marchers', *BA* (June 1920), p. 5.

162. *BA* (August 1920), p. 7.

163. Minutes, EC Meeting, London, 19–21 June 1920, p. 4. WCML, WCir.

164. *Ibid.*

165. 'Luton's Sympathy Aroused', *Luton News & Bedfordshire Advertiser*, 22 April 1920, p. 11.

166. The 1936 march is discussed in Chapter 4. 'Justice not Charity: An Appeal to the Trade Unionists of Britain from their Blind Colleagues', NLB, undated (1959). MRC, MSS292/91/27.

167. *Advocate*, Special Edition (November 1998). http://www.community-tu.org/information/100308/100310/history/ [last accessed 18 October 2012].

3   Mutually Exclusive Principles? Trade Unionism and Charity

1. Advisory Committee on the Welfare of the Blind, Third Annual Report, 1921–2, p. 1. TNA, HO 45/166545/2.

2. Lysons, 'The Development of Social Legislation', pp. 308–11.

3. The last appointment nominated by the League was Alice L. Wallace. 'New Members of the Central Advisory Committee', *BA* (January 1920), p. 3. Minutes, EC Meeting, London, 30 September–2 October 1922, p. 2. WCML, NEC Minutes 1920–37. J. Wheatley, the first Labour politician to become Minister of Health, likewise argued that institutional representation on the

Advisory Committee was not possible, but the League was allowed to nominate an individual to sit on the Committee in 1924. 'Report of a Deputation from the National League of the Blind to the Ministry of Health on July 1st, 1924', p. 2. WCML, WCir. Memo for Mr. Beckett, W. Bramhall, Ministry of Health, 8 December 1944. TNA, PIN 8/53. On the importance of this committee see Phillips, *The Blind in British Society*, pp. 384–6.

4. C. F. Ritchie, Charity Commission, to J. E. Gregory, Gen. Sec., NLB, 3 January 1923, reprinted in Circular, J. E. Gregory, Gen. Sec., NLB, January 1928. WCML, WCir.

5. 'Re the Blind Persons Act', Circular to Branch and District Council Sec. and Members, D. B. Lawley, President, NLB, and J. E. Gregory, Sec., NLB, February 1921. WCML, WCir.

6. Purse, *The British Blind*, p. 8.

7. *Ibid.*, p. 9.

8. *Ibid.*, p. 4.

9. *Ibid.*, p. 8.

10. NLB, Report and Balance Sheet 1916, p. 8. WCML, WRep.

11. *Ibid.*, pp. 10–11.

12. *Ibid.*, pp. 10–15.

13. *Ibid.*, p. 7.

14. 'Printing and Kindred Trades' Blind Aid Committee, November 1923, p. 9. WCML, WCir.

15. Letter J. Perry, Midland Organiser, NLB, to W. Citrine, TUC, 16 November 1926, pp. 3–4. MRC, MSS292/74/4/1. Purse's new organisation listed 285 members in January 1922. TNA, FS 27/232.

16. The League's Midland Organiser, for example, accused Purse of having defrauded workers through an insurance scheme against blindness after leaving the League. Letter J. Perry, Midland Organiser, NLB, to W. Citrine, TUC, 16 November 1926, pp. 3–4. MRC, MSS292/74/4/1.

17. Purse, *The British Blind*, pp. 2–3.

18. *Ibid.*, pp. 37–8.

19. *Ibid.*, p. 56.

20. Certificate of Registry of Trade Union, in NUPIB Rules, p. 11. See also *ibid.*, p. 1. TNA, FS 27/232.

21. NLB Rules 1924, p. 2. WCML, NLB Rule Books.

22. In cases of doubt applicants could be required to produce a medical certificate which confirmed that their vision was impaired. NUPIB Rules, p. 1. TNA, FS 27/232.

23. NUPIB Rules, pp. 3–4. TNA, FS 27/232.

24. Extract from the *Tribune*, October 1926. MRC, MSS292/91/26. 'History of the League, 1893–1921', p. 2.

25. Extract from the *Tribune*, October 1926. MRC, MSS292/91/26. On the membership of the League see also Phillips, *The Blind in British Society*, p. 308. On the different attitude towards workshops, see Danieli and Wheeler, 'Employment Policy and Disabled People', p. 494.

26. 'Scottish Notes', *BA* (November 1922), pp. 6–7.

27. A. R. and C. P. Griffin, 'The Non-Political Trade Union Movement', in Asa Briggs and John Saville (eds), *Essays in Labour History 1918–1939* (London, 1977), pp. 133–62.

28. In March 1937 the League actually responded to an appeal for funds from the Nottinghamshire Miners' Association 'to enable them to carry on a fight against the imposition of the Spencer Union at the Harworth Colliery'. Minutes, EC Meeting, London, 20–23 March 1937, p. 8. WCML, NEC Minutes 1920–37.

29. David Gilbert, 'The Landscape of Spencerism: Mining Politics in the Nottingham Coalfield, 1910–1947', in Alan Campbell, Nina Fishman and David Howell (eds), *Miners, Unions and Politics, 1910–47* (Aldershot, 1996), pp. 175–97; Clegg, *A History of British Trade Unions since 1889*, Vol. II, pp. 417 and 445–9.

30. Letter Asst. Registrar to B. Purse, Hon. Gen. Sec., NUPIB, 6 January 1933; Letter B. Purse, Hon. Gen. Sec., NUPIB, to Registrar of Friendly Societies, 9 January 1933; Memo of meeting B. Purse, NUPIB, with Mr Cunning, Registry of Friendly Societies, 21 January 1933, all in TNA, FS 27/232.

31. Letter B. Purse, Hon. Gen. Sec., NUPIB, to F. Bramley, Gen. Sec., TUC, 3 June 1924. MRC, MSS292/91/26. NUPIB's annual returns list approximately 816 members at the end of 1923 and approximately 906 members at the end of 1924. TNA, FS 27/232.

32. Letter J. E. Gregory, Gen. Sec., NLB, to F. Bramley, Gen. Sec., TUC, 23 June 1924. MRC, MSS292/91/26.

33. 'Application for Affiliation', Letter A. S. Firth, Group Sec., TUC, to B. Purse, Hon. Gen. Sec., NUPIB, 26 June 1924. MRC, MSS292/91/26.

34. 'Application for Affiliation', Letter B. Purse, Hon. Gen. Sec., NUPIB, to F. Bramley, Gen. Sec., TUC, 9 July 1924. MRC, MSS292/91/26.

35. 'Application for Affiliation', Letter A. S. Firth, Group Sec., TUC, to B. Purse, Hon. Gen. Sec., NUPIB, 10 July 1924; 'Application for Affiliation', Letter B. Purse, Hon. Gen. Sec., NUPIB, to F. Bramley, Gen. Sec., TUC, 2 February 1925, both in MRC, MSS292/91/26.

36. Letter B. Purse, Hon. Gen. Sec., NUPIB, to W. Citrine, Gen. Sec., TUC, 18 May 1926. MRC, MSS292/91/26.

37. 'Application of Professional and Industrial Blind for Affiliation', Letter J. E. Gregory, Gen. Sec., NLB, to W. Citrine, Gen. Sec., TUC, 17 July 1926. MRC, MSS292/91/26.

38. 'Application for Affiliation by National Union of Blind', Letter W. Citrine, Gen. Sec., TUC, to O. Lister, NLB, 25 November 1926. MRC, MSS292/91/26.

39. Extract from the *Tribune*, September 1926. MRC, MSS292/91/26.

40. Letter O. Lister, Sec., NLB, to W. Citrine, Gen. Sec., TUC, 8 January 1927. MRC, MSS292/91/26.

41. Robert Taylor, *The TUC: From the General Strike to New Unionism* (Basingstoke, 2000).

42. Neil Riddell, 'Walter Citrine and the British Labour Movement, 1925–1935', *History* Vol. 85(278) (April 2000): 285–306 (293).

43. 'Application for Affiliation', Letters from Asst. Sec. TUC, to B. Purse, Hon. Gen. Sec., NUPIB and O. Lister, Sec., NLB, 9 March 1927, both in MRC, MSS292/91/26. A request from the Glasgow branch in 1929 to start fusion talks with NUPIB was somewhat ironically rejected by the Executive with the argument that NUPIB was 'not a recognised Trade Union affiliated to the Labour Party or the B.T.U.C.' Minutes, EC Meeting, Manchester, 8–10 June 1929, p. 4. WCML, NEC Minutes 1920–37.

44. 'Application for Affiliation', Letter B. Purse, Hon. Gen. Sec., NUPIB, to W. Citrine, Gen. Sec., TUC, 22 March 1927; Letter Gen. Sec., NLB, to W. Citrine, Gen. Sec., TUC, 13 April 1927, both in MRC, MSS292/91/26.
45. The League's two Birmingham branches had followed Purse into NUPIB. A new League branch was only formed in November 1926, which then challenged NUPIB's right to maintain its affiliation with the local Trades Council. 'National League of the Blind and the N. U. Professional and Industrial Blind', Letter F. W. Rudland, Sec., Birmingham TC & Labour Party, to W. Citrine, Gen. Sec., TUC, 15 November 1926. MRC, MSS292/74/4/1.
46. Letter J. Perry, Midland Organiser, NLB, to W. Citrine, Gen. Sec., TUC, 19 November 1926. MRC, MSS292/74/4/1.
47. Resolution, Birmingham branch, NLB, 27 January 1927, pp. 1 and 4. MRC, MSS292/74/4/1.
48. Letter Hon. Sec., Birmingham branch, NUPIB, to W. Citrine, Gen. Sec., TUC, 9 July 1927. MRC, MSS292/91/26.
49. *Ibid.*
50. Minutes, EC Meetings, London, 12–15 September 1931, pp. 5–6 and London, 12–15 December 1931, p. 7, both in WCML, NEC Minutes 1920–37.
51. Minutes, EC Meeting, Manchester, 17–20 September 1932, p. 1. WCML, NEC Minutes 1920–37. Letter B. Purse, NUPIB, to Registrar of Friendly Societies, 18 March 1933. TNA, FS 27/232.
52. Letter V. Tewson, Asst. Sec., TUC, to A. Henderson, Gen. Sec., NLB; 16 May 1945; Letter A. Henderson, Gen. Sec., NLB, to W. Citrine, Gen. Sec., TUC, 3 July 1945, both in MRC, MSS292/91/27. Quotation in Memo of Meeting Mr Wilson and Mr Holdwell, NABW, with Mr Cunning, Registry of Friendly Societies, 4 July 1945. TNA, FS 27/232. The final audit and distribution of the NABW's assets took considerable time due to a number of circumstances and were only completed in 1949. Letter Mann, Judd & Co., Chartered Accountants, to Management Committee, NABW, 5 July 1949; Letter Mathieson, King & Co., Chartered Accountants, to Chief Registrar of Friendly Societies, 18 July 1949, both in TNA, FS 27/232.
53. Oliphant, 'Empowerment and Debilitation', p. 63; June Rose, *Changing Focus*, pp. 30–8.
54. Coles, *Blindness and the Visionary*, pp. 21–4, quotation p. 24.
55. 'Editorial', *BA* (April 1950), p. 4.
56. Minutes, EC Meeting, London, 23–4 June 1962, p. 2; Minutes, EC Meeting, London, 23–5 March 1963, p. 14, both in WCML, NEC Minutes 1951–64.
57. J. A. Clydesdale, 'N.U.B.', *BA* (January 1922), p. 7.
58. The penalty was a fine of up to £100 or imprisonment for up to three months. Circular, NLB, to Branch and District Council Secretaries and Members Re the Blind Persons Act, signed by D. B. Lawley, President, and J. E. Gregory, Sec., February 1921, WCML, WCir.
59. *Barber v. Chudley*, Judgement, Royal Courts of Justice, 19 December 1922. WCML, WCir. See also NLB, 'Verbatim Report of the Proceedings at the Tower Bridge Police Court, London. In the case of Messrs. Barber and Dale, prosecuted by the Commissioner of Police for raising funds on behalf of the principles and objects of the National League of the Blind', pamphlet (1923). TUCL, HD6661z.

60. Letter Pattinson & Brewer, Solicitors, to J. E. Gregory, Gen. Sec., NLB, 3 November 1923. WCML, WCir.
61. Minutes, EC Meetings, London, 3–5 March 1923, p. 3 and Manchester, 12–14 January 1924, p. 1; Report, Sub-Committee Meeting, 23 April 1923, all in WCML, NEC Minutes 1920–37.
62. Letter A. Henderson, Gen. Sec., NLB, to W. Citrine, Gen. Sec., TUC, 12 October 1933. MRC, MSS292/91/27. Memo, A. Henderson, T. Rainbird and C. Hird, EC, NLB, January 1925. WCML, WCir.
63. Circular, E. Fuller, Hon. Sec., NLB Haslingden, 3 September 1932 and leaflet 'Why You Should Join the National League of the Blind', undated, both in TNA, CHAR 7/56.
64. 'Re Blind Persons Act, 1920', Report by P. S. T. W. Hodkinson, Haslingden, 14 October 1932. TNA, CHAR 7/56.
65. Letter Insp. H. F. Graves, Haslingden, to Superintendent J. S. McCrone, Rawtenstall, 21 November 1932. Forwarded to the Chief Constable of Lancashire 22 November 1932. TNA, CHAR 7/56.
66. 'Blind Persons Act, 1920', Letter Superintendent J. S. McCrone, Rawtenstall, to Chief Constable of Lancashire, 15 October 1932; 'Re Blind Persons Act, 1920', Report by P. S. T. W. Hodkinson, Haslingden, 14 October 1932; 'Blind Persons Act, 1920', from Insp. H. F. Graves, Haslingden, to Superintendent J. S. McCrone, Rawtenstall, 21 November 1932, forwarded to the Chief Constable of Lancashire, 22 November 1932, all in TNA, CHAR 7/56.
67. Letter Chief Constable of Lancashire to Sec., Charity Commission, London, 21 December 1932; 'In the Matter of the Charity called or known as the Haslingden Branch of the National League of the Blind of Great Britain and Ireland', Charity Commission, 6 January 1933; 'National League of the Blind', Minute Paper, Charity Commission, all in TNA, CHAR 7/56.
68. The defendants were fined 10s. each and had to pay 5s. costs each. 'National League of the Blind – Haslingden Branch', Superintendent J. S. McCrone, Rawtenstall, to Chief Constable of Lancashire, 7 March 1933. TNA, CHAR 7/56. 'Excerpts from the "Haslingden Observer" of 7th March regarding a case which was defended by the League Solicitor'. MRC, MSS292/91/27.
69. Letter Chief Constable of Lancashire to the Secretary, Charity Commission, 13 April 1933. TNA, CHAR 7/56. 'Excerpts from the "Manchester Guardian" of 13th April regarding the appeal made by the League against the convictions by the Haslingden magistrates on 6th March 1933'. MRC, MSS292/91/27.
70. Circular to branch secretaries, J. Grierson, President, and A. Henderson, Gen. Sec., NLB, 18 May 1933. WCML, WCir.
71. *Ibid.*
72. The branches which had voted against registration had 1,443 members, those which had voted for it 2,255 members. Another branch voted in favour of registering after the results of the ballot were published. Letter R. Barber, Sec., Bradford TC, to V. Tewson, Asst. Sec., TUC, 19 February 1934, p. 2; Letter A. Henderson, Gen. Sec., NLB, to W. Citrine, Gen. Sec., TUC, 12 October 1933, both in MRC, MSS292/91/27. Minutes, EC Meetings, London, 17–22 June 1933, pp. 6–7 and London, 2–7 December 1933, p. 7, both in WCML, NEC Minutes 1920–37.
73. Hilton et al., *A Historical Guide to NGOs in Britain*, p. 351.

74. Letter R. Barber, Sec., Bradford TC, to V. Tewson, Asst. Sec., TUC, 19 February 1934, p. 2. MRC, MSS292/91/27. Minutes, EC Meeting, London, 17–22 June 1933, p. 7. WCML, NEC Minutes 1920–37.

75. Resolution No. 4, Agenda, Special Conference to be held in the Cooperative Hall, York; Letter R. Barber, Sec., Bradford TC, to V. Tewson, Asst. Sec., TUC, 19 February 1934, pp. 3–4, both in MRC, MSS292/91/27.

76. Resolution No. 9, Agenda, Special Conference to be held in the Cooperative Hall, York. MRC, MSS292/91/27.

77. Minutes, EC Meeting, York, 19 August 1933. WCML, NEC Minutes 1920–37.

78. Minutes of a special National Conference held in the Cooperative Hall, York on 19 and 20 August 1933. WCML, CRP.

79. Letter A. Henderson, Gen. Sec., NLB, to W. Citrine, Gen. Sec., TUC, 12 October 1933. Henderson also personally explained the situation to Vincent Tewson, Asst. Sec., TUC, on the same day. 'Registration of National League of the Blind under the War Charities Act, 1920 [*sic*]', Memo of Interview, 11.30 a.m., 12 October 1933. Both in MRC, MSS292/91/27. See also Minutes, Special EC Meeting, London, 7–8 October 1933, pp. 1–2. WCML, NEC Minutes 1920–37.

80. Letter W. Citrine, Gen. Sec., TUC, to A. Henderson, Gen. Sec., NLB, 26 October 1933. MRC, MSS292/91/27.

81. Letter A. Briggs, Hon. Sec., Leeds branch, NLB, to W. Citrine, Gen. Sec., TUC, received 3 October 1933. MRC, MSS292/91/27.

82. Letter A. S. Hardy, Sec., Stockport Blind Union, to W. Citrine, Gen. Sec., TUC, undated. MRC, MSS292/91/25.

83. Letter H. Kneeshaw, Gen. Sec., Hull and District TC, to W. Citrine, Gen. Sec., TUC, 2 October 1933. MRC, MSS292/91/27.

84. Letter W. Short, Gen. Sec., Newcastle and District TC, to W. Citrine, Gen. Sec., TUC, 3 December 1933; Letter C. E. Benton, Hon. Sec., York and District TC, to W. Citrine, Gen. Sec., TUC, 14 December 1933, both in MRC, MSS292/91/27.

85. Letter V. Tewson, Asst. Sec., TUC, to T. G. Reed, Hon. Gen. Sec., AUBB, 19 March 1935; Letter T. G. Reed, Hon. Gen. Sec., AUBB, to V. Tewson, Asst. Sec., TUC, 20 March 1935, both in MRC, MSS292/91/25.

86. Clinton briefly mentions the episode in his monograph but claims that the split took place in 1934, gives the wrong title for the breakaway union and claims inaccurately that 'it was the Leeds Trades Council that arranged a meeting between the warring groups that settled the dispute'. Alan Clinton, *The Trade Union Rank and File: Trades Councils in Britain, 1900–40* (Manchester, 1977), pp. 173–4.

87. Clegg, *A History of British Trade Unions since 1889*, Vol. II, pp. 452–5; Henry Pelling, *A History of British Trade Unionism* (London, 1992), p. 187; Fraser, *A History of British Trade Unionism*, pp. 168–9.

88. Letter W. Citrine, Gen. Sec., TUC, to T. P. Reed, Sec. pro tem, AUBB, 2 November 1933. MRC, MSS292/91/27.

89. Clinton, *Trades Councils in Britain*, pp. 138–56; Richard Stevens, 'Containing Radicalism: The Trades Union Congress Organisation Department and Trades Councils, 1928–1953', *Labour History Review* Vol. 62(1) (Spring 1997): 5–21.

90. 'Nat. Union of Professional & Industrial Blind', Letter V. Tewson, Asst. Sec., TUC, to A. Henderson, NLB, 15 June 1927. MRC, MSS292/74/4/1.
91. Letter F. W. Rudland, Sec. Birmingham TC & Labour Party, to W. Citrine, Gen. Sec., TUC, 30 December 1926. MRC, MSS292/74/4/1.
92. Riddell, 'Walter Citrine', p. 294; Martin, *TUC*, pp. 218–22 and 233–6. On the role the Trades Councils were to play within this new framework see Taylor, *TUC*, p. 27.
93. Circular 17 requested the trade unions to enforce the ban within their own organisation; Clinton, *Trades Councils in Britain*, p. 152.
94. Letter H. Kneeshaw, Gen. Sec, Hull and District TC, to W. Citrine, Gen. Sec., TUC, 27 December 1933. MRC, MSS292/91/27.
95. *Ibid.*
96. Letter C. E. Benton, York and District TC, to W. Citrine, Gen. Sec., TUC, 4 January 1933. MRC, MSS292/91/27.
97. These were the Trades Councils in Hull, Bradford and York. The information was based on a report in the northern edition of the *Daily Herald* on 19 January 1934. Letter W. Short, Gen. Sec., Newcastle and District TC, to W. Citrine, Gen. Sec., TUC, 29 January 1934; Letter W. Citrine, Gen. Sec., TUC, to W. Short, Gen. Sec., Newcastle and District TC, 20 January 1934; Letter A. Henderson, Gen. Sec., NLB, to W. Citrine, Gen. Sec., TUC, 7 February 1934, all in MRC, MSS292/91/27.
98. Letter J. Walker, Sec., Middlesbrough Trades and Labour Council, to W. Citrine, Gen. Sec., TUC, 5 February 1934. MRC, MSS292/91/27.
99. See, for example, Letter W. Citrine, Gen. Sec., TUC, to W. Short, Gen. Sec., Newcastle and District TC, 30 January 1934; Letter V. Tewson, Asst. Sec., TUC, to R. Barber, Sec., Bradford TC, 10 February 1934. When the Secretary of the TUC's Organisation Department stated in a letter to the Yorkshire Federation that it was 'of course ... in the competence of the Trades Councils themselves to determine' which organisations they wanted to affiliate, he was forced to retract that statement. Letter E. P. Harries, Sec., Organisation Dept., TUC, to R. Barber, Bradford TC, 21 February 1934. All in MRC, MSS292/91/27.
100. Letter R. Barber, Sec., Bradford TC, to V. Tewson, Asst. Sec., TUC, 19 February 1934, p.4. MRC, MSS292/91/27.
101. Letter R. Barber, Sec., Bradford TC, to V. Tewson, Asst. Sec., TUC, 5 March 1934, p. 2. MRC, MSS292/91/27.
102. Letter R. W. Hanlon, President, AUBB, and T. P. Reed, Sec. pro tem, AUBB, to W. Citrine, Gen. Sec., TUC, 30 October 1933. MRC, MSS292/91/27.
103. Letter F. Warburton, Hon. Sec., Leeds branch No. 2, NLB, to V. Tewson, Asst. Sec., TUC, undated. MRC, MSS292/91/25.
104. Letter R. W. Hanlon, President, AUBB, and T. P. Reed, Sec. pro tem, AUBB, to W. Citrine, Gen. Sec., TUC, 30 October 1933. MRC, MSS292/91/27.
105. TUC General Council, extract from Letter R. Barber, Yorkshire Federated Trades Councils, to Secretary's Dept., TUC, 1 February 1934. MRC, MSS292/91/27.
106. Copy of Resolution passed at Annual Meeting of Federation, held on Saturday, 27 January 1934. MRC, MSS292/91/27.
107. Letter W. Short, Gen. Sec., Newcastle and District TC, to W. Citrine, Gen. Sec., TUC, 4 March 1934. MRC, MSS292/91/27. On William Short and the

Council's activities in the 1930s, see the pamphlet Newcastle and District Trades Council, '1873–1973: A Centenary History' (Newcastle upon Tyne, 1973), pp. 33–6. York also passed a resolution which asserted that the National League was 'really the "breakaway" Union'. Resolution, attachment to Letter C. E. Benton, Sec., York and District TC, to W. Citrine, Gen. Sec., TUC, 6 April 1934. MRC, MSS292/91/27.

108. Letter C. E. Benton, Sec., York and District TC, to Newton [*sic*], Gen. Sec., TUC, 21 February 1934. MRC, MSS292/91/27.

109. Letter V. Tewson, Asst. Sec., TUC, to A. Henderson, Gen. Sec., NLB, 10 February 1934. Letters from V. Tewson, Asst. Sec., TUC, to R. Barber, Sec., Bradford TC; C. E. Benton, York and District TC; H. Kneeshaw, Gen. Sec., Hull and District TC, all 10 February 1934. Letter A. Henderson, Gen. Sec., NLB, to V. Tewson, Asst. Sec., TUC, 13 February 1934. All in MRC, MSS292/91/27.

110. 'Memorandum of Interview', A. Henderson, Gen. Sec., NLB with V. Tewson, Asst. Sec., TUC, 21 February 1934. However, the Secretary of Bradford Trades Council argued that the number of rebels was considerably higher. Letter R. Barber, Bradford TC, to V. Tewson, Asst. Sec., TUC, 5 March 1934, p. 2. Both in MRC, MSS292/91/27.

111. 'National League of the Blind and The Amalgamated Union of British Blind', Extracts from Minutes of Finance and General Purpose Committee, TUC, 26 February 1934. Letter C. E. Benton, York and District TC, to W. Citrine, Gen. Sec., TUC, 10 March 1934. MRC, MSS292/91/27.

112. By October 1934 the Honorary Secretary argued that 'this is not a case of recognition of a "breakaway" Union but one of serious maladministration of an affiliated Union'. Letter C. E. Benton, Hon. Sec., York and District TC, to E. P. Harries, Sec., Organisation Dept., TUC, 8 October 1934, p. 2. MRC, MSS292/91/27.

113. Letter F. Wolstencroft, Gen. Sec., ASW, to W. Citrine, Gen. Sec., TUC, 24 July 1934; Letter J. Marchbank, Gen. Sec., NUR, to W. Citrine, Gen. Sec., TUC, 14 September 1934; Letter A. G. Walkden, Gen. Sec., RCA, to W. Citrine, Gen. Sec., TUC, 4 October 1934; Letter R. Barber, Sec., Yorkshire Federated Trades Councils, to W. Citrine, Gen. Sec., TUC, 14 August 1934, all in MRC, MSS292/91/27.

114. Circular, J. Horsley, President, York Branch AUBB, and L. W. Ward, Sec., York Branch AUBB, undated, p. 2; attachment to Letter J. Marchbank, Gen. Sec., NUR, to W. Citrine, Gen. Sec., TUC, 3 August 1934, both in MRC, MSS292/91/27.

115. Letter R. Barber, Sec., Bradford TC, to W. Citrine, Gen. Sec., TUC, 22 March 1934; Letter H. Kneeshaw, Gen. Sec., Hull and District TC, to W. Citrine, Gen. Sec., TUC, 16 April 1934; Letter J. L. Ellis, Hon. Sec., Hull branch, NLB, to W. Citrine, Gen. Sec., TUC, 19 April 1934; Letter J. Walker, Sec., Middlesbrough Trades and Labour Council, to W. Citrine, Gen. Sec., TUC, 17 March 1934, all in MRC, MSS292/91/27.

116. '27. Affiliation to Trades Councils', Minutes of Trades Councils Joint Consultative Committee, 17 May 1934. MRC, MSS292/91/27.

117. Letter C. E. Benton, York and District TC, to E. P. Harries, Sec., Organisation Dept., TUC, 11 June 1934; Letter J. Hallsworth, Industrial Gen. Sec., National Union of Distributive and Allied Workers, to W. Citrine, Gen. Sec., TUC, 21 June 1934; Letter V. Tewson, Asst. Sec., TUC, to C. E. Benton, York

and District TC, 29 October 1934; Letter C. E. Benton, York and District TC, to E. P. Harries, Sec., Organisation Dept., TUC, 8 November 1934, all in MRC, MSS292/91/27.

118. Letter R. Barber, Sec., Bradford TC, to W. Citrine, Gen. Sec., TUC, 23 June 1934. MRC, MSS292/91/27.

119. Letter E. P. Harries, Sec., Organisation Dept., TUC, to R. Barber, Sec., Bradford TC, 28 June 1934. MRC, MSS292/91/27.

120. 'Amalgamated Union of British Blind', Circular by R. Barber, Sec., Bradford TC, 26 June 1934; Letter R. Barber, Sec., Bradford TC, to W. Citrine, Gen. Sec., TUC, 20 July 1934, both in MRC, MSS292/91/27.

121. Letters H. Kneeshaw, Gen. Sec., Hull and District TC, and E. P. Harries, Organisation Dept., TUC, 18 July 1934 and 19 August 1934; Letter M. C. Brown, Asst. Sec., Hull branch, NLB, to W. Citrine, Gen. Sec., TUC, 11 November 1934, all in MRC, MSS292/91/27. Letter J. D. Nicholson, Gen. Sec., Hull and District TC, to W. Citrine, Gen. Sec., TUC, 21 March 1935. MRC, MSS292/91/25.

122. Letter E. P. Harries, Sec., Organisation Dept., to J. Walker, Sec., Middlesbrough TC, 17 October 1934. MRC, MSS292/91/27. Frustrated by the AUBB's inability to gain recognition as a trade union, its Middlesbrough branch independently reorganised itself as a branch of the National League. Letter A. Dickinson, Middlesbrough branch, AUBB, to W. Citrine, Gen. Sec., TUC, 30 March 1935. MRC, MSS292/91/25.

123. Minutes, Special EC Meetings, London, 14–19 July 1934, p. 5 and London, 13–16 October 1934, p. 5, both in WCML, NEC Minutes 1920–37. Letter A. Henderson, Gen. Sec., NLB, to V. Tewson, Asst. Sec., TUC, 30 July 1934. MRC, MSS292/91/27. Resolution No. 6, Triennial Conference, Morecambe, 22–4 September 1934; Minutes Triennial Conference, Morecambe, 22–4 September 1934, p. 4, both in WCML, CRP.

124. 'Report of Meeting of Representatives of the National League of the Blind and the Amalgamated Union of British Blind, held under the Auspices of the General Council of the Trades Union Congress, at the Trades Hall, Leeds, on Saturday, November 17th, 1934, at 11 a.m.'; 'Report of Meeting of Representatives of the National League of the Blind and the Amalgamated Union of British Blind, held under the Auspices of the General Council of the Trades Union Congress, at the Trades Hall, Leeds, on Saturday, January 26th, 1935, at 11 a.m.'; Report of Meeting of Representatives of the National League of the Blind and the Amalgamated Union of British Blind, held at the Co-Operative Hall, York, on Saturday, July 13th, 1935, at 10 a.m.', all in MRC, MSS292/91/27. See also Minutes, EC Meeting, London, 8–11 December 1934, pp. 3–5. WCML, NEC Minutes 1920–37.

125. 'Report of Meeting of Representatives of the National League of the Blind and the Amalgamated Union of British Blind, held under the Auspices of the General Council of the Trades Union Congress, at the Trades Hall, Leeds, on Saturday, January 26th, 1935, at 11 a.m.' MRC, MSS292/91/25. Minutes, Special EC Meeting, London, 16–19 February 1935, pp. 5–6. WCML, NEC Minutes 1920–37.

126. The result was 1,538 votes for and 1,578 against registration, although a majority of branches had actually voted for registration (26 against 16).

Minutes, EC Meeting, London, 7–12 December 1935, p. 7. WCML, NEC Minutes 1920–37.

127. For registration, 2,848 votes; against registration, 1,265 votes, spoilt and blank papers, 31 votes. 'Re-Establishment of Unity – Ballot Re Registration', 10 May 1935. The AUBB had 394 members at the time of the ballot, of which 368 voted against registration. Letter T. G. Reed, Hon Gen. Sec., AUBB, to A. Henderson, Gen. Sec., NLB, 20 June 1935; Letter and Resolution from A. Henderson, Gen. Sec., NLB, to V. Tewson, Asst. Sec., AUBB, 27 June 1935. All in MRC, MSS292/91/25. See also Minutes, EC Meeting, London, 22–6 June 1935, pp. 3–4. WCML, NEC Minutes 1920–37.

128. Letters from H. Vokes, Sec., Hull branch, AUBB, to W. Citrine, Gen. Sec., TUC, 22 March 1935 and 28 March 1935, both in MRC, MSS292/91/25.

129. 'Report of Meeting of Representatives of the National League of the Blind and the Amalgamated Union of British Blind, held at the Cooperative Hall, York, on Saturday, July 13th, 1935, at 10 a.m.' MRC, MSS292/91/27.

130. Letter H. Vokes, Sec., and C. Dickinson, Sec., Hull branch No. 2, NLB, to W. Citrine, Gen. Sec., TUC, 16 November 1935. MRC, MSS292/91/25.

131. Letter H. Vokes, Sec., Hull branch No. 2, NLB, to V. Tewson, Asst. Sec., TUC, 1 December 1935, p. 2. MRC, MSS292/91/25.

132. Letter F. Warburton, Hon. Sec., Leeds branch No. 2, NLB, to A. Henderson, Gen. Sec., NLB, 4 November 1935, p. 1. MRC, MSS292/91/25.

133. Minutes, EC Meeting, London, 7–12 December 1935, p. 5. WCML, NEC Minutes 1920–37. Letter A. Henderson, Gen. Sec., NLB, to V. Tewson, Asst. Sec., TUC, 18 December 1935. MRC, MSS292/91/25.

134. Letter F. Warburton, Hon. Sec., Leeds branch No. 2, NLB, to V. Tewson, Asst. Sec., TUC, 27 December 1935; Letter B. Morton, Sec., Leeds branch, NLB, to V. Tewson, Asst. Sec., 7 January 1936, both in MRC, MSS292/91/25.

135. Letter V. Tewson, Asst. Sec., TUC, to A. Henderson, Gen. Sec., NLB, 4 February 1936; Letter V. Tewson, Asst. Sec., TUC, to H. Vokes, Hon. Sec., Hull branch No. 2, NLB, 5 February 1936, both in MRC, MSS292/91/25.

136. 'Basis of Fusion of the two Branches of the National League of the Blind in Hull, agreed by the Committees of both Branches at a Joint Meeting held in the Cooperative Institute, Hull, on Friday, 21st February, 1936', W. Kean and V. Tewson, 28 February 1936; see also 'Re-Establishment of Unity-Ballot re Registration', from W. Citrine, Gen. Sec., TUC, to Branch Secretaries, 30 March 1935; Letter T. G. Reed, Hon. Gen. Sec., AUBB, to A. Henderson, Gen. Sec., NLB, 15 October 1935, all in MRC, MSS292/91/25.

137. Letter A. S. Hardy, Sec., Stockport Blind Union, to W. Citrine, Gen. Sec., TUC, undated. MRC, MSS292/91/25.

138. The result of this ballot is unfortunately not recorded. Letter V. Tewson, Asst. Sec., TUC, to A. S. Hardy, Sec., Stockport Blind Union, 18 February 1936; Letter A. S. Hardy, Sec., Stockport Blind Union, to V. Tewson, Asst. Sec., TUC, received 24 February 1936, both in MRC, MSS292/91/25.

139. Minutes, EC Meeting, York, 20–4 June 1936, p. 3. WCML, NEC Minutes 1920–37. It is not possible to verify if this organisation is one and the same as the Ulster Blind Persons' Movement mentioned in Ó Catháin, 'The Blind Workers' Struggle in Derry', pp. 14–15. The League was apparently unaware of the Derry Organized Association of the Blind or the Londonderry Local Association of the Blind.

140. Minutes, EC Meeting, London, 8–11 December 1934, p. 5. WCML, NEC Minutes 1920–37.
141. *Ibid.*
142. Nevertheless, the Unemployed Movement did apparently decide to reject a fusion with the League. Minutes, EC Meeting, London, 11–15 September 1937, p. 1. The minutes of the League's Executive meeting in March 1937 mention another organisation which was involved in the fusion talks but do not mention its name. Minutes, EC Meeting, London, 20–3 March 1937, p. 3 and London, 19–23 June 1937, pp. 2–3. All in WCML, NEC Minutes 1920–37.
143. Problems were, for example, experienced with the South London branch in 1932 and Swansea branch in 1944. Letter A. Healy, Hon. Sec., South London branch, NLB, to W. Citrine, Gen. Sec., TUC, 9 May 1932; Letter T. Parker, Sec., H. Ellis, Chairman, and E. Williams, Vice Chairman, Swansea branch, NLB, to W. Citrine, Gen. Sec., TUC, received 7 October 1944, both in MRC, MSS292/91/27.
144. See, for example 'Report and Recommendation of General Council's Representatives as to the Terms of Fusion'. W. Kean, Chairman, and V. Tewson, Asst. Sec., TUC, 23 July 1935, p. 1. MRC, MSS292/91/25.
145. Fraser, *A History of British Trade Unionism*, pp. 152–76; Clegg, *A History of British Trade Unions since 1889*, Vol. II, pp. 449–51.
146. 'Application for Affiliation', Letter B. Purse, Hon. Sec., NUPIB, to F. Bramley, Gen. Sec., TUC, 9 July 1924. MRC, MSS292/91/26. Purse did not even mention that the Regional Organisers also claimed expenses. As a result they actually received between £287 6s. 2d. (Turner) and £344 10s. 5d. (Clydesdale) in 1924. NLB, Statement of Income and Expenditure for the Year ending 31st December 1924. WCML, NLB, Statements of Income. As pointed out in Chapter 1, many members of the League shared his criticism.
147. 'Report and Recommendation of General Council's Representatives as to the Terms of Fusion'. W. Kean, Chairman, and V. Tewson, Asst. Sec., TUC, 23 July 1935, p. 1. In October 1933 Henderson had named 6d. as the weekly contribution which would allow the NLB to become self-sufficient but pre-dicted that this would mean a loss of members. 'Registration of National League of the Blind under the War Charities Act, 1920', Memorandum of Interview, A. Henderson, Gen. Sec., NLB, with V. Tewson, Asst. Sec., TUC, 12 October 1933, 11.30 a.m. MRC, MSS292/91/27.
148. The vote was three against four. Minutes, EC Meeting, London, 5–9 December 1936, p. 8. WCML, NEC Minutes 1920–37. The resolutions in 1937 were submitted by the branches in Leicester, Bradford and Bolton. 1937 Triennial Conference Resolutions, p. 2. WCML, CRP.
149. Letter V. Tewson, Asst. Sec., TUC, to H. Vokes, Hon. Sec., Hull branch No. 2, NLB, 3 December 1935, pp. 1–2. MRC, MSS292/91/25.
150. See, for example, Letter C. E. Benton, Hon. Sec., York and District TC, to E. P. Harries, Sec., Organisation Dept., TUC, 25 October 1934. MRC, MSS292/91/27.
151. Clinton, *Trades Councils in Britain*, p. 154.
152. *Ibid.*, pp. 155–6.
153. *Ibid.*, p. 156.

154. de la Mare Rowley, 'Purse', *ODNB*.
155. Minutes, EC Meeting, Liverpool, 13–14 November 1898, printed in *BA* (January 1899), p. 37.
156. May to July. Joseph Slater, 'The Gossip's Bowl', *BA* (September 1899), p. 7.
157. Phillips' claim that it ceased publication after eleven issues is therefore not correct. Phillips, *The Blind in British Society*, p. 306.
158. *Blind Advocate: Official Organ of the National League of the Blind of Great Britain and Ireland* (February 1902).
159. 'Editorial Notes', *BA* (November 1898), p. 5.
160. T. Churchill and T. W. Rich, 'An Appeal', *BA* (September 1898), p. 3; 'Editorial Notes', *BA* (September 1898), pp. 4–5.
161. 'The Outlook', *BA* (June 1899), p. 90. For appeals to increase sales figures see, for example, 'The Gossip's Bowl', *BA* (May 1899), p. 77; Minutes, EC Meetings, Manchester, 12–14 January 1924, p. 2, and Manchester, 17–19 December 1927, p. 6, both in WCML, NEC Minutes 1920–37; Circular M. A. Barrett, Gen. Sec. & Treasurer, NLB, to Branch Secretaries, February 1980. MRC, MSS349/5/4/4.
162. 'Editorial Notes', *BA* (February 1899), p. 43.
163. See, for example, the League's Annual Reports and Balance Sheets for 1905, p. 6; 1906, p. 6 and 1907, p. 6, all in WCML, WRep.
164. 'The *Horizon*', *BA* (June 1922), p. 83.
165. *Ibid.*
166. Minutes, EC Meeting, Manchester, 12–14 January 1924, p. 1. WCML, NEC Minutes 1920–37.
167. Minutes, EC Meetings, Manchester, 31 March–2 April 1926, p. 1 and Manchester, 24–6 July 1926, p. 1, both in WCML, NEC Minutes 1920–37.
168. Minutes, EC Meeting, Manchester, 16–18 June 1928, pp. 2–3. WCML, NEC Minutes 1920–37.
169. Minutes, EC Meeting, Manchester, 15–18 September 1928, p. 7. WCML, NEC Minutes 1920–37.
170. Circular R. Hughes, President, NLB, and A. Henderson, Gen. Sec., to Branch Sec., May 1930. WCML, WCir.
171. Circular A. Henderson, Gen. Sec., NLB, to Branch Sec., 15 January 1934. WCML, WCir.
172. *Ibid.*
173. Minutes, Special EC Meeting, London, 14–19 July 1934, pp. 14–15. WCML, NEC Minutes 1920–37.
174. Resolution No. 18, 1943, Triennial Conference Resolutions, WCML, CRP.
175. 'The Advocate and its Critics', *BA* (March 1944), p. 4.
176. Minutes, Triennial Conference, 2–3 June 1946, p. 4. WCML, CRP.
177. 'Notice to Subscribers', *BA* (November 1948), p. 8.
178. The Irish League also received 20 copies of each issue of the *Horizon* in return. Minutes, EC Meetings, London, 19–22 June 1948, p. 12; London, 18–21 September 1948, p. 9 and London, 11–14 December 1948, p. 5, all in NEC Minutes 1938–50.
179. Minutes, EC Meeting, London, 23–5 March 1963, p. 7. WCML, NEC Minutes 1951–64.
180. M. Barrett, 'Can we afford to produce our Journals?', *Advocate* (December 1988), p. 3.

181. *BA* (September 1898), pp. 3–4; (February 1899), p. 48; (September 1899), p. 11 and (April 1909), p. 2. Purse and Miller were apparently the only two self-employed individuals in the League's leadership.
182. *BA* (January 1909), p. 1.
183. Minutes, Special EC Meeting, London, 16–19 February 1935, p. 8. WCML, NEC Minutes 1920–37.
184. 'Editorial', *BA* (January 1974), p. 1.
185. See advertising rates in *Advocate* (Autumn 1996), p. 13.
186. Letter [illegible signature], Forest Review, Gloucestershire, to Michael [no surname], received 18 July 1983. WCML, NLB, SWD.
187. *Advocate* (December 1986), p. 12; (June 1989), p. 13 and (Spring 1992), pp. 7, 10 and 12.
188. Conference Report, Manchester, 7–9 February 1925, p. 1. WCML, CRP.
189. 1937 Triennial Conference Resolutions, p. 2. WCML, CRP.
190. 'Editorial', *BA* (July 1948), p. 4.
191. Minutes, EC Meeting, London, 23–5 March 1963, p. 16. WCML, NEC Minutes 1951–64.
192. *Ibid.*
193. See, for example, Minutes, EC Meeting, London, 15–16 September 1962, p. 7. WCML, NEC Minutes 1951–64. Minutes, EC Meeting, 18–20 March 1967, p. 13. WCML, NEC Minutes 1965–74.
194. EC Report, 31st Triennial National Delegates Conference, Blackpool, 4–6 June 1994, p. 3. MRC, MSS349/2/3.
195. It was always accepted that the Braille journal *Horizon* would have to be subsidised. M. Barrett, 'Can we afford to produce our Journals?', *Advocate* (December 1988), p. 3.
196. 'Editor's Tribute', *Advocate* (Autumn 1996), p. 16. See also Chapter 6.
197. EC Report, 31st Triennial National Delegates Conference, Blackpool, 4–6 June 1994, p. 6. MRC, MSS349/2/3. A Special Edition of the *Advocate* with the title 'Supported Employment Factories: The Future of Employment for Disabled People', was published in November 1998.
198. M. Barrett, 'Can we afford to produce our Journals?', *Advocate* (December 1988), p. 3.

4   The Limits of Radicalism: Politics and Protest in the 1920s and 1930s

1. 52nd Annual Trades Union Congress, Report of Proceedings, 6–11 September 1920, p. 42 and pp. 78–9. TUCL.
2. See Chapter 3.
3. 'Conferences held between Representatives of Blind Organisations and the Parliamentary Committee', Memo, Research and Economics Department, TUC, 18 July 1935. MRC, MSS292/91/25. Minutes, EC Meeting, London, 19–21 June 1920, p. 3. WCML, WCir.
4. G. Central, 'State Aid, or Municipal Control, Which?' *BA* (January 1920), p. 3.
5. 53rd Annual Trades Union Congress, Report of Proceedings, 5–10 September 1921, p. 844. TUCL.

6. *Ibid.*
7. Minutes, EC Meeting, Manchester, 12–14 January 1924, p. 1. WCML, NEC Minutes 1920–37.
8. *Ibid.*
9. Hansard 174 HC Deb., 14 May 1924, col. 2320.
10. Apprentices would have received 50 per cent of that wage. A Bill to Amend the Blind Persons Act, 1920 (London: HMSO, 1924). TUCL, HV1793/1924. An oversight by the draughtsman meant that the reference to the local authority was omitted from the draft, but the intention was to rectify this before the Bill would come before a Committee of the House. Bill to Amend The Blind Persons Act, 1920, NLB, 22 February 1924; Minutes, EC Meeting, Manchester, 12–14 April 1924, p. 2, both in WCML, WCir.
11. Hansard 174 HC Deb., 14 May 1924, col. 2320. The government only supported the lowering of the pension age for blind people. Cabinet 45(24), 30 July 1924, p. 5. TNA, CAB 23/48/20.
12. Wheatley stated that he had already received two other deputations from organisations of the blind in that week, but does not give their names. 'Report of a Deputation from the National League of the Blind to the Ministry of Health on July 1st, 1924', p. 2. WCML, WCir.
13. *Ibid.*
14. *Ibid.*
15. A Bill to Amend the Blind Persons Act, 1920 (London: HMSO, 1925). TUCL, HV1793/1925.
16. Minutes, EC Meeting, Manchester, 31 March–2 April 1925. WCML, NEC Minutes 1920–37; Minutes, EC Meeting, London, 4 May 1925, p. 1. WCML, WCir.
17. P. D. Trevor-Roper, 'Fraser, (William Jocelyn) Ian, Baron Fraser of Lonsdale (1897–1974)', rev. *ODNB* (Oxford University Press, 2004); online edn., January 2011, http://0-www.oxforddnb.com.lib.exeter.ac.uk/view/article/31124 [last accessed 3 December 2012].
18. 'Blind Persons Bill', *The Times*, 9 May 1925, p. 7.
19. *Ibid.*
20. 'Re New Parliamentary Bill', to Branch Secretaries and Members, NLB, December 1925. WCML, WCir.
21. A Bill to Amend the Blind Persons Act, 1920 (London: HMSO, 1926). TUCL, HV1793/1926.
22. A Bill to Amend the Blind Persons Act, 1920 (London: HMSO, 1928). TUCL, HV1793/1928.
23. The National Joint Council of Labour represented the General Council of the TUC, the Executive Committee of the Labour Party and the Parliamentary Labour Party. National Joint Council, *The Blind Persons Act 1920* (London, no date).
24. *Ibid.*, pp. 11–12.
25. The pamphlet is undated. The copy in the Modern Records Centre is marked 'January 1930' although this seems too late since the latest figures cited are from 1921–2 and references to 1922–3 are made in the future tense. MRC, MSS126/TG/Res/X/1041A.
26. Among them were Bradford, Glasgow, Newcastle and Sheffield. Smith (ed.), *Golden Jubilee Brochure*, p. 22.

27. 59th Annual Trades Union Congress, Report of Proceedings, 5–10 September 1927, pp. 288–92. TUCL.

28. Hull and Newcastle upon Tyne had shortly before introduced a weekly allowance of twenty-five shillings for unemployable blind. *Ibid.*, p. 289.

29. *Ibid.*, p. 288.

30. 'Provision for Unemployed Blind Person', Circular No. 7, to all Trades Councils, from W. Citrine, Gen. Sec., TUC, 11 November 1927, p. 1. MRC, MSS292/135.01/1.

31. Letter W. Citrine, Gen. Sec., TUC, to Clerks, County Councils and County Borough Councils, 14 November 1927. MRC, MSS292/135.01/1; Smith (ed.), *Golden Jubilee Brochure*, p. 23.

32. Section 5, Local Government Act, 1929, 19 Geo. 5 1928–9, Chapter 17. See also Lysons, 'The Development of Social Legislation', pp. 312–20.

33. Hansard 250 HC Deb., 24 March 1931, col. 216; Hansard 250 HC Deb., 31 March 1931, cols. 927–8; Hansard 253 HC Deb., 4 June 1931, cols. 339 and 359.

34. 'History of the League, 1893–1921', p. 3. British Library, YA.1992.C48. See also Purse's speech in Birmingham in 1928. 'Help for the Blind', *Daily Mail*, 29 May 1928, p. 16.

35. 'Help for the Blind', *Daily Mail*, 29 May 1928, p. 16. Smith (ed.), *Golden Jubilee Brochure*, p. 23.

36. The only difference was that the unemployment allowance was now set at twenty-seven shillings and sixpence per week. A Bill to Amend the Blind Persons Act, 1920 (London: HMSO, 1930). TUCL, HV1793/1930.

37. The General Secretary estimated that around 100,000 petitions would reach the government and called it the greatest propaganda effort ever undertaken by Central Office. Minutes, EC Meetings, Manchester, 13–15 December 1930, p. 9 and Manchester, 29 March–1 April 1930, pp. 4–5, both in WCML, NEC Minutes 1920–37.

38. Andrew Thorpe, *Britain in the 1930s: The Deceptive Decade* (Oxford, 1992), pp. 62–70; John Stevenson and Chris Cook, *The Slump: Society and Politics during the Depression* (London, 1977), pp. 54–73.

39. Richard Overy, *The Morbid Age: Britain and the Crisis of Civilisation* (London, 2009).

40. Communist Party membership peaked at around 18,000 people in 1939. Overy, *Morbid Age*, pp. 266–68; Thorpe, *Britain in the 1930s*, pp. 41–58; Stevenson and Cook, *The Slump*, pp. 125–44.

41. Letter A. F. Barber, Hon. Sec., London & Home Counties District Council, to Sec. of Trades Councils & Labour Parties in Greater London, undated. WCML, WCir. 'Minutes of Meeting of the Executive Committee of the London Labour Party held at the House of Commons on Thursday, 6 March 1930', p. 1. TUCL. 'Trades Councils' Delegates Decide to Organise Demonstration', *BA* (May 1930), p. 7.

42. 'Re. Parliamentary Candidate', circular to all NLB branches, J. E. Gregory, Gen. Sec., NLB, July 1924. WCML, WCir.

43. Dr E. Whitfield was also a member of the Labour Party and the ILP. He contested St Marylebone in 1931 and was comfortably defeated by the Conservative incumbent. Minutes, EC Meeting, Manchester, 13–15 September 1930, p. 6. WCML, NEC Minutes 1920–37.

44. Andrew Thorpe, *A History of the British Labour Party* (3rd edn., Basingstoke, 2008), p. 87.
45. Minutes, EC Meeting, London, 14–18 September 1935, pp. 3–4. WCML, NEC Minutes 1920–37. Lysons, 'The Development of Social Legislation', pp. 459–60.
46. Labour Publications Department, *The Blind Persons Charter* (London, September 1935). MRC, MSS126/TG/Res/X/1041A.
47. *Ibid.*, p. 2.
48. *Ibid.*, p. 8 (in the original this was printed in bold type).
49. Thorpe, *History of the British Labour Party*, pp. 91–3.
50. Minutes, EC Meeting, London, 9–13 September 1933, pp. 11–12 and Special EC Meeting, London, 14–19 July 1934, p. 8, both in WCML, NEC Minutes 1920–37.
51. Tom Parker, 'The March', *BA* (June 1936), p. 7. Neil Evans, ' "South Wales has been Roused as Never Before": Marching Against the Means Test, 1934–36', in David W. Howell and Kenneth O. Morgan (eds), *Crime, Protest and Police in Modern British Society: Essays in Memory of David J. V. Jones* (Cardiff, 1999), pp. 176–206.
52. Parker was joined by A. McAlpine and J. Dixon. Minutes, EC Meeting, London, 22–6 June 1935, pp. 9–10. WCML, NEC Minutes 1920–37.
53. Minutes, EC Meeting, London, 14–18 September 1935, pp. 8–9. WCML, NEC Minutes 1920–37.
54. Minutes, EC Meeting, London, 7–12 December 1935, pp. 2–3. WCML, NEC Minutes 1920–37.
55. *Ibid.*, p. 3.
56. Called the National Joint Council until 1934 it acquired a more important role after Labour's defeat in 1931. Minutes, National Council of Labour Meeting, 17 December 1935, Point 17; Minutes, National Council of Labour Meeting, 21 January 1936, Point 32, both in Labour History Archive, Manchester, National Joint Council of Labour Minutes, Memoir etc., 25 April 1933–21 October 1936, Box II. The support of the Northern Ireland Labour Party was secured by a deputation from the Belfast No. 2 branch to the Party's conference on 29 August 1926. 'Movement to Amend Blind Persons Act', *BA* (October 1936), p. 3.
57. Minutes, March Committee Meeting, London, 16 February 1936, p. 1, WCML, NEC Minutes 1920–37.
58. Minutes, EC Meeting, London, 2–7 December 1933, p. 4. WCML, NEC Minutes 1920–37.
59. Minutes, EC Meetings, Manchester, 8–10 December 1928, p. 5 and Manchester, 16–18 March 1929, p. 1, both in WCML, NEC Minutes 1920–37.
60. Minutes, EC Meeting, Manchester, 25–9 March 1933, p. 5; special EC Meeting, London, 14–19 July 1934, p. 3 and EC Meeting, London, 19–23 June 1937, p. 2, all in WCML, NEC Minutes 1920–37.
61. T. H. Smith, 'Retirement of Organiser J. A. Clydesdale', *BA* (July 1951), pp. 6–7; 'James A. Clydesdale: a Tribute by the General Secretary', *BA* (January 1963), pp. 6–7; 'Army of the Blind to March to London', *Daily Express*, 27 July 1936, clipping in TNA, MH 55/607.
62. Memo C. R. Kerwood, MoH, to Beckett, 15 February 1936, TNA, MH 55/607.

63. Minutes, March Committee, London, 16 February 1936, p. 1. WCML, NEC Minutes 1920–37.
64. The Committee voted 5 to 3 against the Chairman's ruling. *Ibid.*
65. Quotas for the Scottish area, the North East, North West, Midlands and South West areas were fixed at 44 marchers respectively, in addition to 5 marchers requested from Ireland. The March Committees in these areas would obtain the names of prospective marchers from the League's branches, select the most suitable persons and submit the list to the National March Committee. *Ibid.*
66. *Ibid.*, pp. 1–2.
67. Memo AdM [de Montmorency] to G. Chrystal, 20 February 1936. TNA, MH 55/607.
68. In an election address in 1929 Baldwin had promised to lower the qualifying age for a blind pension from fifty to forty years. 'Blind Persons Act, 1920, National League of the Blind, Proposed March of blind persons to London', Memo, no date, p. 4. TNA, MH 55/607. This had also been recommended by the Advisory Committee on the Welfare of the Blind in 1929. *Advisory Committee on the Welfare of the Blind, Report of the Sub-Committee on the Unemployable Blind, Ministry of Health* (London: HMSO, 1935), p. 7.
69. *Ibid.*
70. Lysons, 'The Development of Social Legislation', pp. 462–3.
71. Memo AdM [de Montmorency] to G. Chrystal, 20 February 1936. TNA, MH 55/607.
72. 'Blind Persons Act, 1920, National League of the Blind, Proposed March of blind persons to London', Memo, no date, p. 1. TNA, MH 55/607.
73. The total cost to the Exchequer was estimated at £105,000 in England and Wales, £18,000 in Scotland and £5,000 in Northern Ireland. *Ibid.*, p. 5.
74. The new committee consisted of A. Henderson, J. Grierson, J. Brighty, R. Hanlan, A. Hoy, A. McAlpine and H. Savage. Minutes, EC Meeting, London, 28–31 March 1936, p. 6. WCML, NEC Minutes 1920–37.
75. Minutes, EC Meeting, London, 28–31 March 1936, p. 6. WCML, NEC Minutes 1920–37.
76. T. J. Parker, 'The March must go on', *BA* (April 1936), p. 7. According to Parker the District Council explained its reasons in a circular. Unfortunately, no copy of it was found in the League's archive.
77. Minutes, EC Meetings, York, 28–31 March 1936, p. 6 and York, 20–4 June 1936, p. 5, both in WCML, NEC Minutes 1920–37.
78. Letter J. A. Clydesdale, NLB, to C. R. Kerwood, MoH, 31 March 1936. TNA, MH 55/607.
79. Letter J. A. Clydesdale, NLB, to C. R. Kerwood, MoH, 4 April 1936. TNA, MH 55/607.
80. *Ibid.*
81. *Ibid.*
82. T. J. Parker, 'The March must go on', *BA* (April 1936), p. 7.
83. *Ibid.*
84. J. A. Clydesdale, 'Why March?' *BA* (May 1936), p. 8. Parker denied that Clydesdale's concerns were legitimate. See T. J. Parker, 'The March', *BA* (June 1936), p. 7.

85. Letter B. Speed, 10 Downing Street, to A. N. Rucker, Private Sec., Minister of Health, 7 April 1936. TNA, MH 55/607.
86. The Ministry of Health claimed that 'we succeeded in getting it suggested to the Executive Committee of the League that the first step, at any rate, should be to ask the Minister of Health to receive a deputation'. Letter A. N. Rucker, Private Sec., Minister of Health, to B. Speed, 10 Downing Street, 20 April 1936, PRO, MH 55/607.
87. *Ibid.* Minutes, EC Meeting, York, 20–4 June 1936, p. 4. WCML, NEC Minutes 1920–37.
88. Letter I. Fraser, MP, to E. Campbell, MP, MoH, 12 May 1936. TNA, MH 55/607.
89. The MPs were Sir Francis Edward Fremantle and Lt. Col. John Sandeman Allen (Conservative), William Gallacher (CPGB) and Henry Graham White (Liberal). 'Deputation from the National League of the Blind', 19 May 1936, p. 1. TNA, MH 55/607. 'Welfare of the Blind. Deputation to Minister of Health', *The Times*, 21 May 1936, p. 12.
90. Soldiers blinded during the war received twenty-seven shillings and six-pence a week, whereas civilians received only ten shillings a week. 'Deputation from the National League of the Blind', 19 May 1936, pp. 1–2. TNA, MH 55/607.
91. *Ibid.*, p. 4.
92. The question of piecework was under consideration by the Advisory Com-mittee and also under negotiation between the National League of the Blind and the Association of Workshops. A provisional agreement had been reached which the Association had referred to the individual workshops. *Ibid.*, pp. 3–4.
93. *Ibid.*, pp. 4–5.
94. 'Protest Demonstration. March to London. To the Members; Trades Coun-cils, Labour Parties, Trade Union Branches, Cooperative Societies, Men's and Women's Guilds', A. Henderson, Gen. Sec., NLB, Approved by General Council, TUC on 23 July 1936. TNA, MH 55/607.
95. 'Protest Demonstration: March to London', A. Henderson, Gen. Sec., NLB, no date. WCML, WCir.
96. 'Protest Demonstration. March to London. To the Members; Trades Coun-cils, Labour Parties, Trade Union Branches, Cooperative Societies, Men's and Women's Guilds', A. Henderson, Gen. Sec., NLB, Approved by General Council, TUC on 23 July 1936. TNA, MH 55/607.
97. 'Protest Demonstration: March to London', A. Henderson, Gen. Sec., NLB, no date. WCML, WCir.
98. 'Army of the Blind to March on London', *Daily Express*, 27 July 1936; 'March on London', *Daily Herald*, 27 July 1936, both clippings in TNA, MH 55/607.
99. 'The National League of the Blind. Proposed March on London', Memo C. R. Kerwood, MoH, to Beckett, 1 August 1936. TNA, MH 55/607.
100. J. A. Clydesdale, 'N.U.B.', *BA* (January 1922), p. 7.
101. 'The National League of the Blind. Proposed March on London', Memo C. R. Kerwood, MoH, to Beckett, 1 August 1936. TNA, MH 55/607.
102. Kerwood also suggested reminding the League that 'the Minister received a deputation in order to avoid the hardship and inconvenience involved in a march and that their representations are under consideration'. *Ibid.*

103. Letter K. Wood, Minister of Health, to J. Simon, Home Sec., 11 August 1936, p. 3. TNA, HO 45/16545.
104. *Ibid.*
105. Letter J. Simon, Home Sec., to K. Wood, Minister of Health, 26 August 1936, p. 1. TNA, HO 45/16545.
106. Special Branch reported in July 1936 that the NUWM had decided after weeks of deliberations to organise another Hunger March to London in October or November that year. The first suggestion for a march from Jarrow to London was also made in the same month. 'National March on London', Memo, A. Canning, Superintendent, Special Branch, Metropolitan Police [hereafter: SB, MePo], 25 July 1936. TNA, AST 7/138. Ellen Wilkinson, *The Town that was Murdered: The Life Story of Jarrow* (London, 1939), p. 198.
107. Quotation: 'Copy of Report from Mr. Farrow', Minute Sheet, Ministry of Health, 25 September 1936, p. 2. TNA, MH 55/607.
108. *Ibid.*, pp. 4–5. For the discussion in 1932 see 'Cabinet Committee on the Hunger Marchers', TNA, CAB 27/497.
109. Letter K. Wood, Minister of Health, to J. Simon, Home Sec., 29 August 1936. TNA, HO 45/16545. Cabinet 56(36), 2 September 1936, pp. 42–3. TNA, CAB 23/85/9. Minutes, EC Meeting, London, 19–22 September 1936, p. 7. WCML, NEC Minutes 1920–37.
110. Minutes, EC Meeting, London, 19–22 September 1936, p. 7. WCML, NEC Minutes 1920–37.
111. Letter S. F. S. Hearder, Private Sec., Minister of Health, to A. Henderson, Gen. Sec., NLB, 6 October 1936, pp. 2–3. TNA, MH 55/607. The drafting of the letter was ordered on 28 September. 'Blind Persons' March', for Mr. Maude, Minute Sheet, MoH, 28 September 1936. TNA, MH 55/607.
112. Letter A. Henderson, Gen. Sec., NLB, to S. F. S. Hearder, Private Sec., Minister of Health, 13 October 1936. TNA, MH 55/607.
113. The Leeds contingent, for example, had 40 men from Aberdeen, Hull, Newcastle, Sunderland and Bradford in its ranks, while only 12 came from Leeds itself. '62 Blind Men Set out on March to London', *Daily Worker*, 13 October 1936, clipping in PRO, HO 45/16545.
114. 'March on London', *Daily Herald*, 27 July 1936, clipping in TNA, MH 55/607; 'Midland Notes', *BA* (December 1936), pp. 5–6.
115. The League had 4,012 male and 1,608 female members in 1936. NLB, Annual Returns. TNA, FS 12/141. The *Manchester Guardian* incorrectly stated on 13 October 1936 that 'blind men and women' were marching to London. Clipping in TNA, HO 45/16545.
116. 'Start of 275 Miles Trek', *North Mail*, 6 October 1936, clipping in TNA, MH 57/213.
117. 'Blind Men's Three-Weeks March to London', *Yorkshire Observer*, 26 August 1936, clipping in TNA, MH 55/607.
118. 'Marching to Nottingham To-day', *Nottingham Evening News*, 17 October 1936, clipping in LHA, CP/IND/HANN/05.
119. Minutes, EC Meetings, London, 5–9 December 1936, pp. 2–3 and London, 20–3 March 1937, p. 5, both in WCML, NEC Minutes 1920–37.
120. The March Committee had recommended that single men should receive their weekly income up to a limit of 25*s.* whereas married men would receive their weekly income up to a limit of £2 12*s.* 0*d.* Any additional

income received by a marcher during the march would be deducted from this amount. Because the Executive Council had decided in June 1935 that the League would guarantee the marchers' income, the Executive referred the matter back to the March Committee. It was then decided to give the March Committee plenary powers to determine the amount to be paid to the marchers. Minutes, EC Meeting, London, 19–22 September 1936, pp. 2–3. WCML, NEC Minutes 1920–37.

121. 'Blind Men's Three-Weeks March to London', *Yorkshire Observer*, 26 August 1936, clipping in TNA, MH 55/607.

122. 'National League of the Blind: March of Blind Persons to London', Memo, MoH, no date. TNA, MH 57/212. T. J. Parker, 'Blind March to London', *BA* (December 1936), p. 7.

123. Minutes, EC Meeting, London, 19–22 September 1936, pp. 6–7. WCML, NEC Minutes 1920–37.

124. £9 7s. 6d. 'The Blind Marchers', *Cheshire Daily Echo*, 13 October 1936, clipping in LHA, CP/IND/HANN/05.

125. 'National League of the Blind Meeting', Inspector V. Wright, SB, MePo, 1 November 1936, p. 3. TNA, HO 45/16545. The annual return for 1936 shows an income of £2,895 12s. 5d. NLB, Annual Returns, TNA, FS 12/141.

126. T. J. Parker, 'The March must go on', *BA* (April 1936), p. 7. The expenditure of the March Fund was £1,589 0s. 2d. Statement of Income and Expenditure of Central Office for the Year Ending 31 December 1936, WCML, NLB, Reports and Balance Sheets and Agendas 1905–45.

127. 'They March in Darkness through Autumn Beauty', *Express & Star*, 16 October 1936, clipping in LHA, CP/IND/HANN/05.

128. 'Blind "Army" Undaunted', *Daily Independent*, 15 October 1936, clipping in LHA, CP/IND/HANN/05.

129. 'Marching to Nottingham To-day', *Nottingham Evening News*, 17 October 1936, clipping in LHA, CP/IND/HANN/05.

130. '62 Blind Men Set out on March to London', *Daily Worker*, 13 October 1936, clipping in PRO, HO 45/16545. 'They March in Darkness through Autumn Beauty', *Express & Star*, 16 October 1936, clipping in LHA, CP/IND/HANN/05.

131. 'Marching with Arms Linked', *Star* (no date); see also 'Blind "Army" Undaunted', *Daily Independent*, 15 October 1936, both clippings in LHA, CP/IND/HANN/05. Picture of marchers in *Nottingham Evening News*, 16 October 1936, clipping in LHA, Ellen Wilkinson – Scrapbooks, LP/WI/7. See also picture in *Bristol Evening Post*, 19 October 1936, p. 10.

132. For a public acknowledgement see, for example, 'Blind Marchers', *Evening Advertiser* [Wiltshire], 23 October 1936, p. 1. In addition, Henderson expressed his gratitude to the Commissioner of Police via an Inspector of the Metropolitan Police's Special Branch after the march. 'National League of the Blind march to London', Inspector V. Wright, SB, MePo, 6 November 1936, p. 4. TNA, HO 45/16545.

133. 'Marching to Nottingham To-day', *Nottingham Evening News*, 17 October 1936, clipping in LHA, CP/IND/HANN/05.

134. 'Protest Demonstration. March to London. To the Members; Trades Councils, Labour Parties, Trade Union Branches, Cooperative Societies, Men's

and Women's Guilds', A. Henderson, Gen. Sec., NLB, Approved by General Council, TUC on 23 July 1936. TNA, MH 55/607.

135. 'Blind Men's Three-Weeks March to London', *Yorkshire Observer*, 26 August 1936, clipping in TNA, MH 55/607.

136. See, for example, 'Four Blind Marchers have to Drop out of Contingent at Leicester', *Leicester Daily Mercury*, 22 October 1936, clipping in LHA, CP/IND/HANN/05.

137. 'The Blind Marchers', *Cheshire Daily Echo*, 13 October 1936, clipping in LHA, CP/IND/HANN/05.

138. See, for example, 'Blind Marchers Leave Nottm.', *Nottingham Evening Post*, 19 October 1936, p. 7.

139. 'Blind "Army" Undaunted', *Daily Independent*, 15 October 1936; see also 'Four Blind Marchers have to Drop out of Contingent at Leicester', *Leicester Daily Mercury*, 22 October 1936, both clippings in LHA, CP/IND/HANN/05.

140. 'Copy of Report from Mr. Farrow', Minute Sheet, MoH, 25 September 1936, p. 1. TNA, MH 55/607.

141. An Inspector of Special Branch estimated that there were no more than 8,000–10,000 people in the Park at any time. His report is, however, openly hostile to the marchers and this figure seems much too low. Kingsford, *Hunger Marchers*, p. 215. 'Hunger March 1936', Inspector V. Wright, SB, MePo, 16 November 1936, p. 3. TNA, MEPO 2/3091. In general, figures given by the police must be considered unreliable during that period. Matt Perry, *Bread and Work: Social Policy and the Experience of Unemployment, 1918–39* (London, 2000), p. 115.

142. 'Hunger March and Demonstration Hyde Park', Memo, Inspector J. M. Mempron, SB, MePo, 8 November 1936, p. 13. TNA, MEPO 2/3053. Matthias Reiss, 'Not all were Apathetic: National Hunger Marches as Political Rituals in Interwar Britain', in Michael Schaich and Jörg Neuheiser (eds), *Political Ritual in the United Kingdom, 1700–2000* (Augsburg, 2006), pp. 93–121 (94).

143. For a critical account of the Jarrow march see Matt Perry, *The Jarrow Crusade: Protest and Legend* (Sunderland, 2005).

144. On this occasion, Councillor James Hanlon, who marched with the men from Jarrow, met his brother Bob, who was with the blind marchers. 'The Marchers' Week-End in Northampton', *Chronicle & Echo*, 26 October 1936, p. 5.

145. 'Marching with Arms Linked', *Star* (no date), clipping in LHA, CP/IND/HANN/05.

146. According to Parker they were 'escorted into the Town [of Watford] by the Banners of the Labour Party, the N.U.W.M., the Communist Party and the Women's Section'. T. J. Parker, 'Blind March to London', *BA* (December 1936), p. 7. According to police sources, this occurred when they left Watford.

147. 'National League of the Blind Protest Demonstration', A. Canning, Chief Constable, SB, MePo, 3 September 1936, pp. 1–2. TNA, HO 45/16545.

148. 'National League of the Blind march to London', Inspector V. Wright, SB, MePo, 6 November 1936, p. 2. TNA, HO 45/16545.

149. *Ibid.*

150. The police reported banners from the League's South London, Greenwich, Tottenham and West London branches; the Southwark Borough and North Southwark Labour Parties; New Cross Men's Cooperative Guild; Paddington Trades Council and Labour Party and the Paddington branch of the NUR. 'National League of the Blind Meeting', PS A. Morrison, SB, MePo, 1 November 1936, p. 1. TNA, HO 45/16545.

151. *Ibid.*

152. They were invited by Mrs. Van der Elst to stay as their guests at the Caledonian Hotel, Harpur Street, W.C. 'National League of the Blind march to London', Inspector V. Wright, SB, MePo, 6 November 1936, p. 3. TNA, HO 45/16545. T. J. Parker, 'Blind March to London', *BA* (December. 1936), p. 8.

153. 'National League of the Blind march to London', Inspector V. Wright, SB, MePo, 6 November 1936, p. 2. TNA, HO 45/16545. T. J. Parker, 'Blind March to London', *BA* (December 1936), p. 8.

154. Minutes, EC Meeting, London, 5–9 December 1936, p. 7. WCML, NEC Minutes 1920–37.

155. 'National League of the Blind march to London', Inspector V. Wright, SB, MePo, 6 November 1936, p. 1. TNA, HO 45/16545. The League admitted 691 new members in 1935 and 885 in 1936. The annual average from 1921 to 1934 was only 302 new members. NLB, Annual Returns. TNA, FS 12/141.

156. Minutes, Sub Executive, London, 6–8 November 1937, p. 4. WCML, NEC Minutes 1920–37.

157. The Act furthermore required local authorities to take the needs of dependants into account when determining the scale of assistance provided for visually impaired individuals. It allowed local authorities to pay or contribute towards the funeral costs of blind persons or their dependants and regulated the administration of the Means Test for blind people. Blind Persons Act, 1938, 1 & 2 Geo. 6 1937–38, Chapter 11. 'Blind Persons Bill', Circular 1681 to County Councils, County Borough Councils, and Common Council of the City of London, from Ministry of Health, 14 March 1938. Both in TUCL, HV1793/1938. Rooff, *Voluntary Societies and Social Policy*, pp. 214–15.

158. Circular to the Clerks of County Councils and Town Clerks, from A. Henderson, Gen. Sec., NLB, May 1935. WCML, WCir.

159. 59th Annual Trades Union Congress, Report of Proceedings, 5–10 September 1927, p. 291. TUCL.

160. Minutes, EC Meeting, London, 22–6 June 1935, p. 2. Despite the decision taken in June 1935 the complaint was apparently first launched in writing and the deputation was ordered to only insist on a meeting with the Executive of the Labour Party in case the reply of the latter should be unsatisfactory. Minutes, EC Meeting, London, 14–18 September 1935, p. 4. Both in WCML, NEC Minutes 1920–37.

161. T. J. Parker, 'The March', *BA* (June 1936), p. 7. In Parker's view the League was also let down by the Labour press. After the 1936 March he complained 'that the greatest misfortune of all' was the insufficient publicity the *Daily Herald* had provided for the event. T. J. Parker, 'Blind March to London', *BA* (December 1936), p. 7.

162. Minutes, EC Meeting, London, 4–7 December 1937, pp. 6–7. WCML, NEC Minutes 1920–37.
163. Resolution No. 15, 1940 Triennial Conference Resolutions; see also Resolution No. 13, 1943 Triennial Conference Resolutions, both in WCML, CRP.
164. 'North-Eastern Notes', *BA* (July 1950), p. 5. See also, for example, 'Midland Notes', *BA* (July 1945), pp. 4–5 and 'London Notes', *BA* (July 1946), p. 6. Even when the Labour Party had abandoned the policies spelled out in *The Blind Persons Charter* the League continued to urge their implementation. Minutes, EC Meeting, 17–19 June 1967, p. 16. WCML, NEC Minutes 1965–74.
165. Minutes, EC Meeting, London, 11–15 September 1937, pp. 11–12. WCML, NEC Minutes 1920–37.
166. Letter I. Fraser, MP, to E. Campbell, MP, MoH, 12 May 1936, p. 3. TNA, MH 55/607.
167. Deakin and Davis Smith, 'Labour, Charity and Voluntary Action' in Hilton and McKay (eds), *The Ages of Voluntarism*, p. 75.

5   Success at Last? The League and the Consolidation of the Welfare State

1. Minutes, EC Meeting, Manchester, 24–6 July 1926. WCML, NEC Minutes 1920–37.
2. Minutes, EC Meetings, Manchester, 21–3 June 1930, p. 4; Manchester, 13–15 December 1930, p. 8 and Manchester, 28–31 March 1931, p. 9, all in WCML, NEC Minutes 1920–37.
3. The Advisory Council had fifteen seats in total. 'London Notes', *BA* (September 1943), p. 8.
4. Minutes, Special EC Meetings, London, 14–19 July 1934, p. 11 and London, 13–16 October 1934, p. 3; Minutes, EC Meeting, London, 8–11 December 1934, p. 5, all in WCML, NEC Minutes 1920–37. Minutes, EC Meeting, London, 11–14 December 1948, p. 5. NEC Minutes 1938–50.
5. Each Institution was represented by two members from the Board of Management and its General Manager. 'Scottish Notes', *BA* (March 1939), p. 3.
6. Minutes, EC Meeting, London, 4–7 December 1937, p. 7. WCML, NEC Minutes 1920–37.
7. Beveridge, *Voluntary Action*, pp. 246–7; Lysons, 'The Development of Social Legislation', pp. 299–301.
8. Minutes, EC Meeting, Manchester, 28–31 March 1931, p. 4. WCML, NEC Minutes 1920–37.
9. Rose, *Changing Focus*, p. 59.
10. Resolution No. 20, 1943 Triennial Conference Resolutions. WCML, CRP. For a case study see, for example, 'Scottish Notes: Report of the Aberdeen Asylum for the Blind', *BA* (November 1941), p. 5.
11. Untitled clipping from the *Birmingham Post*, *BA* (May 1942), p. 2.
12. 'Sightless Send Up War Output', clipping from *Yorkshire Evening News*, *BA* (November 1943), p. 8.

13. 'Topical Talk by Trotter: The Employment of the Blind', *BA* (March 1944), p. 4. In total some ten thousand blind people were in full employment in Great Britain by 1944, according to the National Institute for the Blind. 'Blind People in Industry', *BA* (October 1944), p. 3.

14. 'Many More Blind are now on War Work', *BA* (November 1944), p. 6. The League claimed that 'over two thousand two hundred blind men and women previously looked upon as incapable of any kind of work have been taken into War factories and many other kinds of industrial activity' during the war. Letter A. Henderson, Gen. Sec., NLB, to G. Isaacs, Minister of Labour and NI, 4 August 1945, printed in NLB, *Report of the Special Committee 1945* (Sandridge, Herts., 1945), p. 19. WCML, WRep.

15. 'The Blind Can Help', *BA* (May 1945), p. 7.

16. Quotation from Resolution No. 33, 1943 Triennial Conference Resolutions. WCML, CRP. 'Topical Talk by Trotter: The Employment of the Blind', *BA* (March 1944), p. 4.

17. Minutes, EC Meeting, London, 11–14 December 1948, pp. 8–9. NEC Minutes 1938–50. However, many quickly returned to their homes. See, for example, 'North-Western Notes', *BA* (February 1940), p. 6.

18. 'North-Eastern Notes', *BA* (November 1941), p. 5. See also 'London Notes', *BA* (November 1939), p. 6; 'Blind Evacuees', *BA* (December 1939), p. 3.

19. The West Ham branch reopened in the County Borough of West Ham in August 1942. 'London Notes', *BA* (October 1942), p. 7; 'London Notes', *BA* (September 1944), p. 3; 'London Notes', *BA* (December 1945), p. 6.

20. 'North-Western Notes', *BA* (June 1941), p. 3; 'Bombed Institution', *BA* (May 1941), pp. 7–8; 'Blind Institution Restart', *BA* (October 1941), p. 6.

21. 'If Your House is Bombed', *BA* (July 1942), p. 8; 'Homes for the Blind', *BA* (November 1943), p. 6; 'New Schemes to Help Blind. Norwich Institution's Ambitious Plans', *BA* (November 1944), p. 8.

22. Resolution No. 2, 1943 Triennial Conference Resolutions. WCML, CRP.

23. Letter Asst. Gen. Sec. to R. W. Hanlan, North East District Council, NLB, 3 June 1965. MRC, MSS292/91/24; Letter Asst. Sec., TUC, to C. E. Dumbleton, 19 February 1943. MRC, MSS292/91/27.

24. Minutes, EC Meeting, London, 19–22 June 1948, pp. 12–14. WCML, NEC Minutes, 1938–50.

25. Minutes, EC Sub-Committee, Glasgow, 30–31 October 1948, p. 1 and EC Meeting, London, 11–14 December 1948, p. 2, both in NEC Minutes 1938–50. The house in 2 Tenterden Road, Tottenham, became the League's Central Office in 1980. Report, NEC to Triennial Conference 1982, p. 3. TUC Library, HD6661z. Report, NEC to Triennial Conference 1985, pp. 26–7. WCML, CRP.

26. See, for example, 'Midland Notes', *BA* (April 1940), p. 6.

27. Statement of Aims on the front page of the *Blind Advocate* in 1940. See also, for example, 'Minimum Wage Wanted for the Blind', *BA* (May 1940), p. 7. The municipal minimum wage campaign had already started in 1920. '1899–1974', *BA* (January 1974), p. 3.

28. 70th Annual Trades Union Congress, Report of Proceedings, 5–9 September 1938, pp. 429–31; 'Falkirk Town Council', *BA* (September 1939), p. 3; 'Scottish Notes', *BA* (December 1939), p. 5.

29. 'Scottish Notes', *BA* (January 1941), p. 6. See also, 'Scottish Notes', *BA* (September 1939), p. 6 and 'Scottish Notes', *BA* (June 1940), p. 3.
30. 'Scottish Notes', *BA* (May 1942), p. 5.
31. Memo from W. Bramhall, MoH, to Beckett, MoNI, 7 December 1944, p. 2. TNA, PIN 8/53. Of the thirteen workshops in the North-Western Area, for example, only Carlisle paid the municipal minimum wage by the end of 1943. 'Workshops and Domiciliary Conditions in the North West Area', *BA* (June 1944), p. 5.
32. By May 1944 'the ever-increasing adoption of the Minimum Wage method of remuneration throughout the Country' was reported as a fact in the *Blind Advocate*. 'Midland Notes', *BA* (May 1944), p. 7.
33. 'Note of a Meeting with Representatives of the National League of the Blind held in Committee Room 1, 3, St James's Square on 20th August, 1945', printed in NLB, *Report of the Special Committee 1945* (Sandridge, Herts., 1945), pp. 6–7. WCML, WRep.
34. See, for example, 'Midland Notes', *BA* (November 1943), p. 5.
35. 'Midland Notes', *BA* (January 1943), p. 5.
36. TNA, Annual Returns, FS 12/141 and FS 28/359. For a short description of a membership drive conducted during that period, see 'Midland Notes', *BA* (May 1945), p. 6.
37. 'North-Eastern Notes', *BA* (September 1940), p. 8.
38. For a dispute successfully mediated by the Ministry of Labour, see 'Scottish Notes: Provisional Settlement at Edinburgh', *BA* (February 1942), p. 2.
39. 'North-Western Notes' and 'Blind Protest at Preston', *BA* (April 1943), pp. 6–8.
40. 'Scottish Notes', *BA* (October 1942), p. 5.
41. 'Midland Notes', *BA* (March 1944), p. 6.
42. The four authorities were the County Boroughs of Middlesbrough and Sunderland and the County Councils of Durham and the North Riding of Yorkshire. 'North-Western Notes', *BA* (October 1943), p. 3.
43. 'Midland Notes', *BA* (April 1944), p. 6.
44. 'Midland Notes', *BA* (October 1942), p. 6. Other examples are Worcestershire County Council; Bury; the Wolverhampton, Dudley and District Society for the Blind; Norfolk County Council as well as a number of local authorities in North Wales. 'Midland Notes', *BA* (July 1942), p. 7; 'North-Western Notes', *BA* (September 1942), pp. 4–5; 'Midland Notes', *BA* (June 1944), pp. 7–8; 'Midland Notes', *BA* (April 1945), p. 5.
45. 'Midland Notes', *BA* (January 1943), p. 5.
46. *Ibid.*, p. 4.
47. 'Midland Notes', *BA* (May 1944), p. 8.
48. 'History of the League, 1893–1921', p. 4. British Library, YA.1992.C48.
49. Minutes, EC Meeting, London, 10–12 December 1949, p. 10. NEC Minutes 1938–50.
50. Letter W. McEagar, Gen. Sec., NIB, to T. H. Smith, Gen. Sec., NLB, 2 November 1949. MRC, MSS349/3/4/9. Minutes, EC Meeting, London, 10–12 December 1949, p. 10. NEC Minutes 1938–50.
51. Peter Baldwin, 'Beveridge in the Long Durée', in John Hills, John Ditch and Howard Glennerster (eds), *Beveridge and Social Security: An International Retrospective* (Oxford, 1994), pp. 38–9.

52. Joint Statement by President Roosevelt and Prime Minister Churchill, 14 August 1941, 5th Point, http://avalon.law.yale.edu/wwii/at10.asp [last accessed 19 January 2015].
53. Nicholas Timmins, *The Five Giants: A Biography of the Welfare State* (London, 2001), pp. 11–25.
54. Timmins, *The Five Giants*, p. 47; Brian Abel-Smith, 'The Beveridge Report: Its Origins and Outcomes', in Hills, Ditch and Glennerster (eds), *Beveridge and Social Security*, pp. 10–22.
55. 'Scottish Notes', *BA* (September 1941), p. 4.
56. 'Scottish Notes', *BA* (June 1942), p. 5. The records of the EC meetings for these years are unfortunately lost.
57. 'Pay for Blind', *BA* (August 1942), p. 5.
58. 'Blind Welfare Service and Social Security. Scheme Submitted to Beveridge Committee', *BA* (October 1942), p. 8.
59. 'Midland Notes', *BA* (October 1942), p. 6.
60. §169, Beveridge Report.
61. §170, Beveridge Report.
62. Resolution No. 31, 1943 Triennial Conference Resolutions. WCML, CRP.
63. Resolution No. 30, *ibid.*
64. Resolution No. 1, *ibid.*
65. Minutes, Special Conference, Blackpool, 30 September–1 October 1944, pp. 1–2. WCML, CRP. The conference also discussed the Pensions and Determination of Needs Act, 1943. *Ibid.*, pp. 2–3.
66. Hansard 403 HC Deb., 27 September 1944, cols. 235–6.
67. NLB, *Report of the Special Committee 1945* (Sandridge, Herts., 1945), pp. 1–2. WCML, WRep.
68. *Ibid.*
69. *Ibid.* 'Midland Notes', *BA* (November 1944), p. 6.
70. See Chapter 4.
71. Letter A. Henderson, Gen. Sec., NLB, to Sir W. Jowitt, Minister of NI, 27 November 1944. TNA, PIN 8/53.
72. Letter J. Whittam, President, NLB, to W. Jowitt, Minister of NI, undated. TNA, PIN 8/53. 'An Appreciation', *BA* (March 1946), p. 6
73. Handwritten note from E. Bearn, MoNI, to J. N. Beckett, MoH, 5 December 1944. TNA, PIN 8/53.
74. Handwritten note from [illegible] to E. Bearn, 8 December 1944. TNA, PIN 8/53.
75. Letter W. Eastwood, Sec., Stockport branch, NLB, to W. Jowitt, Minister of NI, 11 December 1944; handwritten note, W. Jowitt, 14 December 1944, both in TNA, PIN 8/53.
76. Letter M. Riddelsdell, Private Sec. to Minister of NI, to A. Henderson, Gen. Sec., NLB, 13 December 1944. TNA, PIN 8/53.
77. Letter J. N. Beckett, MoH, to R. H. Farrell, MoNI, 4 December 1944. TNA, PIN 8/53.
78. Letter and Memo from A. Henderson, Gen. Sec., NLB, to W. Jowitt, Minister of NI, 23 February 1945. TNA, PIN8/53.
79. Brief for the Minister of NI, from Assistance Board, 3 November 1947, p. 2. TNA, AST 7/977.
80. Letter A. Henderson, Gen. Sec., NLB, to W. Jowitt, Minister of NI, 23 February 1945, pp. 2–3. TNA, PIN 8/53.

81. 'Note on Letter from the NLB dated 23rd February, 7 March 1945', p. 1. TNA, PIN 8/53.
82. *Ibid.*
83. The letter was reprinted in the *Blind Advocate*. Letter W. Jowitt, Minister of NI, to J. Whittam, Bolton branch, NLB, 18 December 1944. TNA, PIN 8/53. 'Letter Received by Bolton Branch Secretary from Sir W. Jowitt', *BA* (February 1945), p. 6.
84. 'National League of the Blind: Note of a deputation to the Minister of National Insurance on 5th April, 1945', p. 2. TNA, PIN 8/53.
85. *Ibid.*
86. §351, Beveridge Report.
87. Memo from A. Patterson to Miss Ambrose, both MoNI, 29 August 1945. TNA, PIN 8/53. Like the League, the National Institute also considered the individual benefit rate suggested in the government's White Paper as too low. Brief for the Minister of NI, from Assistance Board, 3 November 1947, pp. 1–2. TNA, AST 7/977.
88. Minutes of a Meeting with the Minister of NI, 6 November 1947, p. 6. TNA, AST 7/977.
89. Deputation from Blind Associations, 6 November 1947: Brief for the Minister of NI, from Assistance Board, 3 November 1947, p. 1. TNA, AST 7/977.
90. Letter A. Patterson, MoNI, to H. Fieldhouse, Assistance Board, 21 August 1945. TNA, PIN 8/53. Deputation from Blind Associations, 6 November 1947: Brief for the Minister of NI, from Assistance Board, 3 November 1947, p. 3. TNA, AST 7/977.
91. Letter J. E. Bullard, Assistance Board, to A. Patterson, MoNI, 23 August 1945. TNA, PIN 8/53.
92. 'The Special Needs of the Blind', Letter A. Henderson, Gen. Sec., NLB, to Griffiths, Minister of NI, 26 July 1945. TNA, PIN 8/53.
93. 'Savings "Scare": Mr. Morrison's Challenge to Chancellor', *The Times*, 18 June 1945, p. 2. See also Brief for the Minister of NI, from Assistance Board, 3 November 1947, pp. 3–4. TNA, AST 7/977.
94. 'The Return of Bartimeus', *BA* (January 1945), p. 6.
95. 'Midland Notes', *BA* (April 1945), p. 5.
96. 'Lonsdale M.P. and Welfare of the Blind', *BA* (May 1945), p. 8; 'In the House of Commons', *BA* (June 1945), p. 7; Hansard 452 HC Deb., 16 June 1948, col. 574.
97. 'Midland Notes', *BA* (May 1946), p. 3.
98. See, for example, 'North-Western Notes', *BA* (March 1947), p. 5; 'London Notes', *BA* (June 1947), p. 5; 'South-Western Notes', *BA* (July 1947), p. 6.
99. The decision was applied retrospectively with effect from 31 July 1946. Middlesex paid the rate without conditions. 'London Notes', *BA* (August 1947), p. 3; 'London Notes', *BA* (October 1947), p. 3.
100. Letter T. H. Smith, Gen. Sec., NLB, to the Sec., Ministry of Labour and National Service, 29 May 1948. MRC, MSS349/3/3/2.
101. 'London Notes', *BA* (August 1947), p. 3.
102. Hansard 452 HC Deb., 16 June 1948, col. 603.
103. Minutes, EC Sub-Committee, Glasgow, 30–31 October 1948, p. 2 and 11–14 December 1948, p. 2, both in NEC Minutes 1938–50. 'Midland Notes', *BA* (October 1949), p. 6.

104. Letter T. H. Smith, Gen. Sec., NLB, to the Sec., Ministry of Labour and National Service, 29 May 1948. MRC, MSS349/3/3/2. 'Appeal by Blind Worker: Trades Council's Wage Protest', *BA* (October 1949), p. 8. 'Workshops for the Blind: Relations between the Local Authorities Advisory Committee and the National League of the Blind', Memo, 12 May 1955. TNA, LAB 10/1199. Constitution, National Joint Council for Workshops for the Blind, 24 July 1964. WCML, WNJC.
105. National Assistance Board, Board Meeting, London, 21 June 1950, Notes on item 7. TNA, AST 7/977.
106. 'The National Assistance Act: Determination of Need Regulations Adopted', *BA* (July 1948), p. 4. Parker, *Years of Excitement*, pp. 6–7; Smith (ed.), *Golden Jubilee Brochure*, pp. 28–9.
107. Only Section 1 of the 1938 Blind Persons Act, which granted non-contributory old-age pensions to blind people from the age of forty, remained in force. It was repealed by the Social Security Act of 1966. Lysons, 'The Development of Social Legislation', pp. 566 and 568.
108. For a history of these special provisions, see Ann Abel, 'Visually Impaired People', pp. 47–51.
109. 'The National Assistance Act: Determination of Need Regulations Adopted', *BA* (July 1948), pp. 4–5; Hansard 452 HC Deb., 16 June 1948, cols. 575–8.
110. See, for example, 'National Assistance (Determination of Need) Regulations: Proposals for their Amendment', NLB, 20 June 1951, p. 1. TNA, AST 7/977.
111. Minutes of a Meeting with the Minister of NI, 6 November 1947, pp. 1–2. TNA, AST 7/977.
112. The MPs were Ian Fraser, L. W. Joynson-Hicks, E. Evans and F. Messer. Minutes of a Meeting with the Minister of NI, 6 November 1947, p. 1. TNA, AST 7/977.
113. 'Provisions under National Assistance Act', *BA* (July 1948), p. 3.
114. 'Deputation from the National League of the Blind to the National Assistance Board', 21 June 1950, p. 2. TNA, AST 7/977.
115. Brief for the Minister of NI, from Assistance Board, 3 November 1947, pp. 4–5. TNA, AST 7/977. 'The National Assistance Act: Determination of Need Regulations Adopted', *BA* (July 1948), p. 4.
116. 'The National Assistance Act: Determination of Need Regulations Adopted', *BA* (July 1948), p. 5.
117. *Ibid.*
118. 'Local Blind Welfare Services and the National Assistance Act', *BA* (January 1949), p. 5.
119. 'Social Rehabilitation', *BA* (January 1949), p. 5.
120. 'The National Assistance Act: Determination of Need Regulations Adopted', *BA* (July 1948), p. 5.
121. J. E. Rose, 'Training of Blind Workers', reprinted from *Industrial Welfare* in *BA* (July 1947), p. 7.
122. Some 425,000 people were interviewed between 1941 and 1945. Around three-quarters were placed in employment while one-sixth found work on their own account. Harry Malisoff, 'The British Disabled Persons (Employment) Act', *Industrial and Labour Relations Review* Vol. 5(2) (January 1952): 249–57 (250).
123. *Report of the Inter-departmental Committee on the Rehabilitation and Resettlement of Disabled Persons* (London, 1943). Malisoff, 'The British

Disabled Persons (Employment) Act', p. 249; Borsay, *Disability*, pp. 133–5.
124. 1920 Blind Persons Act, Section 1.
125. Disabled Persons (Employment) Act, Section 1(1).
126. 'Employment of Disabled Workers', BA (February 1945), pp. 4–5.
127. The only designated employments were electric passenger lift attendant and car park attendant. Malisoff, 'The British Disabled Persons (Employment) Act', pp. 249–52.
128. J. L. Edwards, 'Remploy: An Experiment in Sheltered Employment for the Severely Disabled in Great Britain', *International Labour Review* Vol. 77(2) (1958): 147–59 (148–9).
129. Malisoff, 'The British Disabled Persons (Employment) Act', p. 255.
130. Borsay, *Disability*, p. 135.
131. Letter A. Henderson, Gen. Sec., NLB, to G. Isaacs, Minister of Labour and NI, 4 August 1945, printed in NLB, *Report of the Special Committee 1945* (Sandridge, Herts., 1945), p. 18. WCML, WRep.
132. *Ibid.*, p. 20.
133. Disabled Persons (Employment) Act, Section 16.
134. Edwards, 'Remploy', p. 153. The author was in charge of the Disabled Persons Branch in the Ministry of Labour and National Service.
135. *Ibid.*
136. 'Wider Employment for the Blind', *Manchester Guardian*, reprinted in BA (November 1944), p. 8.
137. NLB, *Report of the Special Committee 1945* (Sandridge, Herts., 1945), p. 2. WCML, WRep.
138. *Ibid.*, p. 1.
139. 'Note of a Meeting with Representatives of the National League of the Blind held in Committee Room 1, 3, St James's Square on 20th August, 1945', printed in *ibid.*, p. 6. See also Letter A. Henderson, Gen. Sec., NLB, to G. Isaacs, Minister of Labour and NI, 4 August 1945, printed in *ibid.*, pp. 19–20.
140. *Ibid.*, p. 1.
141. Letter A. Henderson, Gen. Sec., NLB, to G. Isaacs, Minister of Labour and National Insurance, 4 August 1945, printed in *ibid.* p. 20.
142. 'Note of a Meeting with Representatives of the National League of the Blind held in Committee Room 1, 3, St James's Square on 20th August, 1945', printed in *ibid.*, p. 7.
143. *Ibid.*, p. 8. See also Griffiths' remarks in 1947: 'Minutes of a Meeting with the Minister of National Insurance, 6 November 1947', p. 7. TNA, AST 7/977.
144. Remploy had over 6,000 employees in around 90 factories. Edwards, 'Remploy', pp. 149 and 152.
145. *Ibid.*, p. 148. 'Remploy Factories and Workshops for the Blind', BA (January 1950), p. 5.
146. Edwards, 'Remploy', p. 152.
147. 'Remploy Factories and Workshops for the Blind', BA (January 1950), p. 5.
148. Edwards, 'Remploy', p. 148.
149. Ministry of Labour, *Report of the Working Party on Workshops for the Blind* (London, 1962), pp. 11–12.

150. *Ibid.*, pp. 49–52.
151. Minutes, EC Meeting, London, 15–16 September 1962, p. 6; Minutes, EC Meeting, London, 8–10 December 1962, pp. 7–8, both in WCML, NEC Minutes 1951–64. Letter M. Barrett, Gen Sec., NLB, to The Registrar, Registry of Friendly Societies, London, 7 November 1962. TNA, FS 24/68.
152. Resolution No. 22, Report, 1964 Triennial Conference, 23–5 May 1964, pp. 13–14. WCML, CRP. Parker, *Years of Excitement*, p. 8.
153. See, for example, George Follows, 'Blind Workers set an Export Pace', *Birmingham Gazette*, reprinted in *BA* (January 1948), p. 3.
154. J. E. Rose, 'Training of Blind Workers', reprinted from *Industrial Welfare* in *BA* (July 1947), p. 7.
155. Report of Working Party on Workshops for the Blind, p. 5. 'More Employment for the Blind', *BA* (April 1951), pp. 4–6.
156. Report of Working Party on Workshops for the Blind, p. 6. The rising age of new entrants was also due to the fact that medical developments reduced blindness in children and young adults. Sight loss therefore became most common between the ages of forty and sixty-five. *Ibid.*, p. 8.
157. Rose, *Changing Focus*, p. 65.
158. 'Our Right to Celebrate', *BA* (April 1948), p. 6.
159. *Ibid.*
160. Frank Prochaska, 'The War and Charity', in Oppenheimer and Deakin (eds), *Beveridge and Voluntary Action*, pp. 36–47.
161. The Institute only changed its name to Royal National Institute five years later, http://www.rnib.org.uk/aboutus/who/historyofrnib/Pages/rnibhistory.aspx [last accessed 28 March 2014].
162. Quoted in 'Editorial', *BA* (January 1949), p. 4.
163. *Ibid.*
164. 'The Golden Jubilee Celebrations', *BA* (July 1949), p. 6. The League also pointed out that many local authorities were creative in their policies as well as sympathetic towards the blind community. 'The Gateshead Blind Centre', *BA* (October 1949), p. 3; 'Quarterly Notes', *BA* (April 1950), pp. 2–3.
165. Lowe, *The Welfare State in Britain since 1945*, p. 285.
166. 'London Notes', *BA* (January 1950), p. 6.
167. NLB Rules 1952, p. 5. WCML, NLB Rule Book.
168. 'Deputation from Blind Associations, 6 November 1947: Brief for the Minister of National Insurance, from Assistance Board, 3 November 1947', p. 1. TNA, AST 7/977.
169. Bill Price, 'Tom Parker – a credit to his people, by Bill Price', *Advocate* (December 1984), p. 8. In an interview with the *Guardian*, Parker claims that this happened when he was twelve. Keith Harper, 'Out of Sight, Out of Mind', *Guardian Extra*, 11 May 1973, p. 14.
170. Bill Price, 'Tom Parker – a credit to his people, by Bill Price', *Advocate* (December 1984), p. 8.
171. *Ibid.*
172. *Ibid.*
173. *Ibid.* National League of the Blind and Disabled: Officers, Manuscript, May 1970, p. 1. MRC, MSS292B/91/14.
174. Minutes, EC Meeting, London, 28–31 March 1936, p. 4. WCML, NEC Minutes 1920–37. Bill Price, 'Tom Parker – a Credit to his People, by Bill Price',

Advocate (December 1984), p. 8. Letter T. J. Parker to T. H. Smith, Gen. Sec., NLB, 7 September 1961. WCML, League for the Blind London and Home Counties District, folder 'Lon. O. Rep. 1961–6'.

175. Minutes, EC Meeting, London, 20–3 March 1937, p. 3. WCML, NEC Minutes 1920–37.

176. J. A. Wall, 'Obituary Thomas J. Parker', http://ourhistory-hayes.blogspot.co. uk/2007/02/tom-parker-councillor-tom-parker-born.html [hereafter: Wall, 'Obituary Parker'] [last accessed 12 November 2012]. Wall was Chairman of the Royal National Institute of the Blind.

177. Letter J. C. Colligan, Sec.-Gen., RNIB, to editor, *The Times*, 23 May 1962, p. 13. 'Mr. T. J. Parker adopted as Parliamentary Candidate', *BA* (October 1950), p. 8; 'Hackney's New Mayor', *BA* (July 1962), pp. 4–5. Baldwinson, *Unacknowledged Traces*, p. 101.

178. 'Hackney's New Mayor', *BA* (July 1962), p. 4.

179. The Conservative F. P. Crowder received 25,295 votes. Parker, who ran as a Labour and Cooperative candidate received 14,491 votes. 'Full Results of General Election', *Manchester Guardian*, 27 October 1951, p. 5.

180. Curran received 20,519 votes, Parker 19,866 votes and the Liberal candidate R. Goodall 6,644 votes. 'First Results in the General Election', *Guardian*, 16 October 1964, p. 4. Bill Price, 'Tom Parker – a Credit to his People, by Bill Price', *Advocate* (December 1984), p. 9.

181. Michael Barrett, 'A Tribute to the Life and Work of Thomas J. Parker O.B.E., June 1909 to August 1995', *Advocate* (Autumn 1996), p. 5.

182. Wall, 'Obituary Parker'.

183. *Ibid.*

184. The rival World Council for the Welfare of the Blind likewise dissolved. *Ibid.* Bill Price, 'Tom Parker – a Credit to his People, by Bill Price', *Advocate* (December 1984), p. 9. Report, NEC to Triennial Conference 1985, p. 34. WCML, CRP.

185. Wall, 'Obituary Parker'.

186. 'Tom Parker reaches 80 not out!' *Advocate* (October 1989), p. 5.

187. Report, NEC to Triennial Conference 1985, p. 34. WCML, CRP.

188. 'Tom Parker gets his Award from Princess Di', *Advocate* (December 1989), p. 5.

189. Wall, 'Obituary Parker'.

190. Michael Barrett, 'A Tribute to the Life and Work of Thomas J. Parker O.B.E., June 1909 to August 1995', *Advocate* (Autumn 1996), p. 5.

191. Unlike Purse, Parker has no entry in the *Oxford Dictionary of National Biography*.

192. Wall, 'Obituary Parker'.

193. For Parker's role in the 1936 march on London, see Chapter 4.

6   A Changing Relationship: The League and Charity in the Post-War Era

1. These and all following figures are taken from: Annual Returns. TNA, FS 12/141 and FS 28/359. Membership figures do not include sighted Associates. Apparently their numbers were not recorded by the League.

2. According to its website, it had around 45 branches in 2013, http://www. community-tu.org/who-we-represent/nlbd-sector.aspx [last accessed 9 July 2013].
3. Phelan, 'Are We Producing the Goods?', p. 71.
4. Parker, *Years of Excitement*, p. 7.
5. 'Quarterly Notes', *BA* (July 1949), p. 5.
6. The TUC and employers both received five seats, but the remaining nineteen were given to individuals not affiliated with either group. 'Employment of Disabled Workers', *BA* (February 1945), pp. 4–5. Trade union representatives were also given quotas on the Local Advisory Committees which were set up once all sections of the Act came into operation in 1945. 'Help for the Disabled', *BA* (July 1945), p. 3.
7. 'National Assistance Act and the Blind Welfare Committee', *BA* (April 1949), p. 4. In addition, some members of the League also found themselves banned from sitting on Local Appeals Tribunals which were set up under the National Injuries Act 1946. The argument was that the work and nature of these tribunals required their members to be sighted. Letter T. H. Smith, Gen. Sec., NLB, to E. Summerskill, MoNI, 1 June 1950; Letter E. Summerskill, MoNI, to E. Evans, MP, 29 June 1951, both in MRC, MSS349/3/5/7.
8. 'National Assistance Act 1948', *BA* (January 1973), p. 7.
9. *Ibid.*, p. 8.
10. Report, 1964 Triennial Conference, 23–5 May 1964, pp. 11–12; Report, 1967 Triennial Conference, 20–2 May 1967, pp. 1–3, both in WCML, CRP. The League had 2,681 members at the beginning of 1991. However, only 65 of them had dual membership: 18 were members of the Banking Insurance and Finance Union and 47 of the National and Local Government Officers Association (later part of UNISON). Report, 1994 Triennial Conference, 4–6 June 1994, p. 23. MRC, MSS349/2/3.
11. See, for example, 'President's Message', Report, 1991 Triennial Conference, 8–10 June 1991, p. 5. MRC, MSS349/2/4.
12. Report, NEC to Triennial Conference 1982, p. 6. TUCL, HD6661z. See also NLBD, *Future Role of the Sheltered Workshops* (London, no date), p. 5. TUCL, HD6661z. Borsay, *Disability*, p. 136.
13. Interview with Joe Mann.
14. Report, 1988 Triennial Conference, 14–16 May 1988, p. 29. TUCL, HD6661z.
15. Interview with Joe Mann.
16. Nicholas Deakin, 'The Perils of Partnership: The Voluntary Sector and the State, 1945–1992', in Smith, Rochester and Hedley (eds), *An Introduction to the Voluntary Sector*, p. 40.
17. Beveridge, *Voluntary Action*, p. 246. Jose Harris, 'Voluntarism, the State and Public-Private Partnerships in Beveridge's Social Thought', in Oppenheimer and Deakin (eds), *Beveridge and Voluntary Action*, pp. 10–11.
18. 'Minutes of a Meeting with the Minister of National Insurance, 6 November 1947', p. 3. TNA, AST 7/977.
19. Lowe, *The Welfare State in Britain since 1945*, p. 289.
20. 'National Assistance Act 1948', *BA* (January 1973), p. 8; '1899–1974', *BA* (January 1974), p. 4; Phelan, 'Are We Producing the Goods?', pp. 71–2.

21. See, for example, 'Charitable Appeals', *BA* (July 1951), p. 8.
22. Resolution No. 6, Report, 1964 Triennial Conference, 23–5 May 1964, p. 6. WCML, CRP. 'Quarterly Notes', *BA* (January 1962), pp. 2 and 3. Minutes, EC Meetings, London, 23–4 June 1962, p. 7 and 15–16 September 1962, p. 15, both in WCML, NEC Minutes 1951–64.
23. NLB, 'The National League of the Blind and its Policy', [*c*.1949]. TUCL, HD6661z.
24. 'Editorial', *BA* (October 1950), p. 4.
25. 'Workshops for the Blind: Two Points of View', *BA* (April 1951), p. 6. See also, for example, 'Scottish Area Notes', *BA* (January 1952), p. 6.
26. Piercy Report, quoted in Report of Working Party on Workshops for the Blind, p. 6.
27. *Ibid.*, pp. 6–7.
28. *Ibid.*, pp. 28–9.
29. *Ibid.*, pp. 9–10.
30. *Ibid.*, pp. 43–9.
31. *Ibid.*, p. 17.
32. *Ibid.*, p. 26. For the national minimum wage, see Parker, *Years of Excitement*, p. 5.
33. Report of Working Party on Workshops for the Blind, pp. 23 and 51.
34. 'Editorial', *BA* (January 1963), pp. 4–6; 'Editorial', *BA* (July 1963), p. 3; 'League Members go to Parliament', *BA* (January 1970), p. 8.
35. 'Those New Trades', *BA* (January 1970), p. 7.
36. However, at least one worker disagreed. Report of Working Party on Workshops for the Blind, pp. 95–6.
37. See, for example, Minutes, EC Meeting, London, 11–14 December 1948, p. 7. WCML, NEC Minutes 1938–50. 'North-Western Notes', *BA* (July 1962), p. 5; 'Those New Trades', *BA* (January 1970), p. 7.
38. Ian Bruce, 'Employment of People with Disabilities', in *Disability and Social Policy* (Policy Studies Institute 1991): 236–49 (238). http://www.psi.org.uk/site/publication_detail/617/ [last accessed 31 May 2014]. Report, 1994 Triennial Conference, 4–6 June 1994, p. 5. MRC, MSS349/2/3.
39. Michael A. Barrett, 'Justice not Charity', *Scottish Trade Union Review* 50 (April–June 1991): 22–3.
40. 'Forward by Jimmy O'Rourke – President NLBD', *Advocate* (November 1998), p. 4. Interview with Joe Mann. Only the Derby branch seemed to have ever contemplated the creation of a cooperative workshop until then. It had requested permission 'to establish workshops for the blind in Derby in the name of the League and also to collect funds for the upkeep' in 1934, but the Executive instructed the District Organiser to press for the establishment of municipal workshops instead. Minutes, Special EC Meeting, London, 13–16 October 1934, p. 9. WCML, NEC Minutes 1920–37.
41. Interview with Joe Mann. Email Joe Mann to author, 16 June 2014.
42. See Case Study C, page 147.
43. 'Ourselves and the Royal National Institute for the Blind', *BA* (April 1962), p. 5. For a history of this dispute see the documents in MRC, MSS349/3/4/13 and MSS349/3/2/13.
44. Composite Resolution 1, Report, 1970 Triennial Conference, 30 May–1 June 1970, p. 6. WCML, CRP.

45. Report, NEC to Triennial Conference 1982, pp. 13–15; Report, 1988 Triennial Conference, 14–16 May 1988, p. 2, both in TUCL, HD6661z.
46. Report of Sub-Committee Meeting of the EC on the Financial Position of NLBD, 9–12 January 1986, p. 4a. WCML, NEC Minutes 1984–87. Report, 1994 Triennial Conference, 4–6 June 1994. MRC, MSS349/2/3.
47. Interview with Joe Mann.
48. Hilton et al., *A Historical Guide to NGOs in Britain*, pp. 39–40.
49. See, for example, Minutes, EC Meeting, London, 15–16 September 1962, pp. 7–8. WCML, NEC Minutes 1951–64; 'The Concession to Blind Tax Payers', *BA* (October 1962), p. 7; 'The League Faces the 70's', *BA* (July 1970), pp. 6–7.
50. Emails G. Davies to author, 7 July and 21 July 2014.
51. Minutes, EC Meeting, London, 15–16 September 1962, p. 14; Minutes, EC Meeting, London, 8–10 December 1962, p. 11, both in WCML, NEC Minutes 1951–64.
52. Minutes, EC Meetings, 18–20 March 1967, pp. 11–12; 17–19 June 1967, p. 14 and 16–18 September 1967, pp. 11–12, all in WCML, NEC Minutes 1965–74.
53. Interview with Joe Mann. Email G. Davies to author, 7 July 2014.
54. See, for example, 'What is the Nature of Your State-Aided System?', *BA* (September 1899), p. 11.
55. Minutes, EC Meeting, London, 19–21 June 1920, p. 1. WCML, WCir.
56. Resolution No. 12, 1934 Triennial Conference Resolutions; Minutes, 1934 Triennial Conference, 22–4 September 1934, p. 5, both in WCML, CRP.
57. Report, NEC to Triennial Conference, 20–2 May 1967, p. 3. WCML, CRP.
58. The visit of the Tanzanian delegates to Britain had been sponsored by the Royal Commonwealth Society for the Blind. 'Report on Visit to Tanzania by Mr. B. Foxall, Midland Area Secretary and National Executive Member of the National League of the Blind and Disabled, 5 November–4 December 1984', p. 1. WCML, CRP.
59. Report, NEC to Triennial Conference 1985, p. 35. WCML, CRP.
60. Report, NEC to Triennial Conference 1982, p. 18. TUCL, HD6661z.
61. Hilton et al., *A Historical Guide to NGOs in Britain*, pp. 22–5.
62. Report on Joint Conference of the National Executive Council and Area Councils, Bishops Stortford, 21–4 October 1983, p. 2. WCML, CRP.
63. Circular to all Branch Sec., M. Barrett, Gen. Sec./Treasurer, NLB, 9 August 1985. MRC, MSS349/3/5/16.
64. *Ibid.* Report of Sub-Committee Meeting of the EC on the Financial Position of NLBD, 9–12 January 1986, p. 8. WCML, NEC Minutes 1984–87.
65. Report, 1994 Triennial Conference, 4–6 June 1994, pp. 3–4. MRC, MSS349/2/3.
66. 'Avoiding an Identity Crisis', *Advocate* (Autumn 1996), p. 13.
67. Michael Bradley and Nick Matthews, 'Big does not necessarily mean beautiful for trade unions', *Advocate* (Autumn 1996), pp. 12–13.
68. Interview with Joe Mann.
69. According to the League General Secretary who supervised the merger, 97 per cent of the League's members voted for it. *Ibid.*
70. Interview with Robert Mooney, President, NLBD, London, 9 November 2014.

71. Hansard 474 HC Deb., 28 April 1950, col. 1286.
72. *Ibid.*, p. 1301.
73. 'Quarterly Notes', *BA* (July 1950), pp. 2–3.
74. http://www.helpforheroes.org.uk/how-we-help/ [last accessed 10 October 2014].
75. Hilton et al., *A Historical Guide to NGOs in Britain*, pp. 204–5. http://www.rnib.org.uk/about-rnib-who-we-are/history-rnib [last accessed 10 September 2014].
76. Donatella della Porta and Mario Diani, *Social Movements: An Introduction* (2nd edn.; Malden, MA, 2006), pp. 5–11; Lowe, *The Welfare State in Britain since 1945*, pp. 289–90; Nicholas Deakin, 'The Perils of Partnership' in Smith, Rochester and Hedley (eds), *An Introduction to the Voluntary Sector*, pp. 48–51.
77. Helen McCarthy and Pat Thane, 'The Politics of Association in Industrial Society', *Twentieth Century British History* Vol. 22(2) (2011): 217–29, quotation on p. 224; Craig Calhoun, ' "New Social Movements" of the early Nineteenth Century', *Social Science History* Vol. 17(3) (1993): 385–427; Christopher Moores, 'The Progressive Professionals: The National Council for Civil Liberties and the Politics of Activism in the 1960s', *Twentieth Century British History* Vol. 20(4) (2009): 538–60; Berridge and Mold, 'Professionalisation' in Hilton and McKay (eds), *The Ages of Voluntarism*, pp. 114–34.
78. 'Lord Freud offers "unreserved apology" for Comment about Disabled People', *Guardian*, online edition, 15 October 2014 [last accessed 15 October 2014].
79. Interview with Joe Mann.
80. Ministry of Labour, *Report of the Working Party on Workshops for the Blind* (London, 1962), p. 2.
81. For Lysons, for example, the League and its leaders were a crucial reason why blind people had a more privileged position than deaf people in Britain before the consolidation of the welfare state after the Second World War. Lysons, 'The Development of Social Legislation', pp. 586–99.

Bibliography

Archival sources

British Library
YA.1992.C48: 'History of the League, 1893–1921', anonymous typescript manuscript, 19 December 1947 [4 pp.].

Labour History Archive and Study Centre, Manchester (LHA)
Communist Party, Industrial Papers:
  CP/IND/HANN/05
Labour Party:
  LP/WI/7: Ellen Wilkinson – Scrapbooks
  National Joint Council of Labour Minutes, Memoir etc., 25 April 1933–21 October 1936, Box II.

London School of Economics Archive (LSE)
Independent Labour Party:
  ILP 4
  ILP 5

Modern Records Centre, University of Warwick (MRC)
Transport and General Workers' Union:
  MSS126/TG/Res/X/1041A
TUC:
  MSS292/74/4/1
  MSS292/91/24
  MSS292/91/25
  MSS292/91/26
  MSS292/91/27
  MSS292/135.01/1
  MSS292B/91/14
National League of the Blind:
  MSS349/2/3
  MSS349/2/4
  MSS349/3/1/2
  MSS349/3/2/13
  MSS349/3/3/2
  MSS349/3/4/9
  MSS349/3/4/13
  MSS349/5/4/4
  MSS349/3/5/7
  MSS349/3/5/16

The National Archives, Kew (TNA)

Records of the Unemployment Assistance Boards, the Supplementary Benefits
Commission and of related bodies:
   AST 7/138
   AST 7/977
Records of the Cabinet Office:
   CAB 23/48/20
   CAB 23/85/9
   CAB 27/497
Records of the Charity Commissioner and Charity Commission:
   CHAR 7/56
Records created or inherited by the Registry of Friendly Societies:
   FS 12/141
   FS 24/68
   FS 27/232
   FS 28/97
   FS 28/359
Records created or inherited by the Ministry of Pensions and National Insurance
and of related, predecessor and successor Bodies:
   HO 45/16545
Records of Departments responsible for Labour and Employment Matters and
related Bodies:
   LAB 10/1199
Records of the Metropolitan Police Office:
   MEPO 2/3053
   MEPO 2/3091
Records created or inherited by the Ministry of Health and successors, Local
Government Boards and related Bodies:
   MH 55/607
   MH 57/212
   MH 57/213
Records created or inherited by the Ministry of Pensions and National Insurance
and of related, predecessor and successor Bodies:
   PIN 8/53

Parliamentary Archives

The Lloyd George Papers:
   LG/F/230/3

Working Class Movement Library (WCML)

National League for the Blind:
   Circulars 1918–45, 1969–71 [cited as: WCir]
   Conference Reports and Papers [cited as: CRP]
   London and Home Counties District
   London and Home Counties, National Joint Council for Workshops for Blind
      [cited as: WNJC]
   NEC Minutes 1920–37

NEC Minutes 1938–50
NEC Minutes 1951–64
NEC Minutes 1965–74
NEC Minutes 1984–7
Pamphlets [cited as: WPamph]
Reports and Balance Sheets and Agendas 1905–45
Reports and Balance Sheets 1946–82 [cited as: WRep]
Rule Books, Contribution Cards, Agreements [cited as: NLB Rule Books]
NLB Statements of Income 1921–52

London Metropolitan Archives

A/FWA/C/D/285/1

TUC Library (TUCL)

HD6661z
HV1744
HV1793/1924
HV1793/1925
HV1793/1926
HV1793/1928
HV1793/1930
HV1793/1938

22nd Annual Trades Union Congress, Report of Proceedings, 2 September 1889.
52nd Annual Trades Union Congress, Report of Proceedings, 6–11 September 1920.
53rd Annual Trades Union Congress, Report of Proceedings, 5–10 September 1921.
59th Annual Trades Union Congress, Report of Proceedings, 5–10 September 1927.
70th Annual Trades Union Congress, Report of Proceedings, 5–9 September 1938.
Minutes of Meeting of the Executive Committee of the London Labour Party held at the House of Commons on Thursday 6 March 1930.

Acts

Blind Persons Act, 1920, 10 & 11 Geo. 5 1920–1, Chapter 49.
Blind Persons Act, 1938, 1 & 2 Geo. 6 1937–8, Chapter 11.
Disabled Persons (Employment) Act, 1944, 7 & 8 Geo. 6, Chapter 10.
Local Government Act, 1929, 19 Geo. 5 1928–9, Chapter 17.
National Assistance Act, 1948, 11 & 12 Geo. 6, Chapter 29.

Interviews

Emails from Gareth Davies, retired President, NLBD, 7 July and 21 July 2014.
Email from Joe Mann, retired Gen. Sec., NLBD, 16 June 2014.
Interview with Joe Mann, retired Gen. Sec., NLBD, Tipton St John, Devon, 10 June 2014; tape in possession of the author.
Interview with Robert Mooney, President, NLBD, London, 9 November 2014; no tape.

Newspapers and Journals

Aberdeen Journal
Aberdeen Weekly Journal
Advertiser
Advocate
Birmingham Gazette
Blind Advocate
Bristol Evening Post
Carlisle Evening News
Cheshire Daily Echo
Chronicle & Echo
Cumberland News
Daily Express
Daily Herald
Daily Independent
Daily Mail
Daily Worker
Derby and Chesterfield Reporter
Derby Daily Express
Derby Daily Telegraph
Derby Mercury
Dundee Courier & Argus and Northern Warder
Evening Advertiser
Evening Standard
Express & Star
Glasgow Herald
Guardian
Leeds Mercury
Leicester Daily Mercury
Leicester Mercury
Lloyd's Weekly Newspaper
Luton News & Bedfordshire Advertiser
Macclesfield Courier and Herald
Manchester Guardian
Mansfield and North Notts. Advertiser
Market Harborough Advertiser
Northampton Mercury
North-Eastern Daily Gazette
North Mail
Nottingham Evening News
Nottingham Evening Post
Sheffield Daily Telegraph
South Wales Echo
Staffordshire Sentinel
Star
The Times
West Herts Post & Watford Echo
Worcestershire Echo

Yorkshire Evening Post
Yorkshire Observer
Yorkshire Post
Yorkshire Weekly Post

Radio

Northam, Gerry, 'Before Jarrow', BBC Radio 4 FM, Friday, 8 April 2005, 11:00–11:30 a.m.

Websites

Community: The Union for Life:
> http://www.community-tu.org/information/100308/100310/history/ [last accessed 17 September 2012].
> http://www.community-tu.org/who-we-represent/nlbd-sector.aspx [last accessed 9 July 2013].

Hansard 1803–2005:
> http://hansard.millbanksystems.com/
>> 341 HC Deb. 21 February 1890
>> 59 HC Deb. 11 March 1914
>> 121 HC Deb. 25 November 1919
>> 122 HC Deb. 11 December 1919
>> 125 HC Deb. 13 February 1920
>> 126 HC Deb. 12 March 1920
>> 128 HC Deb. 22 April 1920
>> 128 HC Deb. 26 April 1920
>> 129 HC Deb. 14 May 1920
>> 131 HC Deb. 25 June 1920
>> 174 HC Deb. 14 May 1924
>> 250 HC Deb. 24 March 1931
>> 250 HC Deb. 31 March 1931
>> 253 HC Deb. 4 June 1931
>> 403 HC Deb. 27 September 1944
>> 452 HC Deb. 16 June 1948
>> 474 HC Deb. 28 April 1950

Hayes Peoples History:
> http://ourhistory-hayes.blogspot.co.uk/2007/02/tom-parker-councillor-tom-parker-born.html [last accessed 12 November 2012].

Help for Heroes:
> http://www.helpforheroes.org.uk/how-we-help/ [last accessed 10 September 2014].

Huffington Post:
> http://www.huffingtonpost.co.uk/dr-simon-duffy/austerity-cuts-disabled-people_b_3248615.html [last accessed 10 July 2013].

Measuring Worth.com:
   http://www.measuringworth.com/ukcompare/ [last accessed 27 May 2014].
National League of the Blind of Ireland Trust:
   http://nlbit.wordpress.com/ [last accessed 9 July 2013].
The Official Website of the British Monarchy:
   http://www.royal.gov.uk/HMTheQueen/QueenCharities/Overview.aspx   [last accessed 28 May 2014].
Royal National Institute of Blind People:
   http://www.rnib.org.uk/aboutus/who/historyofrnib/Pages/rnibhistory.aspx [last accessed 28 March 2014].
   http://www.rnib.org.uk/about-rnib-who-we-are/history-rnib [last accessed 10 September 2014].
Trades Union Congress:
   http://www.tuc.org.uk/the_tuc/index.cfm?mins=49&minors=45&majorsubject ID=19 [last accessed 17 April 2013].

Brochures and Pamphlets

Labour Publications Department, *The Blind Persons Charter* (London, September 1935).
National Joint Council, *The Blind Persons' Act 1920* (London, no date).
National League of the Blind, *Handbook* (London, 1932).
National League of the Blind, *Report of the Special Committee 1945* (Sandridge, Herts., 1945).
Newcastle and District Trades Council, '1873–1973: A Centenary History' (Newcastle upon Tyne, 1973).
Parker, Tom J., *The National League of the Blind and Disabled: 1899–1974. Years of Excitement . . . and Disappointment* (Glasgow, no date.).
Purse, Ben, *The Social and Industrial Conditions of the Blind*, No. 1 (Manchester, 1908).
Smith, Thomas H. (ed.), *National League of the Blind 1899–1949: Golden Jubilee Souvenir Brochure*, foreword by Sir Vincent Tewson (Glasgow, no date).

Reports

Advisory Committee on the Welfare of the Blind, Report of the Sub-Committee on the Unemployable Blind, Ministry of Health (London: HMSO, 1935).
Beveridge, William, *Social Insurance and Allied Services* (London: HMSO, 1942).
Beveridge, William, *Voluntary Action: A Report on Methods of Social Advance* (London: George Allen & Unwin, 1948).
Ministry of Health, Advisory Committee on the Welfare of the Blind, Report of the Sub-Committee on the Unemployable Blind (London: HMSO, 1935).
Ministry of Labour, *Report of the Working Party on Workshops for the Blind* (London: HMSO, 1962).
Report of the Royal Commission on the Blind, the Deaf and Dumb, &c., of the United Kingdom (London: HMSO, 1889).

Report of the Inter-departmental Committee on the Rehabilitation and Resettlement of Disabled Person (London: HMSO, 1943).

Royal Commission on the Poor Laws and Relief of Distress, Appendix Vol. III: Minutes of Evidence (49th to 71st Days) being mainly the Evidence of Critics of the Poor Law and of Witnesses representing Poor Law and Charitable Associations, with Appendix (London: HMSO, 1909).

Oxford Dictionary of National Biography, online edition

Martin, E., 'Steadman, William Charles (1851–1911)' [last accessed 19 October 2012].

Mare Rowley, J. de la, 'Purse, Benjamin Ormond (1874–1950)' [last accessed 20 September 2012].

Trevor-Roper, P. D., 'Fraser, (William Jocelyn) Ian, Baron Fraser of Lonsdale (1897–1974)' [last accessed 3 December 2012].

Secondary sources

Abel, R. Ann, 'Visually Impaired People, the Identification of the Need for Specialist Provision: A Historical Perspective', *The British Journal of Visual Impairment* Vol. 7(2) (1989): 47–51.

Abel-Smith, Brian, 'The Beveridge Report: Its Origins and Outcomes', in John Hills, John Ditch and Howard Glennerster (eds), *Beveridge and Social Security: An International Retrospective* (Oxford: Clarendon Press, 1994), pp. 10–22.

Addison, Paul, and Harriet Jones (eds), *A Companion to Contemporary Britain 1939–2000* (Malden, MA: John Wiley & Sons, 2007).

Anderson, Julie, *War, Disability and Rehabilitation in Britain: 'Soul of a Nation'* (Manchester: Manchester University Press, 2011).

Anderson, Julie and Neil Pemberton, 'Walking Alone: Aiding the War and Civilian Blind in the Inter-War Period', *European Review of History* Vol. 14(4) (2007): 459–79.

Baldwin, Peter, 'Beveridge in the Long Durée', in John Hills, John Ditch and Howard Glennerster (eds), *Beveridge and Social Security: An International Retrospective* (Oxford: Clarendon Press, 1994), pp. 37–55.

Baldwinson, Tony, *Unacknowledged Traces: Exploring through Photographic Records the Self-Organisation of Disabled People in England from the 1920s to the 1970s* (Manchester: TBR Consulting, 2012).

Barasch, Moshe, *Blindness: The History of a Mental Image in Western Thought* (New York: Routledge, 2001).

Barrett, Michael A., 'Justice not Charity: Campaigning for the Blind and Disabled', *Scottish Trade Union Review* 50 (April–June 1991): 22–3.

Beckett, Angharad E., 'Understanding Social Movements: Theorising the Disability Movement in Conditions of Late Modernity', *Sociological Review* Vol. 54(4) (2006): 734–52.

Bergen, Amanda Nichola, 'The Blind, the Deaf and the Halt: Physical Disability, the Poor Law and Charity c.1830–1890, with Particular Reference to the County of Yorkshire' (PhD thesis, University of Leeds, 2004).

Berridge, Virginia and Alex Mold, 'Professionalisation, New Social Movements and Voluntary Action in the 1960s and 1970s', in Matthew Hilton and James McKay (eds), *The Ages of Voluntarism: How we got to the Big Society* (Oxford: Oxford University Press, 2011), pp. 114–34.

Brown, Kenneth D., *Labour and Unemployment 1900–1914* (Newton Abbott: David & Charles, 1971).

Borsay, Anne, *Disability and Social Policy in Britain since 1750* (Basingstoke: Palgrave Macmillan, 2005).

Bruce, Ian, 'Employment of People with Disabilities', in *Disability and Social Policy* (Policy Studies Institute, 1991): 236–49. http://www.psi.org.uk/site/publication_detail/617/ [last accessed 31 May 2014].

Calhoun, Craig, ' "New Social Movements" of the early Nineteenth Century', *Social Science History* Vol. 17(3) (1993): 385–427.

Campbell, Alan, Nina Fishman and David Howell (eds), *Miners, Unions and Politics, 1910–47* (Aldershot: Scolar Press, 1996).

Campbell, Jane and Mike Oliver, *Disability Politics: Understanding or Past, Changing or Future* (London: Routledge, 1996).

'Care of the Blind', *British Medical Journal* Vol. 2(2955) (18 August 1917): 227–8.

Carnevali, Francesca, and Julie-Marie Strange (eds), *Twentieth-Century Britain: Economic, Cultural and Social Change* (2nd edn.; Harlow: Pearson Longman, 2007).

Carter, Peter, 'State Aid – Direct and Complete: The Blind Workers March 1920', *Working Class Movement Library Bulletin* 7 (1997): 11–19.

Clarke, Peter, *Hope and Glory: Britain 1900–2000* (London: Penguin, 2004).

Clegg, Hugh, *History of British Trade Unions since 1889*, Vol. I: 1889–1910 (Oxford: Clarendon Press, 1964).

Clegg, Hugh, *A History of British Trade Unions since 1889*, Vol. II: 1911–1933 (Oxford: Clarendon Press, 1985).

Clinton, Alan, *The Trade Union Rank and File: Trades Councils in Britain, 1900–40* (Manchester: Manchester University Press, 1977).

Coles, John, *Blindness and the Visionary: The Life and Work of John Wilson* (London: Giles de la Mare, 2006).

Danieli, Ardha and Peter Wheeler, 'Employment Policy and Disabled People: Old Wine in New Glasses', *Disability & Society* Vol. 21(5) (2006): 485–98.

Deakin, Nicholas, 'Civil Society', in Paul Addison and Harriet Jones (eds), *A Companion to Contemporary Britain 1939–2000* (Malden, MA: John Wiley & Sons, 2007), pp. 407–26.

Deakin, Nicholas, 'The Perils of Partnership: The Voluntary Sector and the State, 1945–1992', in Justin Davis Smith, Colin Rochester and Rodney Hedley (eds), *An Introduction to the Voluntary Sector* (London: Routledge, 1995), pp. 40–65.

Deakin, Nicholas and Justin Davis Smith, 'Labour, Charity and Voluntary Action: The Myth of Hostility', in Matthew Hilton and James McKay (eds), *The Ages of Voluntarism: How we got to the Big Society* (Oxford: Oxford University Press, 2011), pp. 69–93.

de la Mare Rowley, J., 'Purse, Benjamin Ormond (1874–1950)', rev. Patrick Wallis, *Oxford Dictionary of National Biography*, Oxford University Press, 2004, http://0-www.oxforddnb.com.lib.exeter.ac.uk/view/article/35633 [last accessed 20 September 2012].

della Porta, Donatella and Mario Diani, *Social Movements: An Introduction* (2nd edn.; Malden, MA: Blackwell, 2006).

Edwards, J. L., 'Remploy: An Experiment in Sheltered Employment for the Severely Disabled in Great Britain', *International Labour Review* Vol. 77(2) (1958): 147–59.

Evans, Neil, ' "South Wales has been Roused as Never Before": Marching Against the Means Test, 1934–36', in David W. Howell and Kenneth O. Morgan (eds), *Crime, Protest and Police in Modern British Society: Essays in Memory of David J. V. Jones* (Cardiff: University of Wales Press, 1999), pp. 176–206.

Ferguson, Ronald J., *We Know Who We Are: A History of the Blind in Challenging Educational and Socially-Constructed Policies. A Study in Policy Archaeology* (San Francisco, CA: Caddo Gap Press, 2001).

Fraser, Hamish W., *A History of British Trade Unionism 1700–1998* (Basingstoke: Palgrave Macmillan, 1999).

Gilbert, David, 'The Landscape of Spencerism: Mining Politics in the Nottingham Coalfield, 1910–1947', in Alan Campbell, Nina Fishman and David Howell (eds), *Miners, Unions and Politics, 1910–47* (Aldershot: Scolar Press, 1996), pp. 175–97.

Grant, Brian, *The Deaf Advance: A History of The British Deaf Association 1890–1990* (Edinburgh: Pentland Press, 1990).

Grant, Peter, 'Voluntarism and the Impact of the First World War', in Matthew Hilton and James McKay (eds), *The Ages of Voluntarism: How we got to the Big Society* (Oxford: Oxford University Press, 2011), pp. 27–46.

Griffin, A. R. and C. P. Griffin, 'The Non-Political Trade Union Movement', in Asa Briggs and John Saville (eds), *Essays in Labour History 1918–1939* (London: Croom Helm, 1977), pp. 133–62.

Griffiths, Clare, 'Remembering Tolpuddle: Rural History and Commemoration in the Inter-War Labour Movement', *History Workshop Journal* Issue 44 (Autumn 1997): 145–69.

Halsey, A. H., with Josephine Webb (eds), *Twentieth-Century British Social Trends* (Basingstoke: Palgrave Macmillan, 2000).

Harris, Jose, 'Voluntarism, the State and Public-Private Partnerships in Beveridge's Social Thought', in Melanie Oppenheimer and Nicholas Deakin (eds), *Beveridge and Voluntary Action in Britain and the Wider British World* (Manchester: Manchester University Press, 2011), pp. 9–20.

Hayhoe, Simon, *God, Money, and Politics: English Attitudes to Blindness and Touch from the Enlightenment to Integration* (Charlotte, NC: Information Age Publishing, 2008).

Henderson, Bruce and Noam Ostrander, *Understanding Disability Studies and Performance Studies* (London: Routledge, 2010).

Hills, John, John Ditch and Howard Glennerster (eds), *Beveridge and Social Security: An International Retrospective* (Oxford: Clarendon Press, 1994).

Hilton, Matthew and James McKay (eds), *The Ages of Voluntarism: How we got to the Big Society* (Oxford: Oxford University Press, 2011).

Hilton, Matthew and James McKay, 'The Ages of Voluntarism: An Introduction', in Matthew Hilton and James McKay (eds), *The Ages of Voluntarism: How we got to the Big Society* (Oxford: Oxford University Press, 2011), pp. 1–26.

Hilton, Matthew, Nick Crowson, Jean-Fançois Mouhot and James McKay, *A Historical Guide to NGOs in Britain: Charities, Civil Society and the Voluntary Sector since 1945* (Basingstoke: Palgrave Macmillan, 2012).

Howell, David W. and Kenneth O. Morgan (eds), *Crime, Protest and Police in Modern British Society: Essays in Memory of David J. V. Jones* (Cardiff: University of Wales Press, 1999).

Humphries, Steve and Pamela Gordon, *Out of Sight: The Experience of Disability 1900–1950* (Plymouth: Northcote House Publishers, 1992).

Jackson, Peter W. and Raymond Lee, *The Origins of the British Deaf Association* (Feltham: British Deaf History Society Publications, 2010).

Jenkins, Jess, *Leicester's Unemployed March to London 1905* (Leicester: Friends of the Record Office for Leicestershire, Leicester & Rutland, 2005).

Keating, Peter J. (ed.), *Into Unknown England, 1866–1913: Selections from the Social Explorers* (Manchester: Manchester University Press, 1976).

Kendall, Jeremy and Martin Knapp, 'A Loose and Baggy Monster: Boundaries, Definitions and Typologies', in Justin Davis Smith, Colin Rochester and Rodney Hedley (eds), *An Introduction to the Voluntary Sector* (London: Routledge, 1995), pp. 66–95.

Kingsford, Peter, *The Hunger Marchers in Britain 1920–1939* (London: Lawrence and Wishart, 1982).

Kornbluh, Felicia, 'Disability, Antiprofessionalism, and Civil Rights: The National Federation of the Blind and the "Right to Organize" in the 1950s', *Journal of American History* Vol. 97(4) (March 2011): 1023–47.

Kudlick, Catherine J., 'Disability History: Why We Need Another "Other"', *American Historical Review* Vol. 108(3) (June 2003): 763–93.

Lowe, Rodney, *The Welfare State in Britain since 1945* (3rd edn.; Basingstoke: Palgrave Macmillan, 2005).

Lyons, Pat, *A Place in the Sun: A Brief History of the National League of the Blind in Ireland* (Blackrock, Co. Dublin: Aquaverra Research Limited, 1999).

Lysons, C. Kenneth, 'The Development of Social Legislation for Blind or Deaf Persons in England, 1834–1939' (PhD thesis; London: Brunel University, 1973).

McCarthy, Helen, 'Associational Voluntarism in Interwar Britain', in Matthew Hilton and James McKay (eds), *The Ages of Voluntarism: How we got to the Big Society* (Oxford: Oxford University Press, 2011), pp. 47–68.

McCarthy, Helen and Pat Thane, 'The Politics of Association in Industrial Society', *Twentieth Century British History* Vol. 22(2) (2011): 217–29.

McKay, James, 'Voluntary Politics: The Sector's Political Function from Beveridge to Deakin', in Melanie Oppenheimer and Nicholas Deakin (eds), *Beveridge and Voluntary Action in Britain and the Wider British World* (Manchester: Manchester University Press, 2011), pp. 80–93.

Malisoff, Harry, 'The British Disabled Persons (Employment) Act', *Industrial and Labour Relations Review* Vol. 5(2) (January 1952): 249–57.

Martin, Ross M., *TUC: The Growth of a Pressure Group 1868–1976* (Oxford: Clarendon Press, 1980).

Matson, Floyd, *Walking Alone and Marching Together: A History of the Organized Blind Movement in the United States, 1940–1990* (Baltimore, MD: National Federation of the Blind, 1990).

Mearns, Andrew, *The Bitter Cry of Outcast London: An Inquiry into the Condition of the Abject Poor* (London: James Clarke & Co., 1883).

Mills, Selina, 'Darkness, Visible: The History of Blindness', *History Today* Vol. 63(9) (2013), http://www.historytoday.com/selina-mills/darkness-visible-history-blindness [last accessed 18 October 2014].

Mills, Selina, *Life Unseen: The Story of Blindness* (London: I. B. Tauris, forthcoming).

Moores, Christopher, 'The Progressive Professionals: The National Council for Civil Liberties and the Politics of Activism in the 1960s', *Twentieth Century British History* Vol. 20(4) (2009): 538–60.

Norman, Andrew, *Father of the Blind: a Portrait of Sir Arthur Pearson* (Stroud: History Press, 2009).

Ó Catháin, Maírtín, ' "Blind, But Not to the Hard Facts of Life": The Blind Workers' Struggle in Derry, 1928–1940', *Radical History Review* 94 (Winter 2006): 9–21.

Oliphant, John, *The Early Education of the Blind in Britain, c.1790–1900: Institutional Experience in England and Scotland* (Lewiston, NY: Edwin Mellen Press, 2007).

Oliphant, John, 'Empowerment and Debilitation in the Educational Experience of the Blind in Nineteenth-century England and Scotland', *History of Education* Vol. 35(1) (January 2006): 47–68.

Oliphant, John, ' "Touching the Light": The Invention of Literacy for the Blind', *Paedagogica Historica* Vol. 44(1/2) (February–April 2008): 67–82.

Oliver, W. H., 'Tolpuddle Martyrs and Trade Union Oaths', *Labour History* 10 (May 1966): 5–12.

Oppenheimer, Melanie and Nicholas Deakin, 'Beveridge and Voluntary Action', in Melanie Oppenheimer and Nicholas Deakin (eds), *Beveridge and Voluntary Action in Britain and the Wider British World* (Manchester: Manchester University Press, 2011), pp. 1–8.

Oppenheimer, Melanie and Nicholas Deakin (eds), *Beveridge and Voluntary Action in Britain and the Wider British World* (Manchester: Manchester University Press, 2011).

Overy, Richard, *The Morbid Age: Britain and the Crisis of Civilisation* (London: Penguin, 2009).

Pagel, Martin, *'On Our Own Behalf': An Introduction to the Self-Organisation of Disabled People* (Manchester: GMCDP Publications, June 1998).

Pelling, Henry, *A History of British Trade Unionism* (5th edn.; London: Penguin, 1992).

Perry, Matt, *Bread and Work: Social Policy and the Experience of Unemployment, 1918–39* (London: Pluto Press, 2000).

Perry, Matt, *The Jarrow Crusade: Protest and Legend* (Sunderland: University of Sunderland Press, 2005).

Phelan, Patrick, 'Are We Producing the Goods?', *British Journal of Visual Impairment* Vol. 2(3) (Autumn 1984): 70–3.

Phillips, Gordon, *The Blind in British Society: Charity, State, and Community, c.1780–1930* (Aldershot: Ashgate Publishing, 2004).

Piven, Frances Fox and Richard A. Cloward, *Poor People's Movements: Why they Succeed, How they Fail* (New York: Vintage Books, 1979).

Powell, Martin, 'The Hidden History of Social Citizenship', *Citizenship Studies* Vol. 6(3) (2002): 229–44.

Priestley, Mark, 'Commonality and Difference in the Movement: An "Association of Blind Asians" in Leeds', *Disability & Society* Vol. 10(2) (1995): 157–70.

Prochaska, Frank, 'The War and Charity', in Melanie Oppenheimer and Nicholas Deakin (eds), *Beveridge and Voluntary Action in Britain and the Wider British World* (Manchester: Manchester University Press, 2011), pp. 36–50.

Purse, Ben, *The British Blind: A Revolution in Thought and Action* (London: Buck Bros. & Harding Ltd., 1928).

Purse, Ben, *Moods and Melodies: A Book of Verse* (London: Buck Bros. & Harding Ltd., 1931).

Purse, Ben, *The Social and Industrial Conditions of the Blind* (Manchester: William Morris Press, 1908).

Reiss, Matthias, 'Forgotten Pioneers of the National Protest March: the National League of the Blind Marches to London, 1920 & 1936', *Labour History Review* Vol. 70(2) (2005): 131–65.

Reiss, Matthias, 'Hartz IV – das britische Beispiel', *Damals: Das Magazin für Geschichte und Kultur* 36 (December 2004): 8–11.

Reiss, Matthias, 'Marching on the Capital: National Protest Marches of the British Unemployed in the 1920s and 1930s', in Matthias Reiss (ed.), *The Street as Stage: Protest Marches and Public Rallies since the Nineteenth Century* (Oxford: Oxford University Press, 2007), pp. 147–68.

Reiss, Matthias, 'Not all were Apathetic: National Hunger Marches as Political Rituals in Interwar Britain', in Michael Schaich and Jörg Neuheiser (eds), *Political Ritual in the United Kingdom, 1700–2000* (Augsburg: Wißner, 2006), pp. 93–121.

Riddell, Neil, 'Walter Citrine and the British Labour Movement, 1925–1935', *History* Vol. 85(278) (April 2000): 285–306.

Rochester, Colin, 'Voluntary Agencies and Accountability', in Justin Davis Smith, Colin Rochester and Rodney Hedley (eds), *An Introduction to the Voluntary Sector* (London: Routledge, 1995), pp. 190–207.

Rooff, Madeline, *Voluntary Societies and Social Policy* (London: Routledge & Kegan Paul, 1957).

Rose, Fred, 'Toward a Class-Cultural Theory of Social Movements: Reinterpreting New Social Movements', *Sociological Forum* Vol. 12(3) (September 1997): 461–94.

Rose, June, *Changing Focus: the Development of Blind Welfare in Britain* (London: Hutchinson, 1970).

Roulstone, Alan, 'Disabling Pasts, Enabling Futures? How Does the Changing Nature of Capitalism Impact on the Disabled Worker and Jobseeker?', *Disability & Society* Vol. 17(6) (2002): 627–42.

Schneer, Jonathan, *Ben Tillett: Portrait of a Labour Leader* (London: Croom Helm, 1982).

Schweik, Susan, *The Ugly Laws: Disability in Public* (New York: New York University Press, 2010).

Smith, Justin Davis, 'The Voluntary Tradition: Philanthropy and Self-Help in Britain 1500–1945', in Justin Davis Smith, Colin Rochester and Rodney Hedley (eds), *An Introduction to the Voluntary Sector* (London: Routledge, 1995), pp. 9–39.

Smith, Justin Davis, Colin Rochester and Rodney Hedley (eds), *An Introduction to the Voluntary Sector* (London: Routledge, 1995).

Snow, David A., 'Framing Processes, Ideology, and Discursive Fields', in David A. Snow, Sarah A. Soule and Hanspeter Kriesi (eds), *The Blackwell Companion to Social Movements* (Malden, MA: Blackwell, 2004), pp. 380–412.

Snow, David A., Sarah A. Soule and Hanspeter Kriesi (eds), *The Blackwell Companion to Social Movements* (Malden, MA: Blackwell, 2004).

Stevens, Richard, 'Containing Radicalism: The Trades Union Congress Organisation Department and Trades Councils, 1928–1953', *Labour History Review* Vol. 62(1) (Spring 1997): 5–21.

Stevenson, John and Chris Cook, *The Slump: Society and Politics during the Depression* (London: Jonathan Cape, 1977).

Taylor, Robert, *The TUC: From the General Strike to New Unionism* (Basingstoke: Palgrave Macmillan, 2000).

Thomas, Mary G., *The Royal National Institute for the Blind, 1868–1956* (Brighton: RNIB, 1957).

Thorpe, Andrew, *Britain in the 1930s: The Deceptive Decade* (Oxford: Blackwell, 1992).

Thorpe, Andrew, *A History of the British Labour Party* (3rd edn.; Basingstoke: Palgrave Macmillan, 2008).

Tickner, Lisa, *The Spectacle of Women: Imagery of the Suffrage Campaign 1907–14* (London: Chatto & Windus, 1989).

Timmins, Nicholas, *The Five Giants: A Biography of the Welfare State* (revised and updated edition; London: HarperCollins, 2001).

Wall, J. A., 'Obituary Thomas J. Parker', http://ourhistory-hayes.blogspot. co.uk/2007/02/tom-parker-councillor-tom-parker-born.html [last accessed 12 November 2012].

Weygand, Zina, *The Blind in French Society from the Middle Ages to the Century of Louis Braille* (Stanford, CA: Stanford University Press, 2009).

Wilkinson, Ellen, *The Town that was Murdered: The Life Story of Jarrow* (London: Victor Gollancz, 1939).

Wrigley, Chris, 'Trade Unions: Rise and Decline', in Francesca Carnevali and Julie-Marie Strange (eds), *Twentieth-Century Britain: Economic, Cultural and Social Change* (2nd edn.; Harlow: Pearson Longman, 2007), pp. 281–92.

Index

Printed and bound by CPI Group (UK) Ltd, Croydon, CR0 4YY